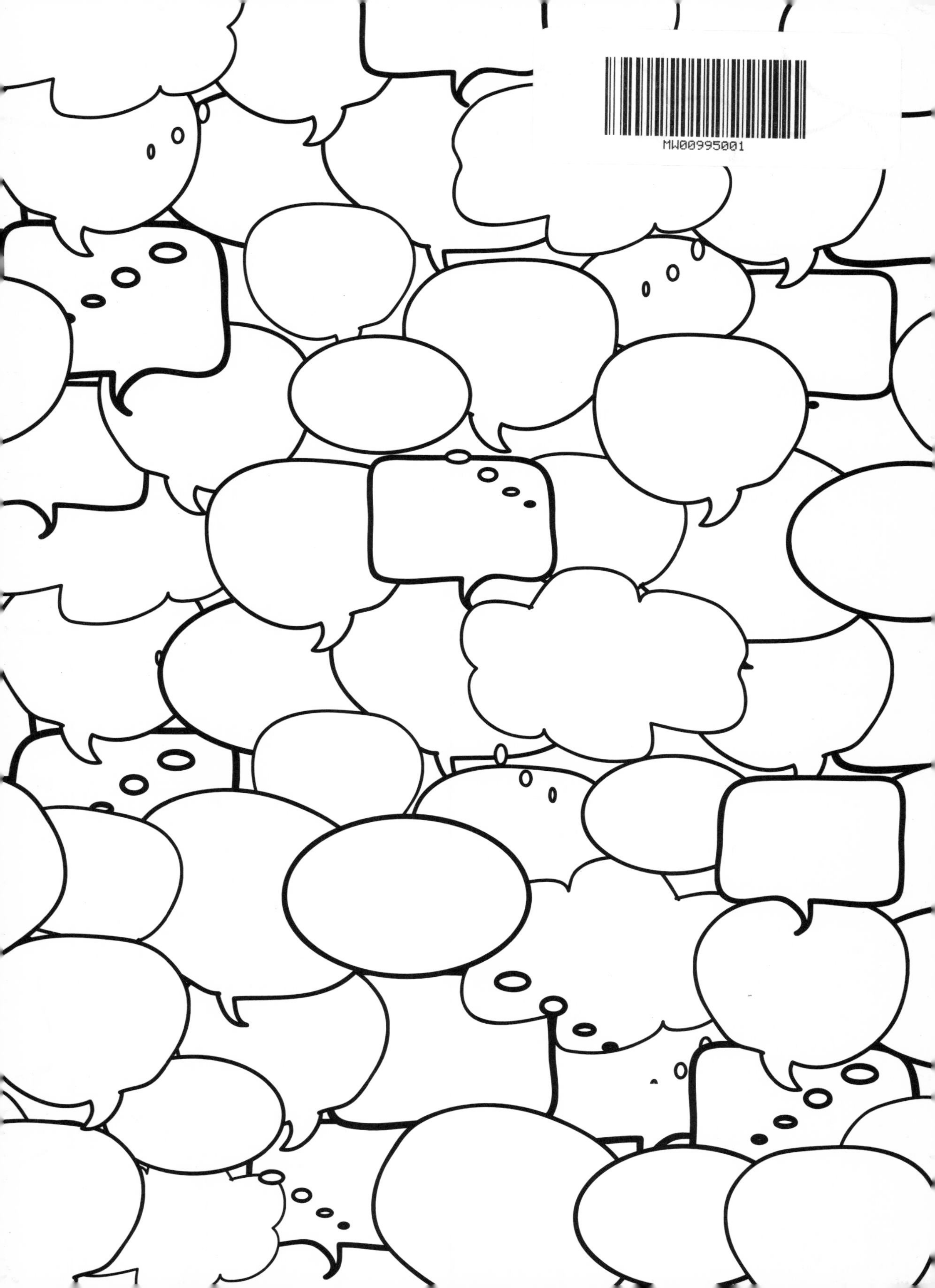

INVADERS FROM
THE NORTH

INVADERS FROM THE NORTH

How Canada Conquered
the Comic Book Universe

John Bell

Foreword by Seth

THE DUNDURN GROUP
TORONTO

Editor: Michael Carroll
Design: Alison Carr
Printer: TRI-GRAPHIC Printing Limited

Library and Archives Canada Cataloguing in Publication

Bell, John, 1952-
Invaders from the north : how Canada conquered the comic book universe / John Bell.

Includes bibliographical references.
ISBN 10: 1-55002-659-3
ISBN 13: 978-1-55002-659-7

1. Comic books, strips, etc., Canadian--History and criticism. I. Title.

PN6731.B443 2006 741.5'971 C2006-904265-9

Conseil des Arts du Canada Canada Council for the Arts

Canada

ONTARIO ARTS COUNCIL
CONSEIL DES ARTS DE L'ONTARIO

1 2 3 4 5 10 09 08 07 06

We acknowledge the support of the **Canada Council for the Arts** and the **Ontario Arts Council** for our publishing program. We also acknowledge the financial support of the **Government of Canada** through the **Book Publishing Industry Development Program** and **The Association for the Export of Canadian Books**, and the **Government of Ontario** through the **Ontario Book Publishers Tax Credit program** and the **Ontario Media Development Corporation.**

Care has been taken to trace the ownership of copyright material used in this book. The author and the publisher welcome any information enabling them to rectify any references or credits in subsequent editions.

J. Kirk Howard, President

Printed and bound in Canada
Printed on recycled paper
www.dundurn.com

Dundurn Press
3 Church Street, Suite 500
Toronto, Ontario, Canada
M5E 1M2

Gazelle Book Services Limited
White Cross Mills
High Town, Lancaster, England
LA1 4XS

Dundurn Press
2250 Military Road
Tonawanda, NY
U.S.A. 14150

To the memory of the artist, writer, and publisher Gene Day (1951–1982), who pursued his own dreams and nurtured those of countless others.

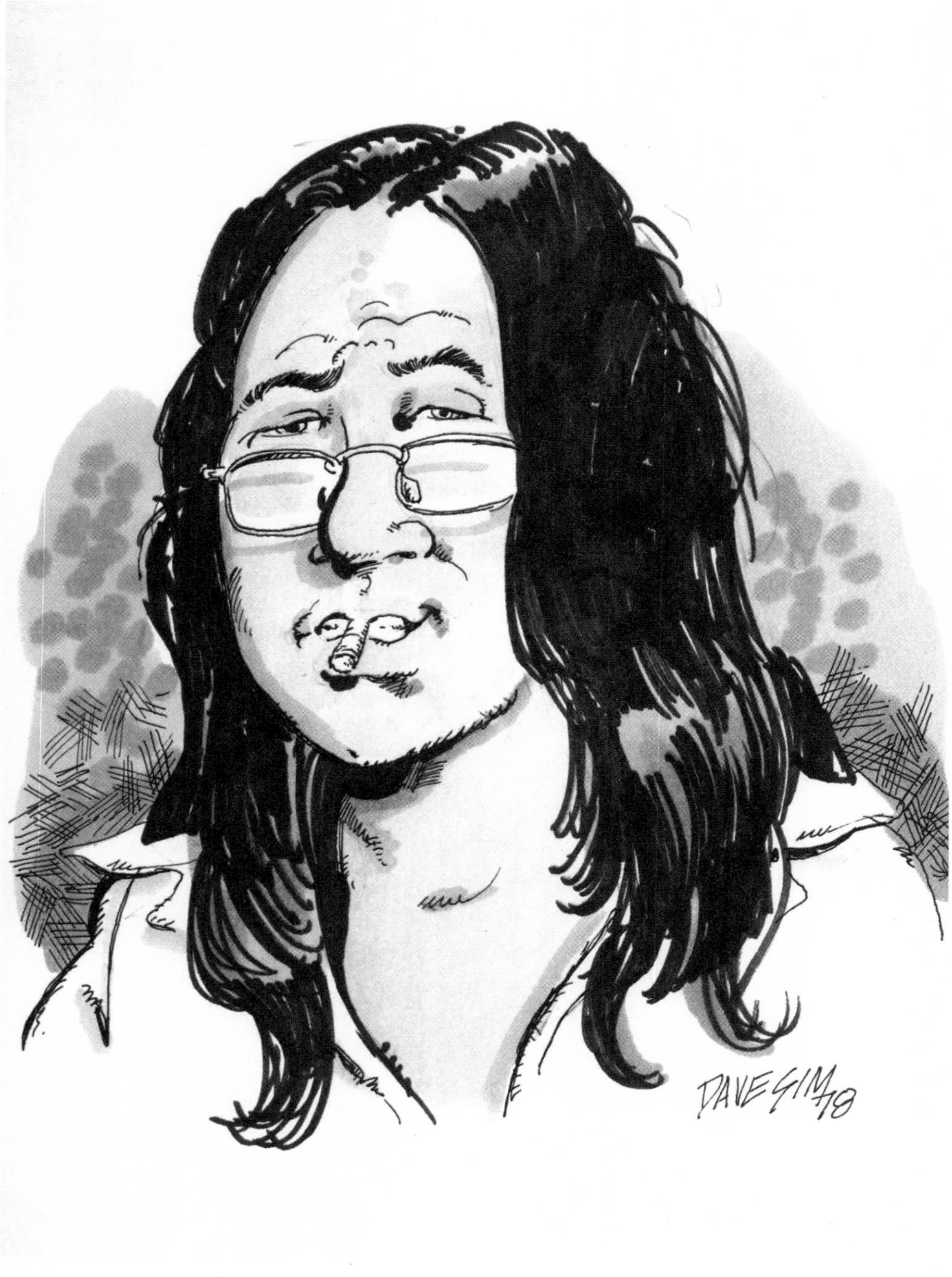
DAVE SIM 78

Portrait of Gene Day, Borealis *No. 1 (Summer 1978). Art by Dave Sim. Copyright © Dave Sim.*

Contents

CANADA, AS A NATION, DOESN'T SEEM VERY INTERESTED IN ITS POPULAR CULTURE.

Don't get me wrong. Canadians are very interested in popular culture in general; it's just that most of the interest seems to be directed south. This becomes very apparent whenever you try to research anything about Canada's pop-culture history. It's hard to find even the basic facts. Most of the time you have nothing but the actual source material to go on. It's surprising how often you discover that no one has ever written a word on the subject. This isn't a problem you're likely to encounter in the United States. No matter how obscure or ephemeral the subject might be, you inevitably find some oddball who has dug up every fact and figure about it. A short trip through American pop culture on the Internet will easily prove this point.

Why is this? That's not an easy question to answer. The most obvious guess would be that Canadians have assumed their own media culture is second-rate, and therefore they direct their interest to the American juggernaut for quality entertainment. Truthfully, much of Canada's junk culture has been just that — second-rate junk — though certainly much of the material crossing the border isn't usually much higher on the quality scale. I might even hazard a guess that Canada has produced as much quality material as the United States (based on some kind of ratio of quality/population chart that I'm incapable of producing).

If you actually take the time to look back over the interesting pile of magazines, television shows, movies, records, comic books, et cetera, that Canadians have produced in the past hundred years, you'll find there is a surprising amount of striking material — a real mix of the great, the clever, the beautiful, and the odd. Of course, you'll also find plenty of the mediocre, the dimwitted, and the down-right embarrassing. The wonderful part of all this material, though, is that it's *ours*. It was made by Canadians for Canadians. It speaks to us when it is brilliant, but it also speaks to us when it is poor.

That alone is a good reason for this book to exist. Here in these pages you will find a doorway into our popular history that has largely gone undocumented. John Bell has taken the time and effort to dig up these dusty, forgotten comic books and figure out their complicated and confusing history. It's fascinating stuff. And it is information that even the most rabid of Canada's comic-book fans know nothing about. They have spent their lives focused on Batman and Spider-Man, hardly realizing that several generations of Canadian cartoonists lived and died here and left behind an interesting body of work. Much of that work is charming and much of it is slight, but some of it rises above its pulpy charms to give us a glimpse of something truly artful.

If this book needs another reason for existing, then its focus on Chester Brown will do. Chester Brown is without doubt one of the most important writers (or artists) in any of Canada's art forms. I have no doubt that time will prove me correct in this prediction, and I am gratified that John Bell obviously thinks so, too.

In the end, I am simply happy to see all this information set down in one place. John Bell has been gathering this information for ages, and though this isn't his first effort to get it out into the world, it seems likely that this book is its most permanent form. Within these pages you will find the names of hard-working artists who seem-ingly left behind nothing but yellowed and ignored piles of paper. John has toiled hard for years to bring these papers and the people who made them back out into the light of day again. I thank him for that.

Seth
July 2006
Guelph, Ontario

NUMEROUS PEOPLE HAVE GENEROUSLY ASSISTED WITH THE PREPARATION OF *INVADERS FROM THE NORTH: How Canada Conquered the Comic Book Universe* and/or with my earlier study of Canadian comics, *Canuck Comics: A Guide to Comic Books Published in Canada* (1986), which served as the primary starting point for this expanded exploration of the graphic-narrative tradition in English Canada.[1]

First of all, I want to thank Seth (Gregory Gallant) for kindly agreeing to prepare a foreword and Dave Cooper for generously providing a cover image. It is very gratifying to have two of Canada's leading masters of comic art associated with this project.

I next want to acknowledge the help that I received from the following individuals: George Allanson, Mark Askwith, Cheryl Avery, Donald A. Baird, Loretta Barber, Les Barker (aka Leo Bachle), Charity Bell, Nicholas Bell, Stanley Berneche, Peter Birkemoe, Barry Blair, Jacques Boivin, David Boswell, Omer Boudreau, Jim Brennan, Michel Brisebois, Jane Britton, Chester Brown, Jim Burant, Leo Burdak, the late Jim Burke (aka T.M. Maple), Chris Butcher, John Robert Colombo, Richard Comely, Jim Craig, Peter Dako, Jeffrey R. Darcey, Dave Darrigo, Dan Day, the late Gene Day, Peter DeLottinville, Gordon Derry, Jennifer Devine, Frank Dobson, Harlan Ellison, Judith Enright, Terry Fletcher, Neil Forsyth, Fiona Foster, Hal Foster, Pierre Fournier, the late Honourable E.D. Fulton, Richard Furness, Dave Geary, Kathy Hall, Peter Hansen, the late George Henderson, Greg Holfeld, Harry Holman, Robert Hough, Jane Howard, Robert Hunter, Christopher Hutsul, Robert Inwood, Calum Johnston, Paul Kowtiuk, Lord Larry, Hope Larson, Phil Latter, Edward Letkeman, Stephen Lipson, Adam

11

McCarron, the late Owen McCarron, Brad Mackay, Trevor W. McKeown, Paul MacKinnon, John MacLeod, Bob MacMillan, Frank McTruck (MacNichol), Vincent Marchesano, Bill Marks, Jamie Martin, Henry Mietkiewicz, Bernie Mireault, Gabriel Morrissette, Carol Mound, Dawn Munroe, Susan North, Chris Oliveros, Owen Oulton, Bill Pelletier, Robert Pincombe, Luc Pomerleau, the late George M. Rae, Dianne Reid, Su Rogers, Harland Ronning, Charles R. Saunders, Mark Shainblum, Dave Sim, J. David Spurlock, Jon Stables, Ken Steacy, Geoffrey Stirling, Scott Stirling, Paul Stockton, Doug Sulipa, Ron Sutton, Jeffrey Taylor, Roy Thomas, Colin Upton, Charles Spain Verral, Michel Viau, James Waley, Kirk Wallace, Randall Ware, and Leonard S. Wong.

I would also like to thank the many staff members of Library and Archives Canada who have provided assistance to me during more than two decades of comics-related research.

As well, I want to acknowledge my debt to the groundbreaking fan writers who were active in the Canadian comics field during the 1970–1974 period, especially Ralph Alfonso, John Balge, Cliff Letovsky, Larry Mitchell, and Dave Sim.

Finally, I would like to express my gratitude to the multitude of largely unsung artists, writers, and publishers who struggled, mostly at the margins of Canadian culture and often against formidable obstacles, to create Canadian comics. Hopefully, *Invaders from the North* will contribute to an appreciation of the rich comic-art heritage that is their legacy.

Introduction

Introduction

The first comic books appeared in 1935. Not having anything connected or literary about them, and being as difficult to read as The Book of Kells, *they caught on with the young.*[1]

— Marshall McLuhan

In book or periodical illustration, art enhances what is essentially a textual narrative. The comics medium, in contrast, combines words and pictures (usually in sequential strips of panels) to create a unique form of storytelling — graphic narrative. According to the noted Canadian artist Harold Town, who contributed to comic books during his youth in the 1940s, this hybrid art form represents an "ultimate form of communication."[2] Certainly, for most of the twentieth century, comics proved to be an immensely popular medium, one that held a special appeal for children and young adults.[3]

In the best comics, text is used with great economy, almost in a poetic fashion, so that much of the story is told visually, with the narrative flow between panels being completed by the reader (for this reason, Canadian communications scholar Marshall McLuhan identified comics as a cool, "participational" medium).[4] Creators shape their narratives — creating dramatic effects or changing mood or pace — through the manipulation of basic design elements such as lighting, perspective, panel and page layout, lettering, and the placement of dialogue (usually within word "balloons"). This marriage of art and text in a singular visual syntax (one that can sometimes be very challenging to the uninitiated) represents a delicate balance and demands considerable unity between the writer and artist. As a result, many of the most successful comic strips and books have been produced by a single creator acting in both roles.[5]

English Canadian comic books first appeared in 1941. Since that time, Canada's comics creators have sought to sustain a national vision within the graphic-narrative medium. This goal has proven to be difficult. Comic-book artists and writers in English Canada have had to contend not only with the pervasive influence of American comics, but also, at times, with powerful forces of censorship.

Although comic books first emerged as an ephemeral form of entertainment for children, today the best Canadian graphic-narrative creators are struggling, often in the face of considerable disdain on the part of mainstream critics and cultural historians, to establish an adult art form of lasting significance. To a considerable degree, they are succeeding. Canadian comics creators are now at the forefront of current graphic-narrative practice, challenging the long-established boundaries between high and low culture. However, despite the considerable achievements of Canada's comics artists, the English Canadian contribution to the comics medium remains decidedly under-explored.[6] *Invaders from the North: How Canada Conquered the Comic Book Universe* is intended to counteract this neglect by providing the most sustained examination of English Canada's comics heritage that has been offered to date.

This book traces the development of comic books in English Canada from their evolution out of earlier forms of cartooning and graphic narrative through to the cutting-edge, internationally renowned comics of artists such as Dave Sim, Chester Brown, Julie Doucet, Seth (Gregory Gallant), and Dave Cooper.[7] In so doing, it sheds considerable light on the multi-faceted relationship between Canadian comics and American comic-book publishing. The book also includes two in-depth studies, or spotlights, one focusing on the somewhat quixotic search for distinctly Canadian superheroes, and the other examining Chester Brown's instrumental role in pushing Canadian graphic narrative well beyond adolescent fantasies of super-heroism.

It is hoped that *Invaders from the North* will inspire a new awareness of English Canada's contribution to the field of comics, particularly in the area of comic books. However, even if this book succeeds in this goal, it is obvious that more work remains to be done in order to create a full picture of the development of Canadian comic art. (This is especially true of the history of Canadian comic strips, which is only touched upon in a brief manner.)

An increasing number of English Canadian academic researchers are already beginning to investigate various facets of comics history, particularly gender and legal issues relating to

Page 67 of Palooka-Ville *No. 18 (2006). Art by Seth. Copyright © Seth (Gregory Gallant) and Drawn & Quarterly.*

Introduction

Canada's role in the anti-comics moral panic of the 1950s. To a large degree, this new attention derives from the realization that comics, like other forms of popular culture such as radio, the pulps, television, film, and the new media, represent a kind of cultural barometer, documenting social attitudes and values. By offering a window on cultural development during various eras, comics serve as valuable artifacts of change.

This growing scholarly interest in comics history might eventually lead to a greater recognition that comics are much more than mere social documents and that the medium is, in fact, a rich field of potential study not only for social historians, but also for art, literary, and cultural historians. Certainly, the more one studies graphic narrative, the more apparent it becomes that the medium deserves to be examined as a powerful art form in its own right, albeit one that has experienced a sometimes difficult and contested evolution.

Of Brownies and Doo Dads: The Precursors, 1849–1928

1

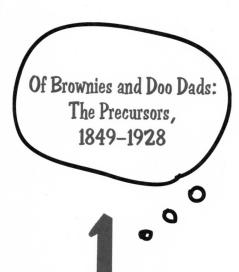

ALTHOUGH THERE ARE MANY EARLY EXAMPLES THROUGHOUT THE WORLD OF WHAT MIGHT BE CALLED GRAPHIC narrative (including, it could be argued, cave paintings and Egyptian hieroglyphics), the first serial cartoons and comic strips began to appear in Europe in the latter part of the eighteenth century and continued to flourish in various forms throughout the nineteenth century (two of the most notable early masters were Rodolphe Töppfer and Wilhelm Busch), first in Europe and then North America. The modern American newspaper strip emerged in the 1890s, and though the precise birth of the U.S. comic strip is difficult to pinpoint due to the fact that its formal conventions (including sequential panels, word balloons, continuing characters, and colour printing) evolved over several years, its origin is most often associated with Richard Felton Outcault's *Hogan's Alley* (later *The Yellow Kid*), which debuted in New York City's *World* newspaper in 1895. However, one can argue that at least two other comics features of the period, James Swinnerton's *The Little Bears* (first called *California Bears*), which appeared in the *San Francisco Examiner* starting in 1892, and Rudolf Dirks's *Katzenjammer Kids*, which was launched in the Sunday supplement of the *New York Journal* in 1897, contributed equally to the form's initial development.

Whatever the case, numerous rival strips soon followed as U.S. newspapers fiercely competed for the growing readership of children and adults drawn to the appealing new art form.[1] English Canadian comic art began to appear not long after and can be viewed, at least in part, as an outgrowth of a distinguished national tradition of political cartooning.

Canadian cartooning started in earnest with the publication in 1849 at Montreal,

1

Cover of Laurier Does Things, Book 2, *a very rare proto-comic issued by the Liberal Party during the Canadian federal election of 1904. Art by an unknown cartoonist.*

Quebec, of John Henry Walker's weekly *Punch in Canada.* Modelled after its famous British namesake, Walker's paper featured cartoons by its multi-talented editor and publisher. Although the periodical was short-lived, it paved the way for a host of similar nineteenth-century journals of humour and satire such as *The Jester, The Grumbler, Grinchuckle,* and *Diogenes.* Most of these papers did not last long, and certainly none approached the success of the country's leading Victorian periodical, the somewhat more staid *Canadian Illustrated News.* Inaugurated in Montreal in 1869, the *News* showcased the work of numerous documentary artists and cartoonists. One of the publication's best early illustrators was the Frenchman Edward Jump, who specialized in finely rendered caricatures of political luminaries. Jump worked at the paper from 1871 until 1873 when he left for the United States, where he apparently committed suicide some years later.[2]

At the same time that Jump was gently lampooning the nation's leaders, a reporter at Toronto's *Globe,* John Wilson Bengough, launched a cartoon weekly entitled *Grip* on May 24, 1873. Luckily for him, the federal Conservative government was soon rocked by the railway-related Pacific Scandal, and Bengough's irreverent periodical was able to exploit the public's growing appetite for a satirical perspective on political shenanigans in Ottawa. The first major English Canadian humour magazine, *Grip* survived for twenty-two years.[3]

While Bengough was probably the most important and prolific cartoonist in Canada before 1900, Henri Julien, who began contributing to *Canadian Illustrated News* and its French edition, *L'Opinion Publique,* in 1874, was unquestionably the most accomplished. Also a noted illustrator, he worked for the leading Canadian journals of his day, as well as for international periodicals such as *Harper's, Century, Le Monde illustré,* and *The Graphic.* In 1888, Julien became the first full-time newspaper cartoonist in the country when the *Montreal Star* hired him as its chief artist. He held the position for two decades.[4]

The only Canadian who rivalled Julien during this period was Palmer Cox, an expatriate. Born near Granby, Quebec, in 1840, Cox moved to the United States, where he became a regular contributor to *St. Nicholas Magazine* and the creator of the Brownies children's characters. Cox's cartoon pixies soon became phenomenally popular. In fact, the first collection of Brownies stories, *The Brownies, Their Book* (1887), sold more than a million copies. Eventually, the Brownies also appeared in a wide array of commercial products such as toys, china, and trade cards. They even lent their name to a new, inexpensive Kodak camera, the famous Brownie, intended to bring photography to the masses.

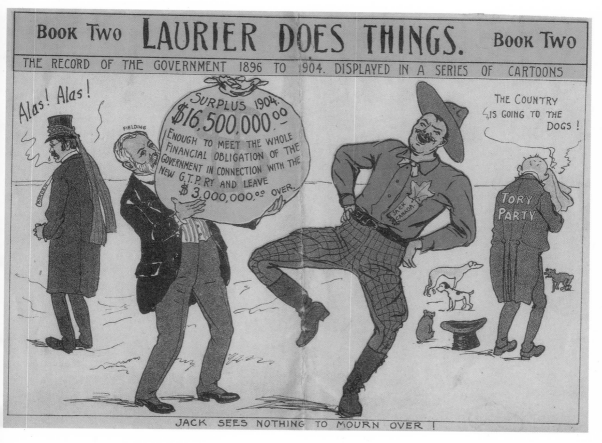

BOOK TWO **LAURIER DOES THINGS.** BOOK TWO

THE RECORD OF THE GOVERNMENT 1896 TO 1904. DISPLAYED IN A SERIES OF CARTOONS

Alas! Alas!

FIELDING

SURPLUS 1904.
$16,500,000.00
ENOUGH TO MEET THE WHOLE FINANCIAL OBLIGATION OF THE GOVERNMENT IN CONNECTION WITH THE NEW G.T.P. RY AND LEAVE $3,000,000.00 OVER.

THE COUNTRY IS GOING TO THE DOGS!

JACK CANADA

TORY PARTY

JACK SEES NOTHING TO MOURN OVER!

Even though the Brownies narratives produced during the late 1880s and the 1890s combined cartoon images with text (poetry), the characters' illustrated adventures did not quite constitute comic art; however, they did later appear in their own spinoff newspaper comic strip, drawn and written by Cox. This *Brownies* strip, which was published from about 1898 to 1907, was one of the earliest examples of non-political comic art by an English Canadian cartoonist (during this same period several French Canadian artists contributed strips to the French-language newspapers *La Presse* and *La Patrie*), though it was only in the last year or so of the strip that Cox actually utilized word balloons. By this time, the artist had returned to Granby, where he lived in his Brownie Castle until his death in 1924.[5]

Another important Quebec cartoonist of the era was Arthur G. Racey, Henri Julien's eventual successor at the *Montreal Star*. Racey produced a memorable series of immigration-related entitled *The Englishman in Canada*. In addition, he contributed to *The Moon*, an influential illustrated humour magazine that debuted in Toronto in 1901.[6] At about the same time the artist J.B. Fitzmaurice initiated his career at Vancouver's *Daily Province*. Fitzmaurice, whose cartoons were often

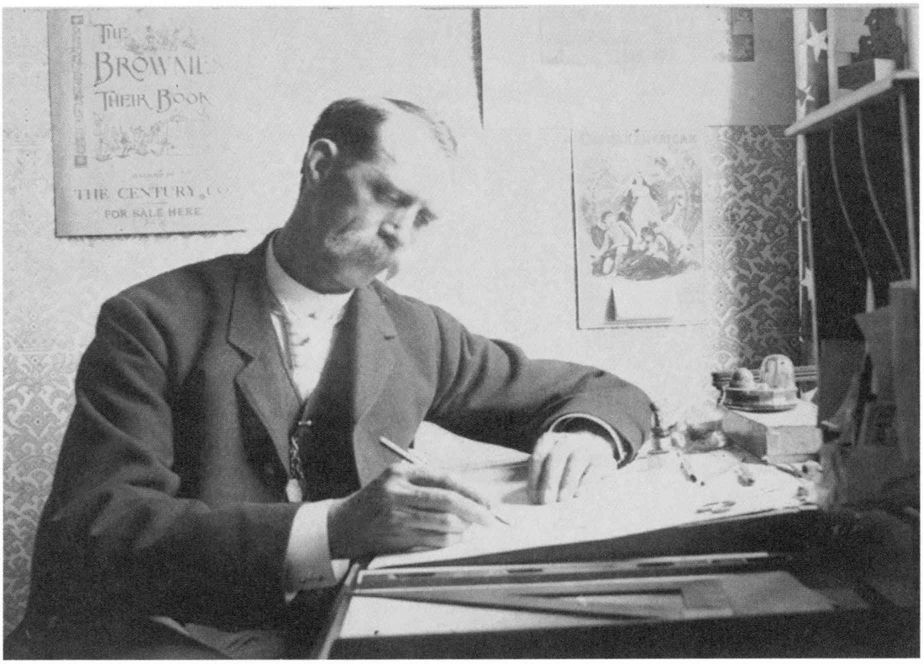
FOR SALE HERE

Cartoonist Palmer Cox drawing the Brownies, circa 1905. Photo courtesy of the website www.freemasonry.bcy.ca/brownies.

Facing page: A colour plate (representing the month of January) from Palmer Cox's Brownie Year Book *(1895). Art by Palmer Cox.*

executed in a comic-strip style (with narrative sustained through several panels or serial cartoons), can be counted among the earliest Canadian comic artists.[7]

A contemporary of Racey's and Fitzmaurice's was Bob Edwards, who launched one of the nation's most irreverent papers, *The Calgary Eye-Opener*, in 1902. While Edwards served as the *Eye-Opener*'s first cartoonist, he later wisely hired professional artists such as Donald McRitchie and Charles H. Forrester. Both the paper and its legendary founder died in 1922.[8] However, eight years later, a somewhat racier version of the publication appeared in the United States. Its art director (and later de facto editor) was a young American cartoonist named Carl Barks, who later worked for Disney, becoming the main Donald Duck comic-book artist and the creator of Uncle Scrooge and many other beloved comic-book characters. Interestingly, Barks later set some of his most memorable Donald Duck adventure stories in Canada.[9] (After Barks's retirement, the Disney duck stories were continued by a number of artists, including the Canadian William Van Horn and his son, Noel.)

By the middle of the first decade of the twentieth century, comic-strip art was still in its infancy in Canada, but nonetheless it was emerging as a lively new art form. During the next two decades, it continued to develop gradually. In English Canada, its growth was shaped by the American newspaper syndicates that dominated the medium. In fact, for many years most aspiring English Canadian comic-strip artists were obliged to pursue their dreams

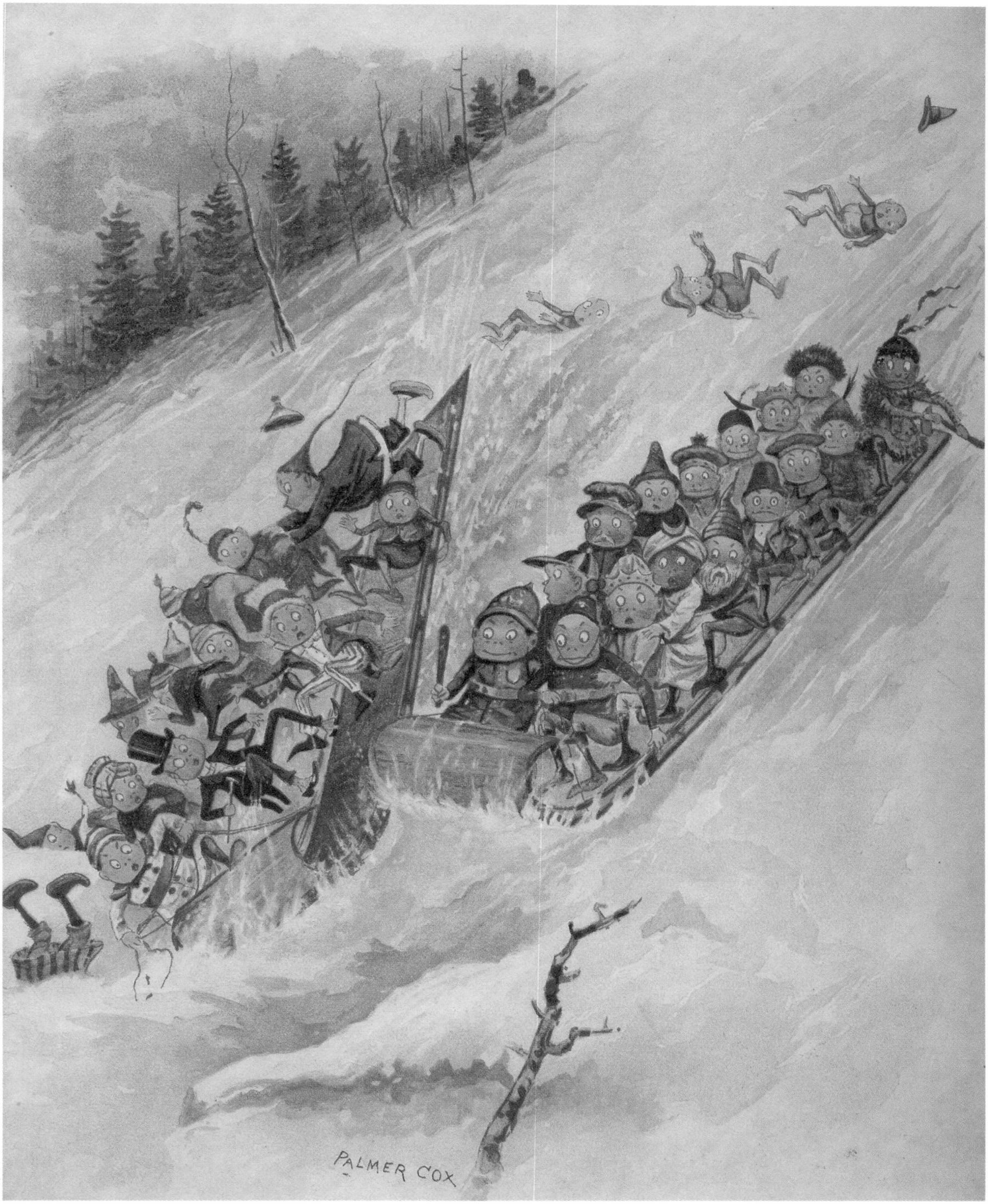
PALMER COX

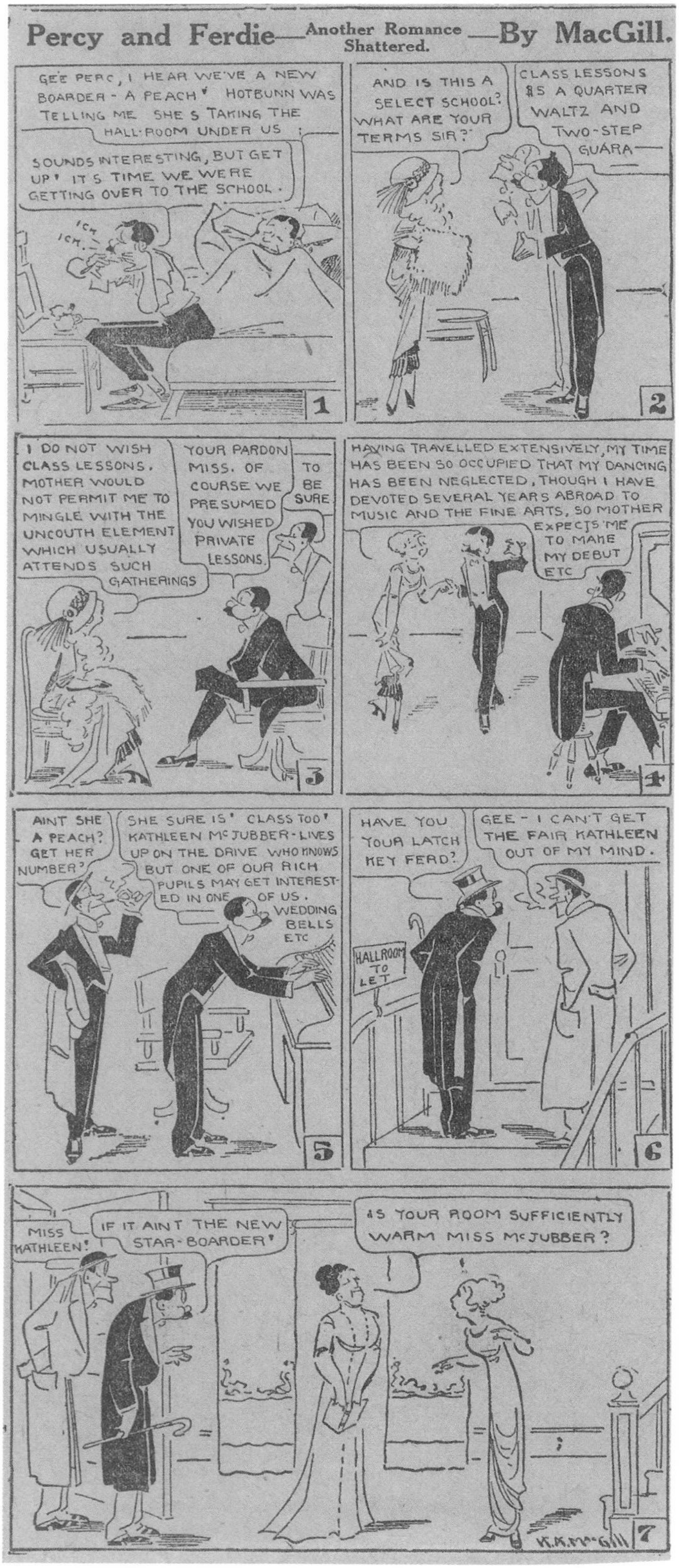
Percy and Ferdie—Another Romance Shattered.—By MacGill.
GEE PERC, I HEAR WE'VE A NEW BOARDER - A PEACH! HOTBUNN WAS TELLING ME SHE'S TAKING THE HALL-ROOM UNDER US :
SOUNDS INTERESTING, BUT GET UP! IT'S TIME WE WERE GETTING OVER TO THE SCHOOL.
ICH ICH.
1
AND IS THIS A SELECT SCHOOL? WHAT ARE YOUR TERMS SIR?
CLASS LESSONS $5 A QUARTER WALTZ AND TWO-STEP GUARA—
2
I DO NOT WISH CLASS LESSONS. MOTHER WOULD NOT PERMIT ME TO MINGLE WITH THE UNCOUTH ELEMENT WHICH USUALLY ATTENDS SUCH GATHERINGS
YOUR PARDON MISS. OF COURSE WE PRESUMED YOU WISHED PRIVATE LESSONS.
TO BE SURE
3
HAVING TRAVELLED EXTENSIVELY, MY TIME HAS BEEN SO OCCUPIED THAT MY DANCING HAS BEEN NEGLECTED, THOUGH I HAVE DEVOTED SEVERAL YEARS ABROAD TO MUSIC AND THE FINE ARTS, SO MOTHER EXPECTS ME TO MAKE MY DEBUT ETC
4
AINT SHE A PEACH? GET HER NUMBER?
SHE SURE IS! CLASS TOO! KATHLEEN M^c JUBBER - LIVES UP ON THE DRIVE WHO KNOWS BUT ONE OF OUR RICH PUPILS MAY GET INTEREST-ED IN ONE OF US. WEDDING BELLS ETC
5
HAVE YOU YOUR LATCH KEY FERD?
GEE - I CAN'T GET THE FAIR KATHLEEN OUT OF MY MIND.
HALLROOM TO LET
6
MISS KATHLEEN!
IF IT AINT THE NEW STAR-BOARDER!
IS YOUR ROOM SUFFICIENTLY WARM MISS M^c JUBBER?
7

south of the border. Consequently, for a time, the main centres of comic art by English Canadians were New York City and Chicago.

Palmer Cox and several Canadian political cartoonists flirted with comic-strip narratives at the turn of the century, but the cartoonist Harold A. MacGill, a Nova Scotian who had moved from his native province to New York, was probably the first English Canadian to work full-time as a comic-strip artist. In 1904, MacGill shifted from political cartooning and turned his attention to newspaper strips, most of which depicted the lives of young workers in the big city. The most popular of these creations, *The Hall-Room Boys* (later retitled *Percy and Ferdie*), first appeared in 1906 and ran for several years before it was collected in book form in 1921 by the noted American comic-strip reprint publisher Cupples and Leon. The strip also inspired a series of short silent films, which were produced by Jack Cohn and starred Sid Smith and Jimmy Adams. The Hall-Room Boys even appeared in their own "Tijuana Bible" (the name given to pirated, cheaply produced eight-page pornographic comics featuring well-known comic-strip characters).[10]

Not long after MacGill's initial success in the United States, an American-born cartoonist who grew up in Canada, Russell Patterson, placed a strip, *Pierre et Pierrette*, with the Montreal paper *La Patrie*. Rejected by the Canadian army at

Facing page: Percy and Ferdie *daily strip (December 12, 1910). Art by Harold A. MacGill.*

the outbreak of World War I, he moved to Chicago, where he became a leading U.S. illustrator and sometime comic-strip artist.[11]

In 1912 another contributor to *La Patrie*, Raoul Barré, a Quebecker then based in New York City, created a strip called *Noah's Ark* for the McClure Syndicate. The following year Barré (who is known in the United States as "Barre") contributed a French-language version of the strip to the Quebec City paper *La Patrie*. Barré's activities as a cartoonist soon ceased, however, as he shifted his attention to film animation, a field in which he became a leading pioneer. In 1914 in New York City, he opened the first true animation studio, where he introduced numerous innovations. Although Barré stopped working on his own newspaper strips, he did produce animated shorts based on Bud Fisher's popular *Mutt and Jeff* strip. In fact, Barré sold his studio to Fisher in 1917.[12]

Another political cartoonist who made the transition to comic art was Arch Dale. While working freelance for both the *Winnipeg Free Press* and the *Grain-Grower's Guide*, he created a comic strip featuring Brownie-like characters called the Doo Dads. After moving to Chicago in 1921, Dale was able to arrange for his strip to be syndicated in more than fifty newspapers throughout North America. Eventually, however, Dale resumed political cartooning in Canada, and *The Doo Dads* strip was largely forgotten. (Dale also worked briefly in 1926 on a strip entitled *Adventures of Dicky Dare*.)[13]

During his time in Chicago, Dale was replaced at the *Grain-Grower's Guide* by Charles Thorson, who also hoped to become a comic-strip artist. Thorson's major comics project, *Cap'n Bill's Fantastic Tales*, did not meet with success, but the artist did eventually make his mark in a related field — animation, where he emerged as an important character designer and worked at most of the major U.S. animation studios, including Walt Disney and Metro-Goldwyn-Mayer. One of Thorson's close friends at Disney was Walt Kelly who, as the creator of *Pogo*, later became a world-famous comic-strip artist. In an interview in 1950, Kelly claimed that he "owed everything to my sainted mother and Charlie Thorson." Today Thorson is probably best remembered as the first artist to design Bugs Bunny.[14]

Unlike MacGill, Patterson, and Dale, who pursued their comic-art careers in the United States, Toronto artist Jimmy Frise was able in 1921 to sell a strip, *Life's Little Comedies*, to the *Star Weekly*, a weekend supplement to the *Toronto Star*. Frise, who was one of Ernest Hemingway's drinking and fishing companions during the latter's Toronto years, soon retitled the strip *Birdseye Centre*, which became the longest-running comic strip ever published in English Canada.[15] After appearing in the *Star Weekly* for twenty-six years, the strip was lured away in 1947 by the *Montreal Standard,* where it was featured in colour with a new title: *Juniper Junction.* The strip also enjoyed a limited degree of syndication prior to Frise's death in 1948. *Juniper Junction* was continued by Doug Wright, who became one of Canada's best post-war comic-strip artists.[16]

The same year that Frise began *Life's Little Comedies,* the humour magazine *The Goblin* was launched in Toronto. During the Roaring Twenties, it featured a number of talented cartoonists, including artists such as Richard Taylor ("Ric") and Lou Skuce, who also drew comic strips. Taylor, a sometime contributor to the Communist Party of Canada paper *The Worker,* later became one of the greatest *New Yorker* cartoonists.[17]

This same era also witnessed the emergence of the Canadian-born cartoonist John Robert Williams, whose family left his native Nova Scotia not long after his birth. In 1922, Williams's single-panel cartoon series about rural and small-town life, *Out Our Way,* was syndicated by the Newspaper Enterprise Association. The cartoon quickly met with success and was soon followed by a Sunday comic strip, *Out Our Way, with the Willits.* At the height of its popularity, *Out Our Way* appeared in more than 700 newspapers. The cartoon series ran for more than fifty years, even outliving its creator, who died in 1957. (Recently, the Ottawa-based publisher Algrove Publishing reissued *The Bull of the Woods,* a well-regarded collection of Williams's cartoons based on his experiences as a machinist.)[18]

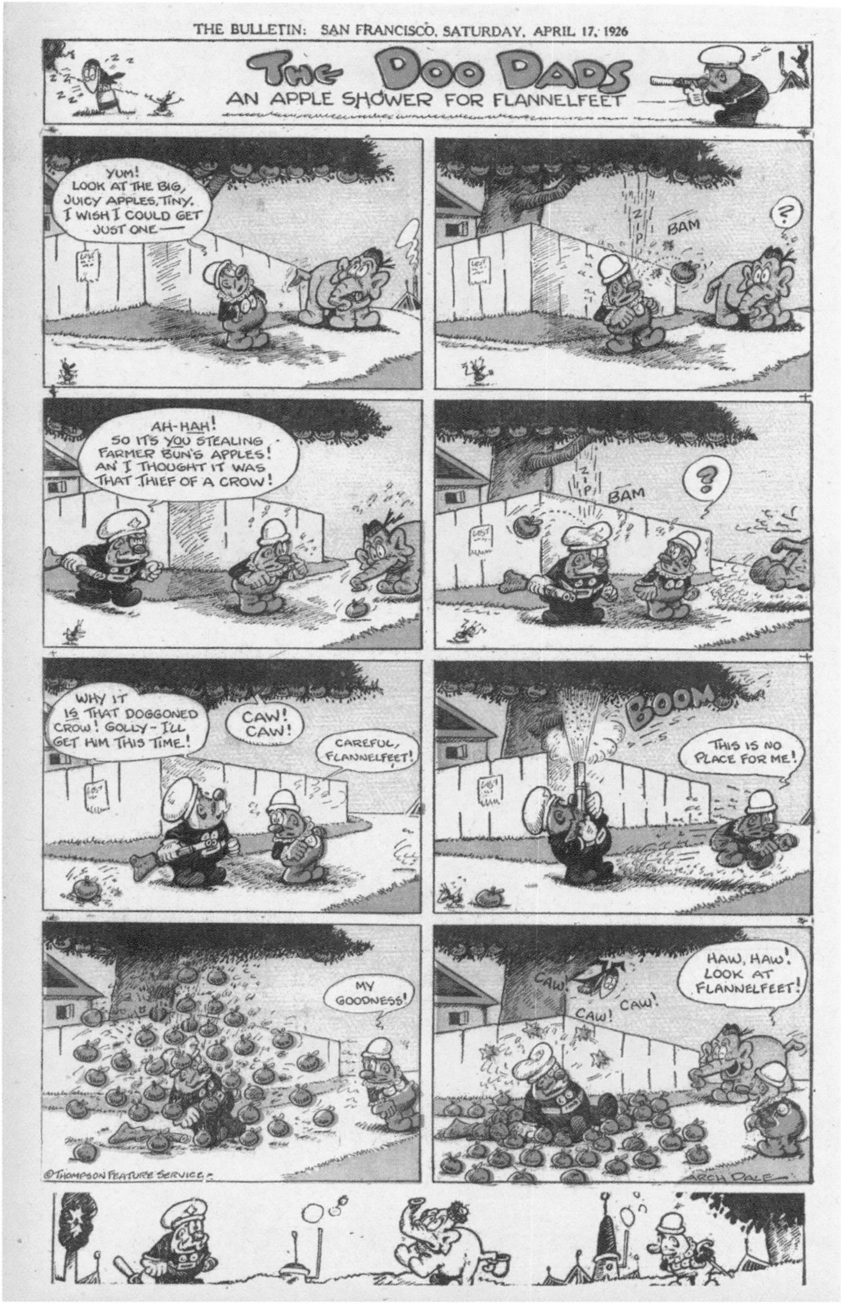
THE BULLETIN: SAN FRANCISCO, SATURDAY, APRIL 17, 1926
THE DOO DADS
AN APPLE SHOWER FOR FLANNELFEET
YUM! LOOK AT THE BIG, JUICY APPLES, TINY. I WISH I COULD GET JUST ONE —
ZIP
BAM
?
AH-HAH! SO IT'S YOU STEALING FARMER BUN'S APPLES! AN' I THOUGHT IT WAS THAT THIEF OF A CROW!
ZIP
BAM
?
WHY IT IS THAT DOGGONED CROW! GOLLY - I'LL GET HIM THIS TIME!
CAW! CAW!
CAREFUL, FLANNELFEET!
BOOM
THIS IS NO PLACE FOR ME!
MY GOODNESS!
© THOMPSON FEATURE SERVICE
CAW!
CAW!
CAW!
HAW, HAW! LOOK AT FLANNELFEET!
ARCH DALE

The Doo Dads *Sunday page, which in this case appeared on a Saturday (April 17, 1926). Art by Arch Dale. Copyright © estate of Arch Dale.*

1

2

Up, Up, and Away:
Dawn of the Comic Book,
1929–1940

By the late 1920s, North American newspaper comic strips — the "funnies" — were an established popular art form, and one, by this point, quite distinct from political and gag cartooning. However, not everyone welcomed the emergence of this new mass entertainment. For instance, the noted Canadian critic and academic Archibald MacMechan decried the pervasiveness of comic strips: "We cannot even invent our own vulgarity," he complained. "The American comic supplement curses the country from the Atlantic to the Pacific. They should all be burnt by the common hangman."[1] Although it would offer little solace to cultural elitists — and nationalists — like MacMechan, the U.S. comics were about to change.

With the advent of the Great Depression, newspaper publishers quickly recognized the public's need for inexpensive escapist entertainment, something the comics could readily deliver. The year 1929 saw the appearance of *Buck Rogers* and *Tarzan*, the first non-humour strips devoted to adventure narratives.[2] The latter strip was drawn by Harold Foster, a native of Halifax, Nova Scotia, who had worked as a catalogue illustrator for both Eaton's and the Hudson's Bay Company before departing for the United States in 1921.[3] These two groundbreaking strips were eventually followed by such adventure classics as *Dick Tracy*, *Flash Gordon*, and *Prince Valiant*. The last strip, set in Arthurian England, was written and drawn by the expatriate Foster and was soon recognized as a masterpiece of comic art. The emergence of the adventure strips meant that comics would no longer be confined to a single genre, even though they would still be frequently referred to as the "funnies."

In 1933, Toronto's *Telegram* began publishing a comic strip entitled *Men of*

Facing page: Brian Kane's critically acclaimed, award-winning biography of Hal Foster, published by Vanguard Productions in 2003, is the first full-scale study devoted to a Canadian comics creator. Copyright © Vanguard Productions.

the Mounted, which drew upon one of the true mainstays of adventure fiction, radio, and film: the intrepid and iconic Mountie bent on bringing justice to the untamed North.[4] Written by Ted McCall and drawn by Harry Hall, *Men of the Mounted* was significant not only because it was the first indigenous adventure strip, but also as a result of its eventual connection with the early Canadian comic-book publisher Anglo-American. The strip was well received and was eventually featured in several Big Little Books and in a set of trading cards issued by Willard's Chocolates of Toronto. Despite this measure of success, McCall's efforts to arrange for international syndication for *Men of the Mounted* were rebuffed. As a result, he abandoned the strip early in 1935, the same year the widely syndicated U.S. strip *King of the Mounted* was launched.[5]

A few months later McCall inaugurated a second strip, *Robin Hood and Company*, illustrated by Charles R. Snelgrove. This time McCall managed to find a syndicate, and *Robin Hood* appeared in Canadian, American, and even some European papers. (Among the strip's most ardent fans was a young Robert Fulford, who eventually became one of Canada's leading critics. "At age five," he later recalled, "my central motive in learning to read was my desire to understand daily strips, in particular 'Robin Hood,' without the intercession of parents or older siblings.") Late in 1939, following Snelgrove's death, the strip went on a brief hiatus as McCall rushed to find a replacement artist. *Robin Hood* eventually resumed publication early in 1940, with art by Syd Stein. Later that year, however, Stein joined the army, putting an end to what was then English Canada's only adventure strip.[6]

Up, Up, and Away: Dawn of the Comic Book, 1929–1940

In addition to new themes, the 1930s witnessed the emergence of a new form of comics. The newspaper comic strip, which had grown out of the political-cartooning tradition, would now, in turn, give birth to a new type of graphic narrative — the comic book. Starting with the U.S. publication *Funnies on Parade* in 1933, a number of entrepreneurs experimented with these new periodicals.[7] Although most of the publishers of the early comics magazines were American, the field did include one Canadian — Windsor, Ontario, businessman Jake Geller. Inspired by the success of *The Funny Wonder and Jester* and other British comics papers, which had been available for several years in so-called overseas editions on some Canadian newsstands, Geller acquired the rights to a few U.K. strips, opened an office in New York, and began publishing a comics weekly entitled *Comic Cuts* (named after one of Britain's most famous comics periodicals). Launched in May 1934, the tabloid lasted for only nine issues (today it counts among the rarest comics publications ever issued in North America).

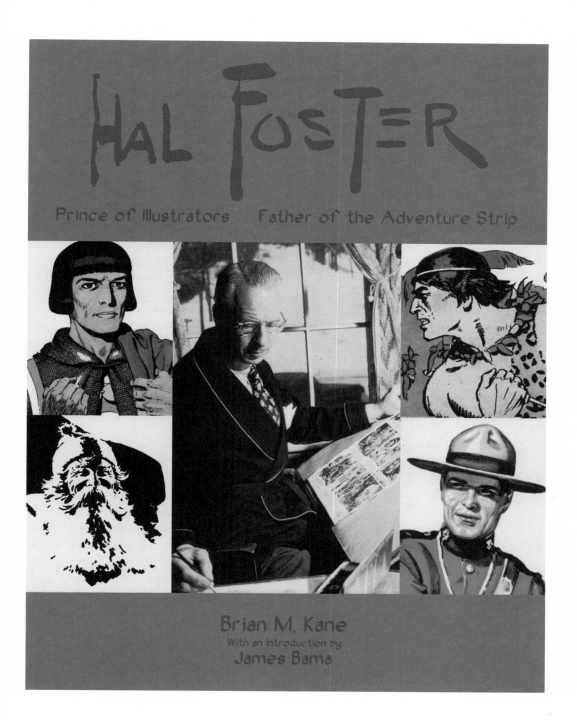

HAL FOSTER

Prince of Illustrators   Father of the Adventure Strip

Brian M. Kane

With an Introduction by
James Bama

Facing page:
Rare trading cards
featuring panels
from the Men of
the Mounted strip,
issued circa 1934.
Art by Harry Hall.
Copyright © estate
of Ted McCall.

**Up, Up, and Away:
Dawn of the Comic
Book, 1929–1940**

Discouraged by the poor reception of *Comic Cuts*, Geller returned to Canada. He would soon regret his departure from the fledgling New York comic-book milieu, which was about to be rocked by the improbable, heroic visions of a young Canadian artist.[8]

The early comics magazines had, for the most part, reprinted U.S. newspaper strips, but increasingly, through 1936 and 1937, more non-reprint titles appeared. At the outset the new comic books were only moderately successful, but their popularity increased dramatically following the release, with a cover date of June 1938, of *Action Comics* No. 1, which featured the adventures of Superman. The first significant comic-book superhero, Superman was co-created by Jerry Siegel and Toronto-born Joe Shuster (the cousin of Canadian comedian Frank Shuster of the noted comedy team of Wayne and Shuster), two young, Cleveland-based science-fiction fans.[9] Although it is now obvious that Superman and comic books were made for each other, the potential of the character was not immediately recognized. In fact, beginning in 1934, the strip was rejected by numerous publishers due to its unrealistic nature. Even the eventual publisher of the character, Harry Donenfeld of National Periodical Publications (later DC), is reputed to have been nervous about the outrageous cover of the debut issue of *Action*, which depicted Superman holding a car above his head![10]

To say the least, Donenfeld's doubts, if any, proved to be unfounded, and *Action* was soon followed by a flood of American superhero comics, which found a huge audience in both the United States and Canada. One of the young Canadians who eagerly devoured the thrilling new publications was Mordecai Richler, who later became one of Canada's most distinguished writers. For Richler, the primal appeal of the early superheroes was obvious: "*Superman, The Flash, The Human Torch*, even *Captain Marvel*, were our *golems*," he later observed. "They were invulnerable, all-conquering, whereas we were puny, miserable, and defeated."[11]

As tens of thousands of kids north of the Forty-ninth Parallel embraced America's most colourful and fantastic export, a handful of Canadians became active in the burgeoning U.S. comic-book field. Among them were the Quebec artist Albert Chartier, who contributed to some Columbia Comics titles, and Charles Spain Verral, a pulp-magazine writer who also wrote for Street and Smith's *Bill Barnes Comics*.[12]

With the advent of war for Canada in September 1939, the popularity of American comics continued to grow. However, as Canadian government officials responded to the overwhelming demands of the war economy, emergency

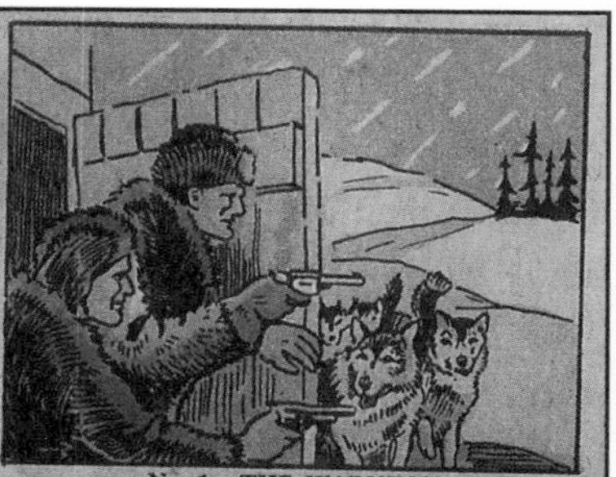
No. 1—THE WARNING

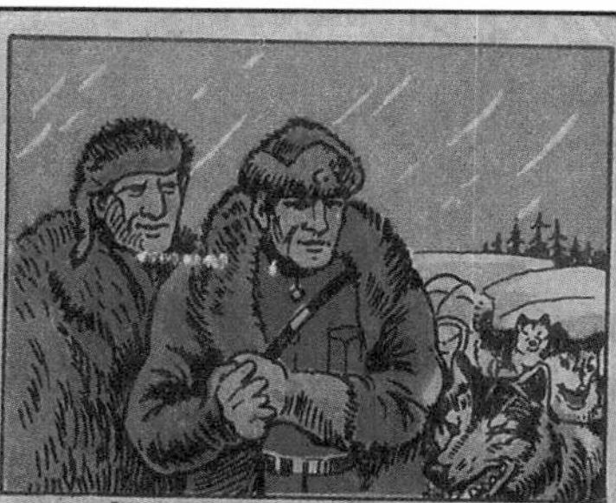
No. 3—THE DANGER TRAIL

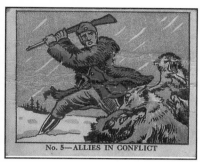

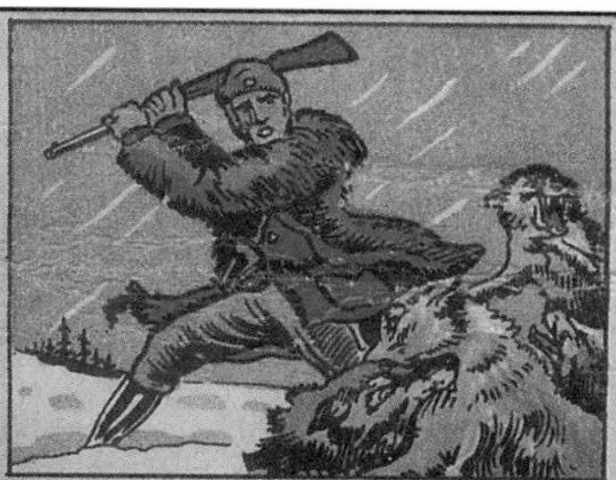
No. 5—ALLIES IN CONFLICT

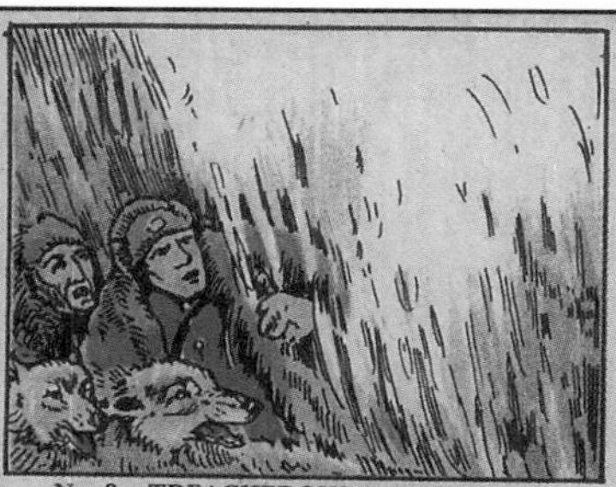
No. 8—TREACHEROUS SNOW-SLIDES

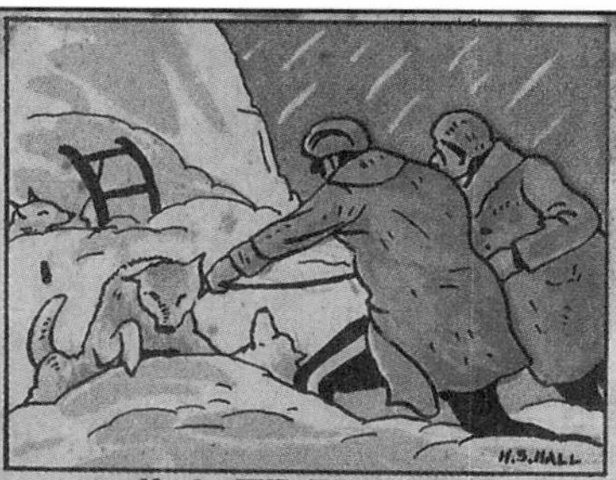
H.S.HALL
No. 9—THE SNOW TRAP

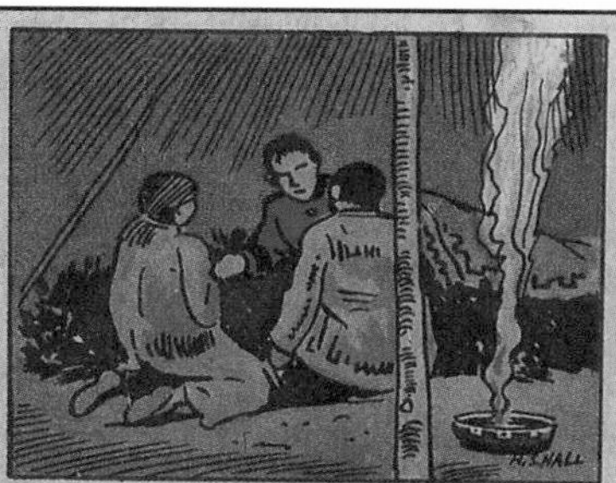
H.S.HALL
No. 16—RECOVERY

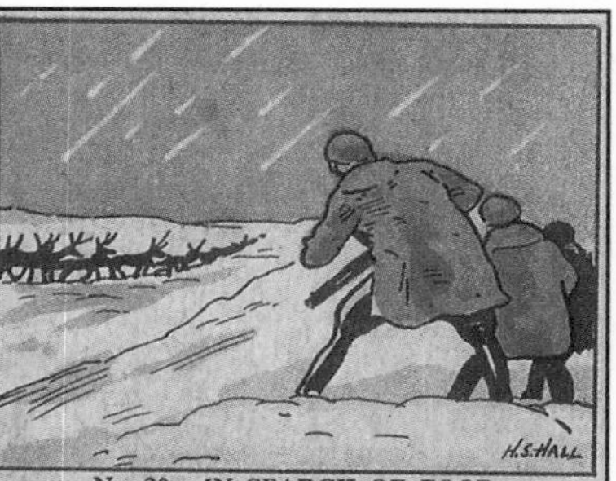
H.S.HALL
No. 20—IN SEARCH OF FOOD

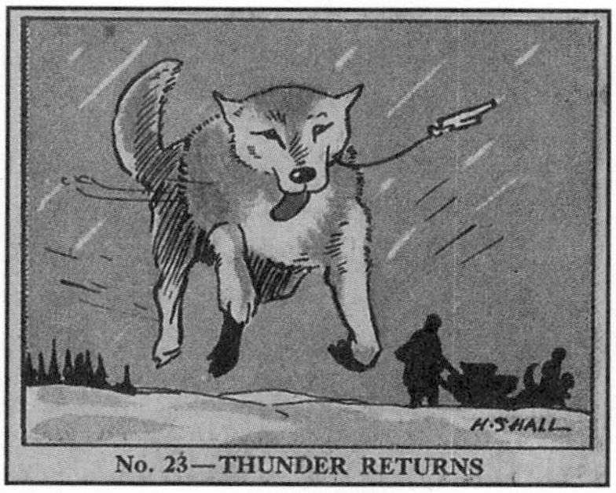
H.S.HALL
No. 23—THUNDER RETURNS

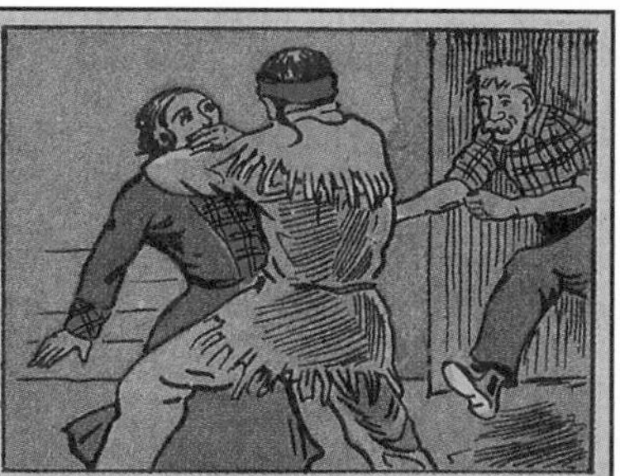
No. 28—IN THE PROWLER'S CLAWS

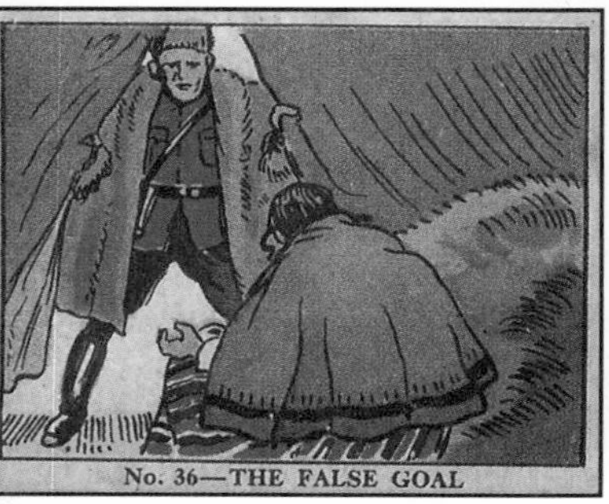
No. 36—THE FALSE GOAL

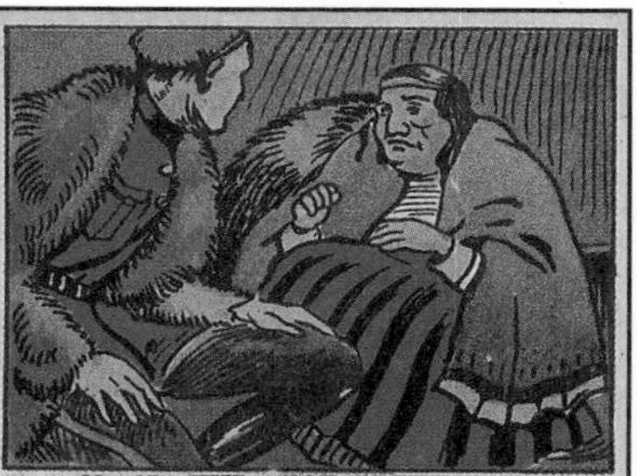
No. 37—THE SHOT IN THE BUSH

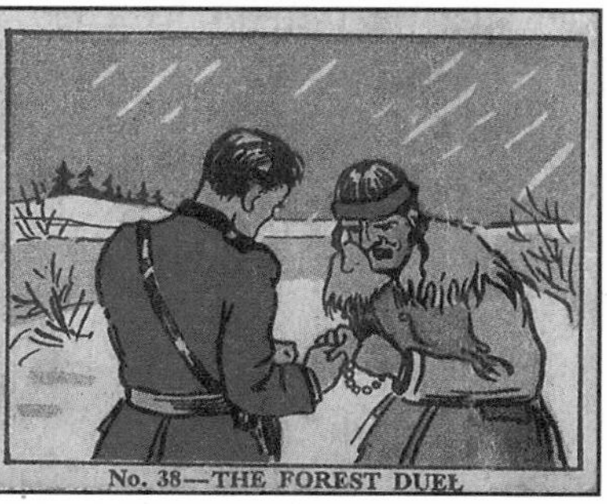
No. 38—THE FOREST DUEL

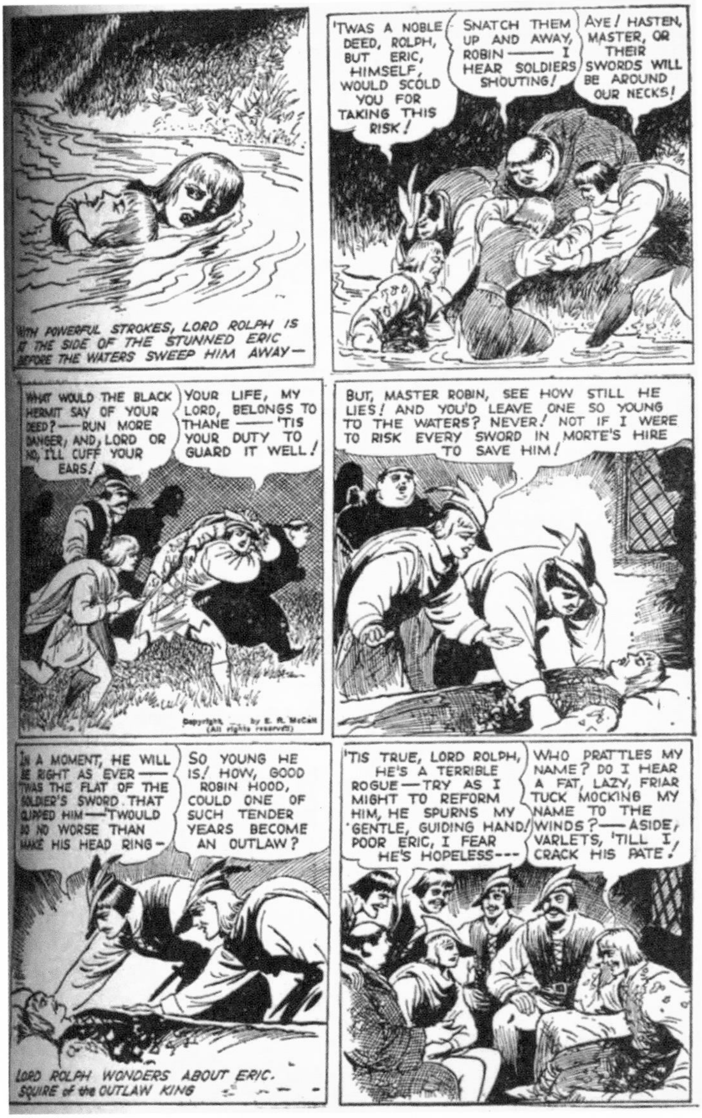
WITH POWERFUL STROKES, LORD ROLPH IS AT THE SIDE OF THE STUNNED ERIC BEFORE THE WATERS SWEEP HIM AWAY—
'TWAS A NOBLE DEED, ROLPH, BUT ERIC, HIMSELF, WOULD SCOLD YOU FOR TAKING THIS RISK!
SNATCH THEM UP AND AWAY, ROBIN —— I HEAR SOLDIERS SHOUTING!
AYE! HASTEN, MASTER, OR THEIR SWORDS WILL BE AROUND OUR NECKS!
WHAT WOULD THE BLACK HERMIT SAY OF YOUR DEED?—RUN MORE DANGER, AND, LORD OR NO, I'LL CUFF YOUR EARS!
YOUR LIFE, MY LORD, BELONGS TO THANE —— 'TIS YOUR DUTY TO GUARD IT WELL!
BUT, MASTER ROBIN, SEE HOW STILL HE LIES! AND YOU'D LEAVE ONE SO YOUNG TO THE WATERS? NEVER! NOT IF I WERE TO RISK EVERY SWORD IN MORTE'S HIRE TO SAVE HIM!
IN A MOMENT, HE WILL BE RIGHT AS EVER —— 'TWAS THE FLAT OF THE SOLDIER'S SWORD THAT CLIPPED HIM—'TWOULD DO NO WORSE THAN MAKE HIS HEAD RING—
SO YOUNG HE IS! HOW, GOOD ROBIN HOOD, COULD ONE OF SUCH TENDER YEARS BECOME AN OUTLAW?
LORD ROLPH WONDERS ABOUT ERIC, SQUIRE of the OUTLAW KING
'TIS TRUE, LORD ROLPH, HE'S A TERRIBLE ROGUE—TRY AS I MIGHT TO REFORM HIM, HE SPURNS MY GENTLE, GUIDING HAND! POOR ERIC, I FEAR HE'S HOPELESS---
WHO PRATTLES MY NAME? DO I HEAR A FAT, LAZY, FRIAR TUCK MOCKING MY NAME TO THE WINDS?—ASIDE, VARLETS, 'TILL I CRACK HIS PATE!

Panels from the Robin Hood *newspaper strip reprinted in Anglo-American Publishing's* Robin Hood and Company *No. 6 (December 1941–January 1942). Art probably by Charles Snelgrove. Copyright © estate of Ted McCall.*

measures were formulated that abruptly deprived kids in Canada of the breathtaking adventures of Superman, Captain Marvel, and the multitude of other American superheroes. From the beginning of its development in the 1890s, comic art in anglophone North America had been largely American. In English Canada that was finally about to change. While U.S. strips still dominated in the newspaper "funnies" sections, strange new comic books soon offered Canadian kids their very own heroes.

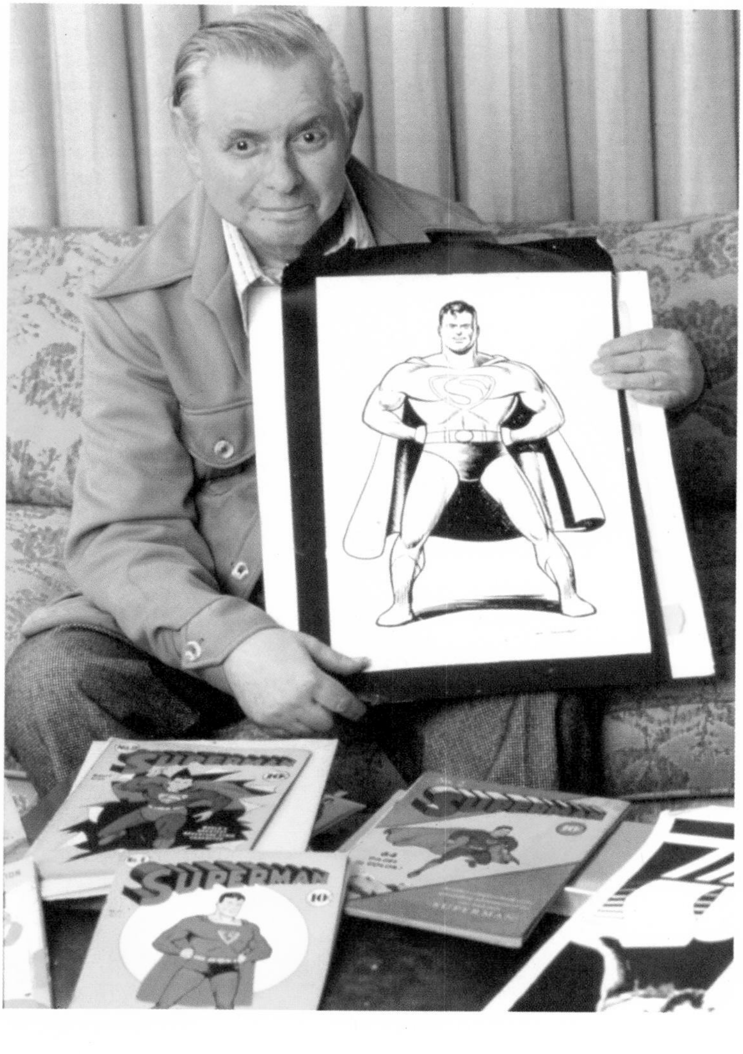
SUPERMAN
SUPERMAN
SUPERMAN

Joe Shuster in his Los Angeles apartment a few months before his death in 1992. Photo by Henry Mietkiewicz. Copyright © Henry Mietkiewicz. Superman and all related characters and symbols copyright © DC Comics, Inc.

2

3

Smashing the Axis:
Canada's Golden Age
of Comics,
1941–1946

On September 15, 1939, shortly after Canada's declaration of war against Germany, the Foreign Exchange Control Board was established to oversee the rationing of foreign currency, something it would do with varying severity until 1951. In December 1940, as Canada's trade deficit with the United States grew, and British gold shipments were curtailed, government intervention in the economy broadened with the introduction of the War Exchange Conservation Act. Aimed at countries outside the sterling bloc, it was primarily designed to conserve American dollars by restricting the importation of non-essential goods from Canada's largest trading partner.[1] Among the items banned were fiction periodicals, a category that encompassed pulps and other newsstand magazines, including comic books. As a result, the government inadvertently laid the groundwork for an indigenous comics industry (this period also saw the publication of Canadian pulps such as *Uncanny Tales* and *Eerie Tales*).[2]

As long as American comic books had flowed freely into Canada, none of the nation's publishers could afford to compete. Printing costs, market size, distribution obstacles, and various other factors all conspired against the possibility of a Canadian firm wresting any appreciable portion of the market from major U.S. publishers like Fawcett and National Periodical Publications. Nevertheless, this did not mean that publishers in Canada had been unaware of the phenomenal popularity that the new medium enjoyed. In fact, several entrepreneurs in various centres across the country were more than a little envious of the obvious success of U.S. comics. However, it was not until the American periodicals were abruptly excluded at the end of 1940 that would-be comics publishers in Canada could

3

Facing page: Cover of Better Comics *Vol. 3, No. 3 (April–May 1945). Art by Jon St. Ables (John Stables). Copyright © Maple Leaf Publishing.*

seriously contemplate the creation of a national comic-book publishing industry.

Working independently of one another, four publishers rushed to take advantage of the vacuum created by the sweeping economic legislation. One company, Maple Leaf Publishing, was located in Vancouver; the other three — Anglo-American Publishing, Hillborough Studio, and Commercial Signs of Canada — were all based in Toronto. Both Maple Leaf and Anglo-American managed to hit the newsstands with comics by March 1941, while Hillborough and Commercial made their debuts in August and September respectively.[3] The voracious appetite that Canadian kids had developed for funny books was about to be assuaged by new heroes.[4]

Maple Leaf's first title, *Better Comics*, was released the same month as the inaugural issue of Anglo-American's *Robin Hood and Company*, but the former was distinguished by its content and format. Unlike its rival, which initially appeared as a tabloid-size collection of reprint strips, *Better Comics* consisted entirely of original material and was published in a regular comic-book format. Consequently, Maple Leaf should probably be viewed as the publisher of the first true Canadian comic book. Whatever the case, *Better Comics* also had the distinction of introducing the first Canadian superhero — Vernon Miller's The Iron Man. Miller, who had returned to British Columbia following a stint with the Walt Disney studio in California, apparently played an instrumental role in launching Maple Leaf, convincing the Vancouver magazine vendor Harry Smith to invest in the promising new comics industry.[5]

Smith and his associates were obviously encouraged by the response to *Better Comics*, as the title was soon followed by three more comic books: *Bing Bang Comics*, *Lucky Comics*, and *Rocket Comics* (initially entitled *Name-It Comics*). Like the majority of pre-1945 comics produced during Canada's Golden Age of Comics (1941 to 1946), all four titles had colour covers and black-and-white interiors, thus giving rise, among young fans, to the term *whites* (actually, the first few issues of *Better Comics* featured some colour). As well, they often relied on serial stories to induce kids to fork out their hard-earned dimes issue after issue.[6]

In addition to Vernon Miller, Maple Leaf employed several other notable artists, including Bert Bushell, Ernie Walker, Ley Fortune, and John Stables, who signed his work "Jon St. Ables." Stables, whose best work surpassed that of most of his North American comic-art contemporaries, was responsible for an elegantly rendered, Edgar Rice Burroughs–like fantasy strip called *Brok Windsor*. Set in the Canadian North, in the "land beyond the mists," *Brok Windsor* debuted in the April-May 1944 issue of

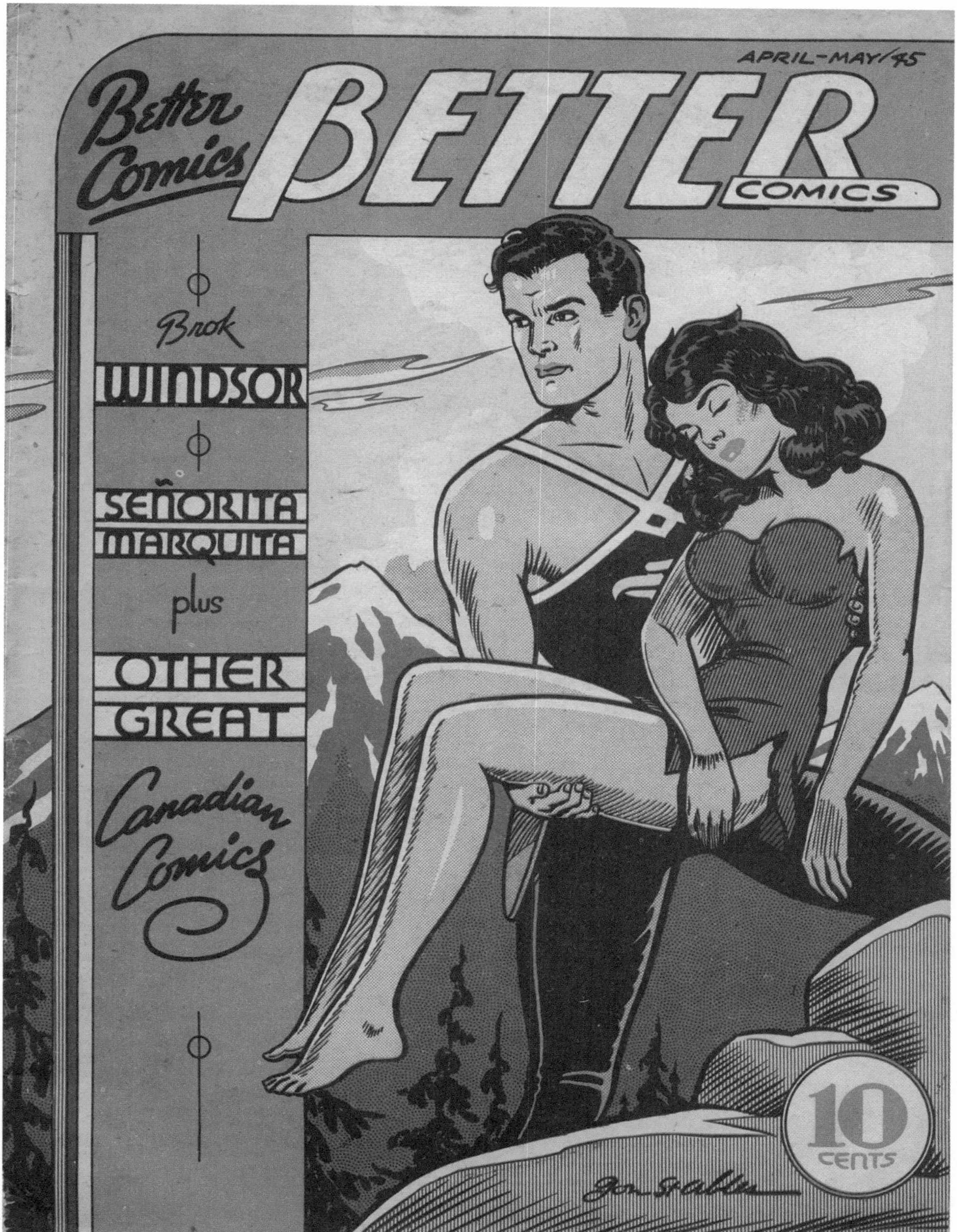
APRIL–MAY/'45
Better Comics
BETTER COMICS
Brok
WINDSOR
SEÑORITA MARQUITA
plus
OTHER GREAT
Canadian Comics
10 CENTS

Facing page: Jon St. Ables (John Stables) working on the strip Bill Speed, *circa 1947. Copyright © Jon Stables. Photo courtesy of Peter Hansen.*

Better Comics. On the whole, Maple Leaf comics were probably the most professional products of Canada's Golden Age. All of the company's titles were well drawn and designed, featuring engaging, rather sophisticated characters such as Deuce Granville, Señorita Marquita, Bill Speed, Stuff Buggs, and Black Wing.

Maple Leaf's first competitor, Anglo-American, was owned and operated by four Toronto businessmen: Thomas H. Sinnott, John M. Calder, John G. Baker, and Edward C. Johnston; but its creative force derived primarily from two creators, Ted McCall and Ed Furness. McCall, the writer responsible for the newspaper adventure strips *Men of the Mounted* and *Robin Hood and Company*, brought both with him when he joined the company. In addition, he worked on a number of original characters with Furness, Anglo-American's talented chief artist. Among the firm's major heroes, which drew upon virtually every adventure genre, were Freelance, Purple Rider, Red Rover, Commander Steel, Terry Kane, and Dr. Destine.[7]

In an effort to bypass the government's restrictive foreign-exchange legislation, Anglo-American also acquired scripts from Fawcett Publications in the United States, producing original Canadian versions of that company's American superhero stories. This arrangement led to some curious results. Commander Yank, for instance, fought his Canadian adventures with a Union Jack emblazoned on his chest. Among the other Fawcett heroes redrawn by Anglo-American were Captain Marvel, Captain Marvel Jr., Bulletman, and Spy Smasher.

Like Maple Leaf, Anglo-American quickly expanded its line of comics. By the end of 1941, it was publishing four more titles: *Freelance, Grand Slam*, *Three Aces*, and *Whiz*. In 1942 these were augmented by *Captain Marvel* and *Spy Smasher*. (Early in 1941, Anglo-American also apparently issued a few reprints of comics published by the U.S. publisher Fox. It is not clear how the firm managed to circumvent the provisions of the War Exchange Conservation Act. In any event, this experiment was short-lived.)[8] Unlike most Canadian companies between 1941 and 1946, Anglo-American avoided serialized stories; nor was its product particularly Canadian. While undeniably patriotic, insofar as it supported the war effort, the firm's comic books lacked the fervent nationalism evident in many Golden Age comics.

A number of artists, among them a very young Harold Town, worked on Anglo-American's titles, but they all tended to emulate the clean, square-jawed, Fawcett style developed by the famous American artist C.C. Beck.[9] This deliberate "house" style resulted in a somewhat homogenized product. Furthermore, Anglo-American's comics were initially the least impressive of the Canadian

Golden Age comic books in terms of production values. Printed slightly oversize on cheap newsprint, they utilized flimsy two-colour covers during the first few years of their existence. Like all Canadian comics, though, they improved markedly over the course of the war.[10]

While both Maple Leaf and Anglo-American represented fairly substantial publishing ventures, the third Canadian publisher to enter the comic-book field, Hillborough Studio, was founded by three unemployed artists, Adrian Dingle and the brothers René and André Kulbach, who were joined by a single anonymous investor. Their primary title, *Triumph-Adventure Comics*, made its

debut in August 1941. It appeared for only a few more issues under the Hillborough imprint (the firm also published one issue of *Top Flight Comics*, which featured art by Dingle, Clayton Dexter, and other artists) until the company's lead creator, Dingle, decided in 1942 to throw in his lot with what became the best-known Canadian comics publisher, Bell Features. Most of Dingle's Hillborough colleagues followed him to Bell. Prior to joining Bell, though, Dingle created one of the most memorable characters of the Golden Age — the superheroine Nelvana of the Northern Lights, the first Canadian national superhero.[11]

Dingle later credited the artist Franz Johnston, a member of Canada's most prestigious art coterie, the Group of Seven, with the concept of Nelvana, who predated Wonder Woman, the best-known U.S. female superhero, by several months. Initially garbed in a fur-trimmed mini-skirt, Nelvana was a very powerful heroine, and her adventures often had a Flash Gordon flavour, an aspect of the strip that Dingle obviously relished as he developed the character further at Bell Features, Canada's fourth Golden Age publisher.[12]

During the 1930s, Cy Bell and his brother, Gene, ran a Toronto-based commercial-art firm called Commercial Signs of Canada. In 1939 they had been approached by a French Canadian artist, Edmund Legault, who hoped to find a publisher for his comic art. The Bells were forced to turn Legault away. However, late in 1940 when Cy Bell learned of the impending ban on U.S. comics, he re-established contact with Legault, acquired capital from businessman John Ezrin, and began work on an adventure comic book entitled *Wow Comics*.[13]

The inaugural issue of *Wow*, which was dated a month later than *Triumph*, was a huge success. Initially, it appeared in poorly registered colour, but eventually, like subsequent Bell titles, it switched to the familiar Canadian "whites" style of black-and-white interiors with colour covers. Early in 1942, around the time

that Commercial absorbed Hillborough Studio, Bell changed his company's name to Bell Features and hired Hillborough's Adrian Dingle as his art director. Shortly thereafter, Bell launched five new titles: *Active, Commando, Dime, The Funny Comics,* and *Joke.* He also later employed, as his managing editor, the Canadian pulp writer John Hollis Mason.[14]

Although somewhat uneven in terms of quality (after all, many of the strips were written and drawn by adolescent comic-book fans), Bell's line of comics was unabashedly Canadian. Among its major heroes were both Nelvana and the Penguin by Dingle, Legault's Dixon of the Mounted, Phantom Rider by Jerry Lazare, Edmond Good's Rex Baxter, and Fred Kelly's Doc Stearne (a character that was resurrected in the 1980s as Mr. Monster by American artist Michael T. Gilbert). Another particularly notable Bell character was Leo Bachle's Johnny Canuck (the second Canadian national superhero), who made his debut in the first issue of *Dime Comics* in February 1942.[15]

More than fifty other freelance artists contributed to Bell's titles, including René Kulbach, Ted Steele, Manny Easson, Jack Tremblay, Mel Crawford, and veteran newspaper cartoonist Leo Skuce. Bell's pool of freelancers also included the artist Doris Slater and the writer Patricia Joudrey, two of the few women involved in Canadian comics during the 1940s. Given the number of contributors to its

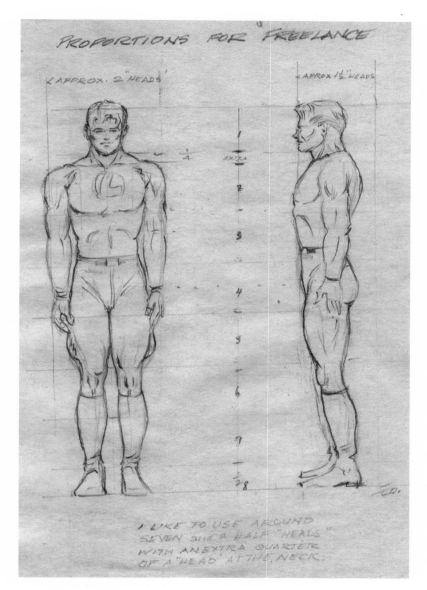

PROPORTIONS FOR FREELANCE

‹APPROX. 2 "HEADS"

‹APPROX 1½ "HEADS"

EXTRA

I LIKE TO USE AROUND
SEVEN AND A HALF "HEADS"
WITH AN EXTRA QUARTER
OF A "HEAD" AT THE NECK.

Sketch of Freelance, probably prepared as a style guide for other Anglo-American artists, circa 1941. Art by Ed Furness. Copyright © Carol Mound and Richard Furness.

3

comic books, it is not surprising that Bell proved to be the most prolific publisher of the Canadian Golden Age, eventually issuing nearly twenty different titles (including several compilations). By the end of 1943, the firm was selling more than 100,000 comics a week.[16]

The success enjoyed by Maple Leaf, Anglo-American, and Bell soon encouraged other publishers. In late 1942, they were joined by a fourth company, Educational Projects of Montreal, which was owned and managed by Harry J. Halperin. Although it adopted the same format as its predecessors, Educational, as its name suggested, sought to produce a more edifying type of periodical for children. As a result, its main title, *Canadian Heroes,* focused on such wholesome fare as profiles of Canadian prime ministers and governors general, historical narratives, and Royal Canadian Mounted Police cases. Never especially inspired, the rather didactic stories found in *Canadian Heroes* were generally handled in a competent fashion by Educational's stable of freelance artists, which included Joseph Hillenbrand, George M. Rae, Sid Barron, and Fred Kelly. In fact, Rae and Barron were among the most accomplished comics artists of the Canadian Golden Age.[17]

While the approach of *Canadian Heroes* appealed to parents and government officials (some issues of *Canadian Heroes* actually featured laudatory endorsements from Canadian cabinet ministers), even the publisher Halperin came to realize that Canadian children had developed an appetite for somewhat more thrilling narratives. As a result, when George M. Rae suggested that *Canadian Heroes* depart from its focus on true stories and feature a fictional character, a national superhero named Canada Jack, Halperin gave him the go-ahead. However, the publisher insisted that the realistic nature of the character be emphasized so as not to detract from his firm's wholesome image.[18]

Assisting Jack in his efforts to protect the Canadian home front from a host of Nazi agents and dupes were the members of the Canada Jack Club (CJC). While many wartime heroes were joined by young sidekicks, the CJC was unique in that it existed both in the pages of *Canadian Heroes* and in the real world. Organized by Educational's publisher, who worked with children before and after the war, the CJC attracted hundreds of members across Canada from among the readers of *Canadian Heroes*. Once the club was up and running, each issue featured CJC news and contests and also a profile of a CJC honour member who had made a signal contribution to the war effort.[19]

In 1943, Maple Leaf, Anglo-American, Bell, and Educational Projects were joined by a fifth publisher, F.E. Howard of Toronto which, taking its cue from Anglo-American's reprint arrangement with Fawcett, acquired the publishing rights to

10¢
Top Flight
COMICS
FEBRUARY
DEXTER
LLOW THE ADVENTURES OF "The Rapier"

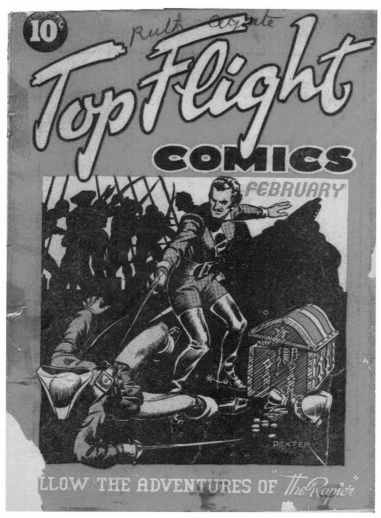

Cover of Top Flight Comics *(February 1942), one of the rarest comics ever published in Canada. Art by Clayton Dexter. Copyright © Hillborough Studio.*

3

material from the U.S. publisher MLJ Magazines. Howard's first title was *Super Comics*, comprising black-and-white and, apparently, partly redrawn versions of stories that had originally appeared in the U.S. comic book *Pep*. Among the popular MLJ characters featured in *Super Comics* were Archie, The Shield, and Captain Commando and the Boy Soldiers. Like Fawcett's Commander Yank, MLJ's The Shield was obliged to alter his ultra-patriotic American costume for his Canadian

Facing page: Cover of Wow Comics *No. 16 (circa 1943). Art by Adrian Dingle. Copyright © Nelvana Limited. Used with permission. All rights reserved.*

adventures, replacing the Stars and Stripes with the Union Jack — at least for his appearances on the covers of *Super Comics*. Howard published a total of six issues of *Super Comics* and later issued several more comics titles, mostly one-shots. (A single undated and unnumbered issue of *Super Comics* was also seemingly issued by Citren News of Canada, which may have been connected with Howard. It is possible that the Citren issue preceded the Howard issues.)[20]

Not surprisingly, the growing popularity of Canadian comics encouraged further publishing ventures. In 1944 yet another Toronto-based publisher, Features Publications, was launched by sometime Bell contributor Edward Schecter. Features Publications' sole title was *Lightning Comics*, a rather amateurish monthly that featured the unrestrained adventures of such characters as Captain Daring, Dr. Future and Pee Wee, and Nemesis and Rover the Wonder Dog.

Although 1945 saw two more new firms, Al Rucker Publications (ARP) and Superior (aka Century) Publishers, become active (it is possible that both Rucker and Superior actually began publishing comics late in 1944), the year proved to be disastrous for the Canadian comics industry.[21] As the Allied victory over Nazi Germany approached, Canada's vulnerable comic-book publishers were all too aware that the war's end would mean the full resumption of U.S. comics distribution in Canada.[22] Some companies revamped their titles in the face of this formidable threat, while others, without the resources to survive American competition, accepted the inevitability of their demise. Two publishers, Educational Projects and Feature Publications, folded almost immediately in the fall of 1945. Maple Leaf, on the other hand, boldly switched to colour in an effort to hold its own on the nation's newsstands. Creating such an expensive product exclusively for the limited Canadian market, though, was not a viable undertaking over the long term. Consequently, Maple Leaf began exporting comics to the United Kingdom. However, by the end of 1946, the firm had failed.[23]

Both Anglo-American and the newcomer Al Rucker Publications tried to avoid Maple Leaf's fate by not only adopting U.S. production values (colour interiors and glossy covers), but also by penetrating the lucrative American market (as well, Rucker appears to have briefly exported to Britain). It was probably the only strategy that might have allowed for the survival of original Canadian comics. The result, in the case of Anglo-American, was a line of polished adventure comic books that received some U.S. distribution (a young Harlan Ellison, who later became a major science-fiction writer, was among the comics' most ardent American fans). Regrettably, their quality did not translate into success on the newsstands. Faced with unsatisfactory sales, the

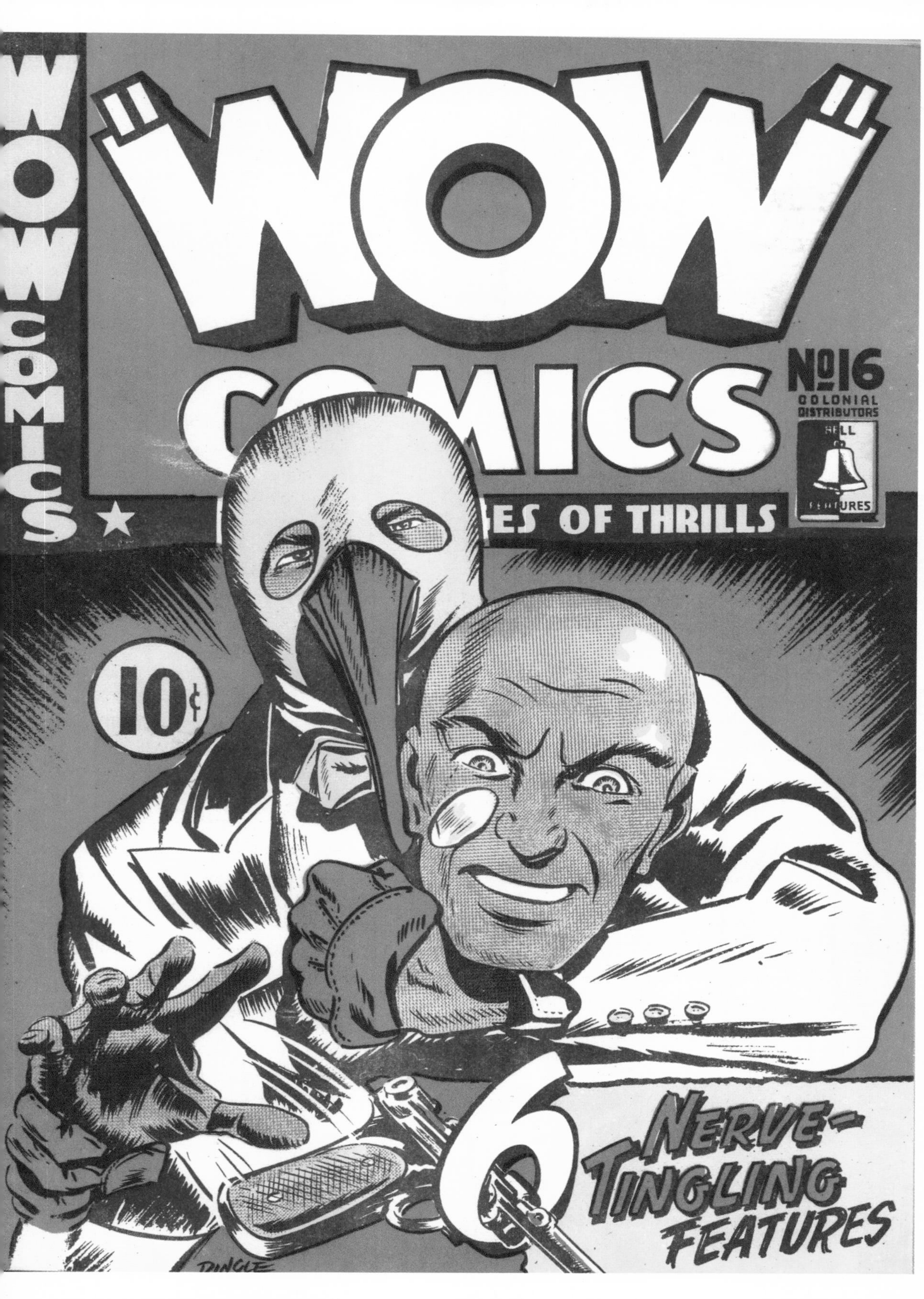

WOW COMICS
"WOW"
COMICS
No 16
COLONIAL DISTRIBUTORS
ES OF THRILLS
10¢
6 NERVE-TINGLING FEATURES
DINGLE

firm was forced by late 1946 to abandon its own titles, as was Rucker Publications. Anglo-American, however, was eventually able to resume comics publishing as a reprint operation.[24]

A more or less similar fate befell Bell Features. As the war neared its end, Cy Bell borrowed $75,000 and purchased a huge offset press from the *Cleveland Plain Dealer*. Determined not to be displaced by the influx of American comics, he issued two colour comic books in 1946, *Dizzy Don Comics* and *Slam-Bang*, and planned for an ambitious line of new titles. He also began to arrange for distribution not only in the United States, but in the United Kingdom, as well. Bell apparently encountered a major obstacle, however, when the federal government refused to authorize the purchase of newsprint in the quantities that his company required. Deterred by this and other problems, Bell Features ceased publishing its own titles and began reprinting U.S. comics for the Canadian and British markets.[25]

Even though Bell, and later Anglo-American, managed to remain, however tenuously, in the comic-book business, by the end of 1946, Canada's Golden Age of Comics was clearly over. Where there once had been five major publishers regularly issuing more than twenty original titles, there were now, with the exception of the relatively untested

Superior Publishers and F.E. Howard, only reprint houses.

Nevertheless, the glory days between 1941 and 1946 would never be forgotten by those who had partaken of their magic. All in all, it had been an exhilarating explosion of Canadian popular culture. At no time since have English Canadian children grown up with such a wide array of indigenous heroes and superheroes. The experience also represented an unprecedented opportunity for dozens of mostly young, struggling artists to emulate mentors such as U.S. comic-art giants Milton Caniff, Will Eisner, C.C. Beck, Alex Raymond, and Lou Fine. Unfortunately, most of the Canadian comics creators of the 1940s drifted into anonymity. A few, though, went on to make their marks both inside and outside the comics field.[26]

Adrian Dingle (Bell Features) and George Rae (Educational Projects), who became friends after the war, both worked as illustrators while pursuing careers as fine artists. Patricia Joudrey, who had written scripts for Bell, became an important playwright, while Harold Town (Anglo-American) later emerged as one of the country's leading abstract painters. Maple Leaf's Bus Griffiths became a commercial fisherman, leaving comics behind until the 1960s when his graphic narratives depicting the logging industry were discovered by the Royal

CANADIAN HEROES
C.D.L.
CANADIAN
HEROES
VOL. 5
NO. 6
68 PAGES
10¢
SIEUR DE LASALLE_
ADVENTURER-EXPLORER
INVEST IN CANADA'S NINTH VICTORY LOAN
9
THE NATIONAL MAGAZINE FOR YOUNG CANADIANS
OFFICE OF PUBLICATION ..... MONTREAL
OCT. 1945

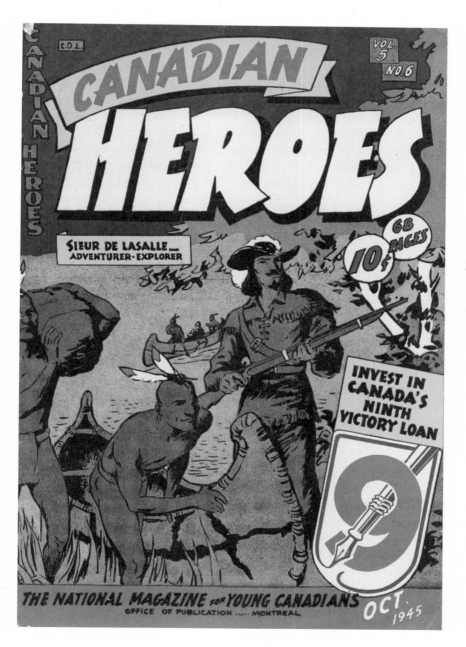

Cover of Canadian Heroes *Vol. 5, No. 6 (October 1945). Copyright © Educational Projects.*

3

British Columbia Museum in Victoria. Jerry Lazare (Bell Features), Vernon Miller (Maple Leaf), and Jack Tremblay (Bell Features and Educational Projects) all became accomplished illustrators, as did Harold Bennett (Bell Features and Al Rucker Publications), who worked in the United States as a paperback-cover artist. Sid Barron (Educational Projects) emerged as one of Canada's foremost political cartoonists.

The few artists who chose to remain in the comics business were largely obliged to pursue their careers south of the border. Edmond Good (Bell Features) worked on such strips as *Scorchy Smith*, *Casey Ruggles*, *Red Ryder*, *Bruce Gentry*, and *Dixie Dugan*. He also freelanced for Quality, DC (where he co-created the character Tomahawk), and a number of other U.S. comics (and pulp) companies before launching his own title, *Johnny Law, Sky Ranger*, in 1955. Johnny Canuck's creator, Leo Bachle (Bell Features), worked for the American firms Prize and Croydon prior to abandoning comics for a career as a comedian and nightclub performer under the name Les Barker. John Alton (Bell Features), co-creator of the *Doodlebugs*, contributed to various EC, Fox, and Gleason comics titles. Most prolific of all the Canadian artists working in the

United States was Mel Crawford (Bell Features), who became one of the major artists at the American firm Western Publishing. Although Crawford entertained thousands of Canadian children throughout the 1950s and 1960s, his Canadian roots were as scarce as copies of the Canadian "whites" to which he had contributed. (Among Crawford's contemporaries in the U.S. comic-book field was another extremely prolific Canadian artist — Winslow Mortimer, who was especially famous for his numerous covers depicting Superman and Batman.)[27]

In the United States, the first post-war decade witnessed a veritable explosion in the comics industry (it is estimated that at the boom's peak, more than sixty million comics were appearing every month). Inexorably, it seemed, comics in anglophone North America (with the exception of a few newspaper strips) were becoming an exclusively American medium.[28] This did not mean, however, that Canadian publishers could not profit from the popularity of U.S. comic books. As had been the case in 1940, growing government concern over Canada's foreign-exchange situation provided the basis for Bell, Anglo-American, and a host of new firms to survive in the comic-book industry.

SPOTLIGHT

JOHNNY CANUCK AND THE SEARCH FOR CANADIAN SUPERHEROES

With the appearance of Superman, the groundbreaking creation of Toronto-born artist Joe Shuster and the writer Jerry Siegel, in *Action Comics* No. 1 (June 1938), it became obvious that superheroes had found the perfect medium — the comic book. Not surprisingly, Siegel and Shuster's character was soon joined by a host of rivals, including Batman, Sub-Mariner, Captain Marvel, and Plastic Man.

Although their unfettered, pulpish adventures were in four colours, the superheroes' moral universe was strictly black and white. And while some adult observers of the new comics genre might have shared Marshall McLuhan's concerns about the uncritical portrayal of "imperfect men, possessing superhuman material power," there was no doubt in the minds of young comic-book fans that their heroes fought for all that was right and good, forcefully opposing evil that, increasingly after the outbreak of World War II, was represented by the Axis powers.[1]

Among the numerous American heroes engaged in the struggle against fascism and militarism was a special kind of superhero — the national superhero, who overtly symbolized America's identity and pride. The first of these figures was The Shield, who appeared in *Pep Comics* No. 1 (January 1940). Next came Uncle Sam, a symbol borrowed from political cartooning, and then Minute-Man. Many more super-patriots eventually followed, including Captain America (the best-known American national superhero), Pat Patriot, and Major Victory.[2]

When the American superheroes, national and otherwise, abruptly disappeared from newsstands in Canada at the end of 1940, the new Canadian publishers that rushed to fill the vacuum were very much aware of the phenomenal success of

Spotlight

59

the U.S. superheroes and of the pressing need to provide Canadian comics fans with new superheroes, including their own national superheroes.[3] Consequently, the first regular-format Canadian comic book, *Better Comics*, which was issued by Vancouver's Maple Leaf Publishing, featured the first Canadian superhero — The Iron Man by Vernon Miller, a former Disney animator.

The Iron Man, who predated the better-known American comic-book character of the same name by twenty-two years, superficially resembled another U.S. superhero, the Sub-Mariner. The sole survivor of a South Seas civilization that had been devastated by an earthquake, The Iron Man lived alone in a sunken city. Summoned by two children and their adult companion, the Major, the patriotic superhero returned to the surface world to combat Nazis and other villains. Although Miller's creation possessed super-strength, was indestructible and, like the original version of Superman, could leap so high that he could virtually fly, he lacked any distinctly Canadian characteristics.

The absence of a Canadian identity also characterized Canada's second superhero, Freelance, who debuted in the first issue of Anglo-American's *Freelance Comics* (July 1941), the third title of the Canadian Golden Age. The invention of writer Ted McCall and artist Ed Furness, Freelance also had his origin in the Southern Hemisphere, having grown up among a lost tribe in a tropical valley in Antarctica. However, unlike those of The Iron Man, Freelance's powers were limited to exceptional athletic ability. Wearing a costume consisting of jodhpurs, knee-high boots, and a sweatshirt emblazoned with the letter *L*, Freelance, with the assistance of his sidekick, Big John Collins, battled the Axis menace all over the world.

However, if The Iron Man and Freelance were devoid of any attributes that could be deemed Canadian, the same was certainly not true of the country's third superhero and first national superhero, Nelvana of the Northern Lights. The creation of Adrian Dingle, Nelvana first appeared in *Triumph-Adventure-Comics* No. 1 (August 1941), issued by Hillborough Studio. Later her adventures were published by Bell Features.

According to Dingle, his friend Franz Johnston, a member of the Group of Seven, contributed to the initial conception of Nelvana. After a trip to the Arctic, Johnston told Dingle about a powerful Inuit mythological figure — an elderly woman called Nelvana. Dingle thought the character had comic-book potential but realized he would have to re-invent her in keeping with the conventions of the superhero genre: "I changed her a bit. Did what I could with long hair and mini skirts. And tried to make her attractive.... Then we had to bring her up to date and

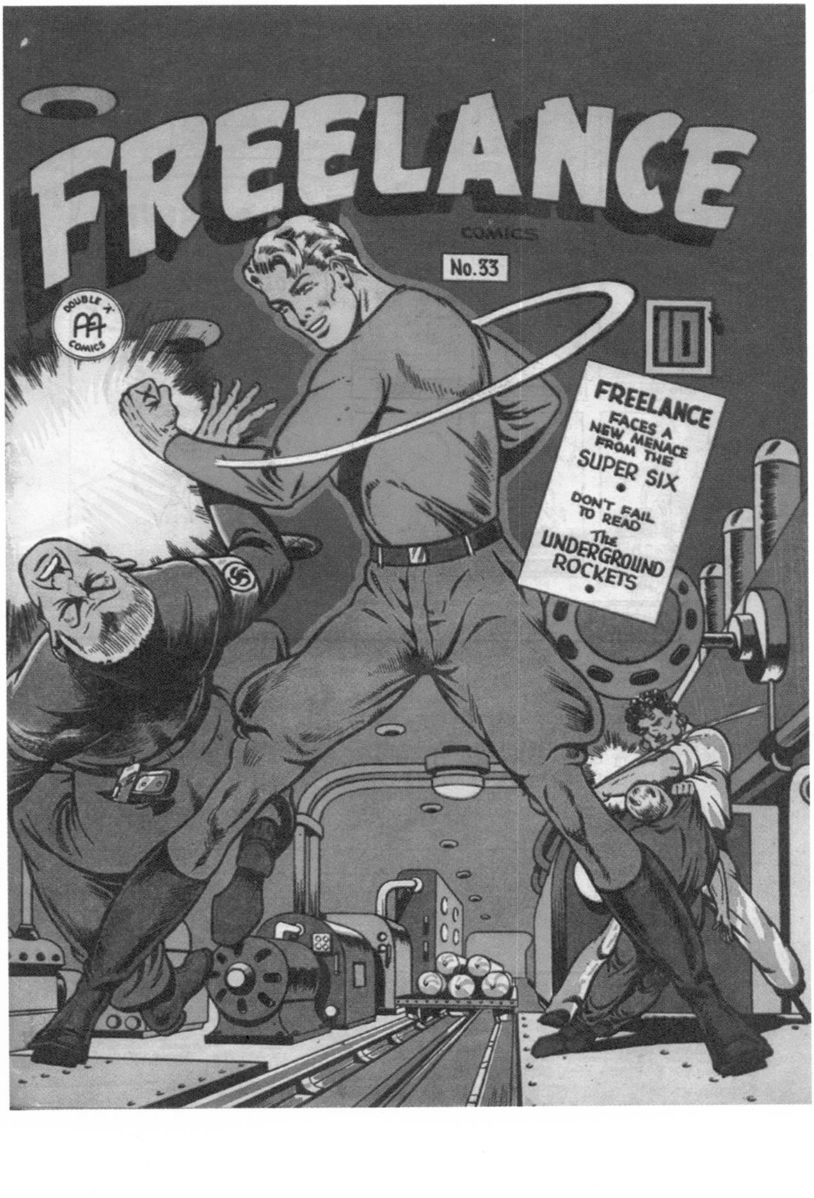
FREELANCE
COMICS
No.33
DOUBLE 'X' AA COMICS
10¢
FREELANCE FACES A NEW MENACE FROM THE SUPER SIX
DON'T FAIL TO READ The UNDERGROUND ROCKETS

Cover of Freelance Comics, *Vol. 3, No. 33 (September 1946). Art probably by Ed Furness. Copyright © Anglo-American Publishing.*

Spotlight

put her into the war effort. And, of course, everything had to be very patriotic."

Nelvana, who was identified as the daughter of Koliak, the King of the Northern Lights, drew her powers from the Northern Lights and was clearly intended to personify the North. This identification was further underscored in issue No. 20 of *Triumph*, in which she goes south and adopts a new identity — Alana North, Secret Agent.[4]

However, while Nelvana personified the North, she was not Inuit, but rather belonged to a long line of white queens and goddesses who had appeared in popular culture since the publication of H. Rider Haggard's classic adventure novel *She* (1887). These alluring, powerful females tended to have names that ended with the letter *a*, were beautiful and immortal, and usually ruled over more "primitive" peoples (often lost races). Prior to Nelvana's appearance, the popular character Sheena, the first of many white jungle queens in American comics, had made her debut in *Jumbo Comics* in 1938. (Although Nelvana succeeded Sheena, she predated Wonder Woman, the best-known female superhero in the United States, by several months.)

Unlike most of the Golden Age artists who were very young men, Dingle was in his thirties when he created Nelvana, bringing to the comics his considerable skills as a graphic artist. His comic art, which was clearly inspired by Milton Caniff's work on the renowned strip *Terry and the Pirates*, was far more sophisticated than that of most of his Canadian contemporaries. Throughout Nelvana's run in the comics, from August 1941 to May 1947, Dingle's artwork was distinguished by its elegant, bold design and by his mastery of chiaroscuro.

Compared to the Canadian national superheroes that followed her, Nelvana was quite formidable. She could fly, travel at the speed of light along a giant ray of the aurora borealis, and call upon other powers of the Northern Lights, including Koliak's powerful ray, which was capable of melting metal and disrupting radio communications. Furthermore, she could make herself invisible, alter her physical form, communicate telepathically with her brother, Tanero, and use her magic cloak to physically transform him from light form to human form. As well, she apparently was immortal.

In fact, the magnitude of Nelvana's powers was problematic. With a real war underway, the creators of superheroes had to offer some explanation as to why their characters didn't use their powers to destroy the Axis forces. Superman's creators solved this conundrum by insisting that the U.S. military was quite capable of defeating the Axis so that Superman could focus his energies on the home front. Dingle's approach to the issue was more inventive: he created otherworld super-villains and Axis super-weapons.

Johnny Canuck and the Search for Canadian Superheroes

62

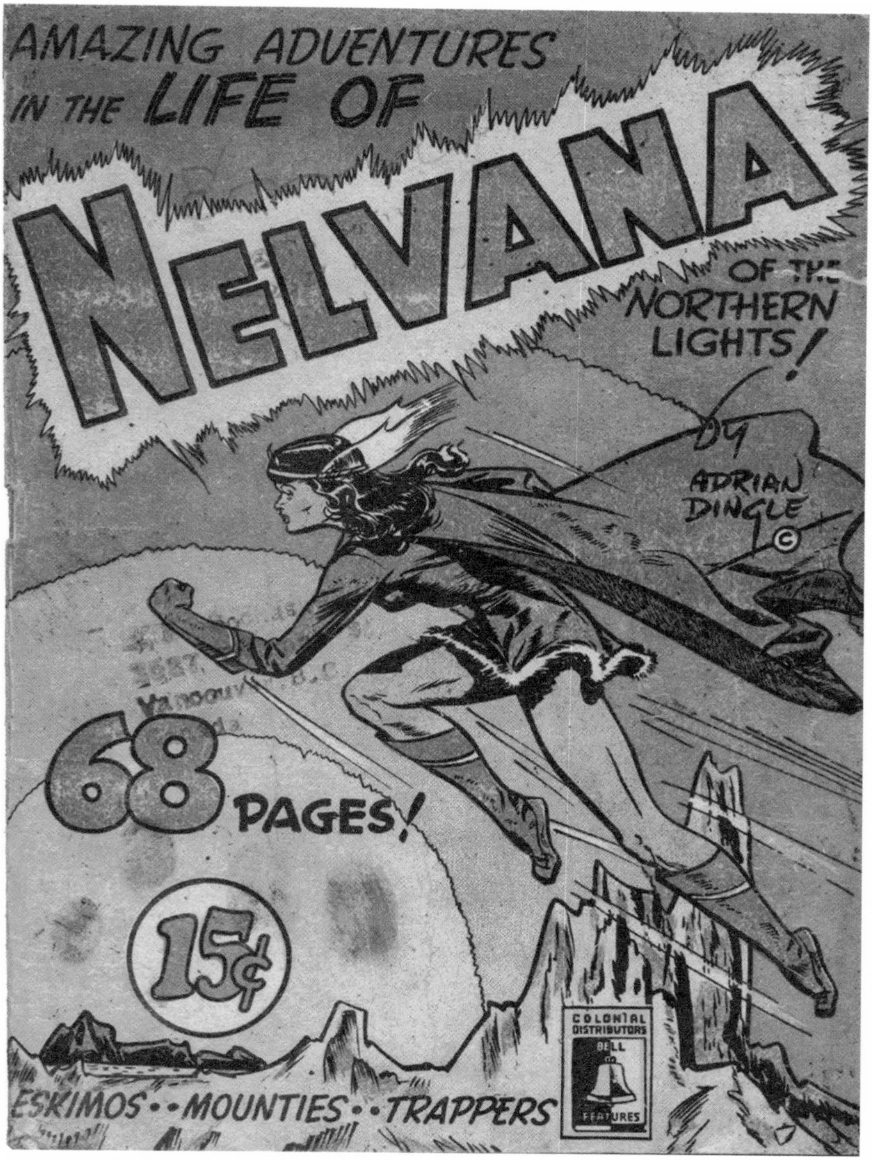
AMAZING ADVENTURES
IN THE LIFE OF
NELVANA
OF THE NORTHERN LIGHTS!
BY ADRIAN DINGLE ©
68 PAGES!
15¢
COLONIAL DISTRIBUTORS
BELL FEATURES
ESKIMOS • • MOUNTIES • • TRAPPERS

Cover of Nelvana of the Northern Lights, *circa 1945. Art by Adrian Dingle. Copyright © Nelvana Limited. Used with permission. All rights reserved.*

Spotlight

Thus, at the same time that Canada's armed forces fought a conventional war, Nelvana protected her country from more far-fetched threats. As a result, her adventures had a decidedly Flash Gordon flavour.

Nelvana's first major escapade centres on her efforts to thwart an Arctic invasion by the Kablunets, Nazi allies armed with Thormite Rays.[5] Her second adventure is even more outré and sees her dispatched to Glacia, a lost world located under the Arctic ice. Here she is drawn into the battle between the Glacians and Vultor, an evil scientist. With Nelvana's help, the Glacians are victorious. However, before she can relish her triumph, Nelvana must return to the Arctic where, in an effort to stop completion of the Alcan Highway, the Japanese have dropped "swarms of savage, starved Manchurian wolves" — an impediment to road construction, but no match for Canada's first national superhero.

The third exploit of Nelvana involves the Nazis' attempts to steal a new Allied secret weapon, the ice-beam, and is most notable for the fact that it brings her south to Nortonville, Ontario, where she assumes her new identity as Alana North. Her next adventure, entitled "Nelvana of the Northern Lights and the Ether People," sees Nelvana and Corporal Keene of the RCMP travel through various stratospheric worlds on their way to Etheria to stop an invasion of the Earth led by Vultor, her old nemesis.

The later Nelvana stories date from the post-war period when comics artists scrambled to find new non-Axis villains and when the English Canadian comic-book industry was on the verge of collapse due to competition from American comics. These narratives generally lacked the verve of the earlier super-science adventures that had made Nelvana one of the most memorable characters of the Golden Age. She lives on, though, in the name and logo of Nelvana Limited of Toronto, one of Canada's leading animation studios.

Among Adrian Dingle's many colleagues at Bell Features was a young man named Leo Bachle. Bachle's involvement with Bell began late in 1941 when, as a sixteen-year-old, he met John Ezrin, the firm's principal investor. Apparently, Ezrin spotted Bachle browsing through some Bell comics and asked the young man for his opinion of the publications. Bachle, an aspiring artist who had been drawing his own strips for several years, criticized some of the artwork. Ezrin was amused by Bachle's brazenness and challenged the young man on the spot to draw two men fighting. Ezrin was sufficiently impressed by Bachle's artistic ability to invite him to dream up a comic-book character and bring his creation to the Bell Features office the next day.[6]

That night Bachle created "Canada's super hero" — Johnny Canuck. The next day Ezrin and Bell Features publisher Cy

"DIME" COMICS
23
JOHNNY CANUCK
JOHNNY CANUCK CANADA'S ANSWER TO NAZI OPPRESSION IS NOW DEVOTING HIS TIME TO THE DESTRUCTION OF HITLER'S WAR MATERIAL FACTORIES IN THE BERLIN AREA.
BY LEO BACHLE
THE BERLIN BLAT
BRONTZ MUNITION FACTORY SABOTAGED
JOHNNY CANUCK BELIEVED RESPONSIBLE
GESTAPO PROMISES ARREST SOON.
ACH! FOOLS...YOU PROMISE ARREST, BUT DOT SVINE CANUCK GOES ON DESTROYING OUR WAR MACHINE!

Page 23 of Dime *No. 2 (March 1942). Art by Leo Bachle.*

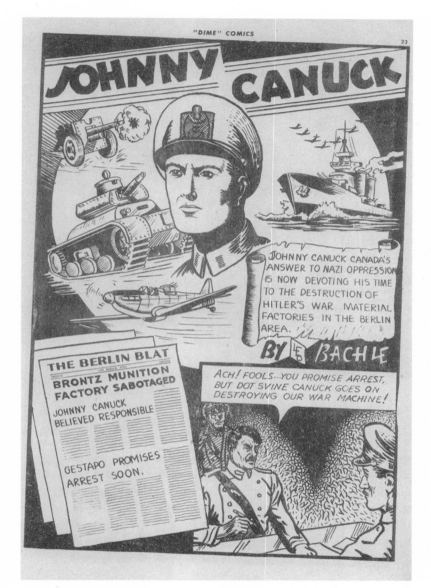

Spotlight

Bell were favourably impressed with Bachle's concept and the young artist joined Bell's growing stable of free-lancers. And while Bachle later worked on several characters in a number of gen-res, Johnny, who made his debut in the first issue of *Dime Comics* in February 1942, remained his most famous and popular creation.

Although the second Canadian nation-al superhero was probably inspired by U.S. superheroes like Captain America, it is apparent that the character also partly derived from the Canadian political-cartooning tradition, in which a Johnny or Jack Canuck figure had long served to symbolize Canada. Created by a high-school student who had to watch the war from the sidelines, Johnny, who bore more than a passing resemblance to Bachle, personified his creator's adoles-cent fantasies of wartime heroism. In fact, Bachle later admitted that he had not been able to resist the temptation to incorporate into his Johnny Canuck stories references to his friends and ene-mies. This was an awesome weapon for a teenager to wield — the ability to trans-form a high-school rival into an Axis villain!

Whereas the ultra-powerful Nelvana's adventures had to be confined to either Canada or fantastic worlds beneath or above the Earth's surface, Johnny, whose powers (including an invincible jaw) more closely resembled those of Freelance, was able to plunge headlong into the war. In fact, as a pilot and secret agent working with partisans and other irregular forces, Johnny travelled to virtually every theatre of war. His only home-front exploit was in a post-war story published in *Dime* No. 28.

While Johnny fought the Axis powers all over the word, his most memorable adventure was probably the early mission that took him to Berlin. In evidence were all the basic Johnny Canuck story ele-ments: a foreign setting, contact with the anti-Axis underground, a foreign beauty, and countless improbable escapes by "Canada's answer to Nazi oppression." What distinguished the Berlin narrative were Johnny's encounters with Adolf Hitler himself. During this rip-roaring saga, the Canadian superhero confronts the Führer no less than three times, each meeting ending with Johnny slugging the Nazi dictator. It is not hard to imagine the thrill for Canadian kids each time their national hero humiliated the ulti-mate villain.

When it came to the quality of his comic art, the teenager Bachle could not compete with a veteran like Adrian Dingle. However, Bachle's strips visibly improved over the course of his career at Bell. Moreover, his artwork compared favourably with most of his contempo-raries during the Golden Age. As well, whatever Bachle might have lacked in sophistication, he compensated for with the sheer audacity of his breathless

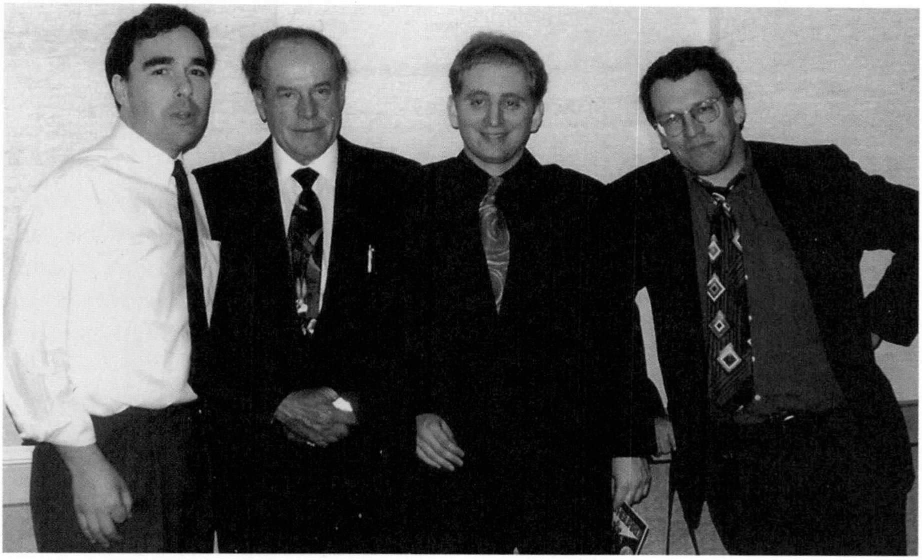

Canadian superhero creators at the launch of Canada Post's Superheroes stamp issue in 1994. Left to right: Richard Comely, Les Barker (Leo Bachle), Mark Shainblum, and Gabriel Morrissette. Copyright © Mark Shainblum.

graphic cliffhangers. Johnny resembled a serial-movie hero who was able to overcome one threat after another, constantly evading the clutches of his enemies. Bachle clearly believed in his character, investing Johnny with a dynamism and integrity that are still apparent more than six decades later.

Bachle's talent was eventually recognized by several American comics publishers who lured him to New York City in 1944. Johnny Canuck, though, was a strong enough character to survive his creator's departure. The hero's final appearances in *Dime* were drawn by André Kulbach and then Paul Dak. Johnny could not, however, outlive the collapse of the English Canadian comic-book industry. Like Nelvana, he succumbed to the onslaught of American comics.[7] Bachle himself left the comics field in the 1950s and became a successful nightclub entertainer, changing his name to Les Barker. In 2005 he was posthumously inducted into the Canadian Comic Book Creator Hall of Fame.[8]

Johnny Canuck, however, was not the only male national superhero of Canada's Golden Age. Educational Projects of Montreal, the fifth Canadian comic-book company of the 1940s, launched a rival character, Canada Jack, in March 1943 in the fifth issue of its main title, *Canadian Heroes*. Unlike its competitors, Educational, which was run

by Harry J. Halperin, viewed comics not as a form of escapist adventure, but rather as an educational medium. Accordingly, issues of *Canadian Heroes* often featured laudatory endorsements from luminaries such as Canadian cabinet ministers.

Nevertheless, Halperin was a businessman and had to be aware of the success his competitors were enjoying with superhero-adventure stories. As a result, when George M. Rae, one of the leading freelance artists who worked for Educational, approached Halperin and proposed that *Canadian Heroes* depart from its focus on narratives about real heroes such as explorers and Victoria Cross winners and feature a fictional character — a national superhero named Canada Jack — Halperin agreed, but with the proviso that the realistic nature of the character be emphasized so as not to detract from his firm's carefully cultivated image as an educational publisher. Thus Canada Jack would be a superhero with very limited powers and with serious constraints on the scope of his adventures. Unlike his Bell Features rivals, Jack would not fight bizarre invaders from other worlds or associate with exotic beauties in the anti-Axis underground.[9]

In many ways, the careers of Canada Jack and Johnny Canuck were complementary. Like Johnny, Jack's very name underscored his Canadian identity. Furthermore, while both heroes were

extremely athletic (and exceedingly lucky), neither was endowed with the kind of super-powers that Superman or Nelvana displayed. However, whereas Johnny had only a single adventure in Canada, Canada Jack had only one adventure abroad. And while Johnny fought the Axis military head on, Jack was a hero for the home front, focusing on the saboteurs and Axis agents who were intent on undermining the war effort in Canada.

A superb horsemen and an expert at jiu-jitsu, Jack was also a first-rate gymnast. His costume thus consisted of a gymnast's outfit with a tank top featuring a Canada Jack crest. Assisting Jack in his adventures were the members of a children's group, the Canada Jack Club (CJC). Many wartime heroes were joined by young sidekicks, but the CJC was unique in that it existed both in the pages of *Canadian Heroes* and in the real world. Organized by Educational's publisher, the CJC drew hundreds of members from the readership of *Canadian Heroes*. Once the club was up and running, each issue of the comic book featured CJC news, contests, and a profile of a club member who had made a signal contribution to the war effort.

Drawn and written by Rae, who signed himself variously as Rae, Geo, and Dez, the Canada Jack stories generally lacked the exoticism that characterized the adventures of the other Canadian

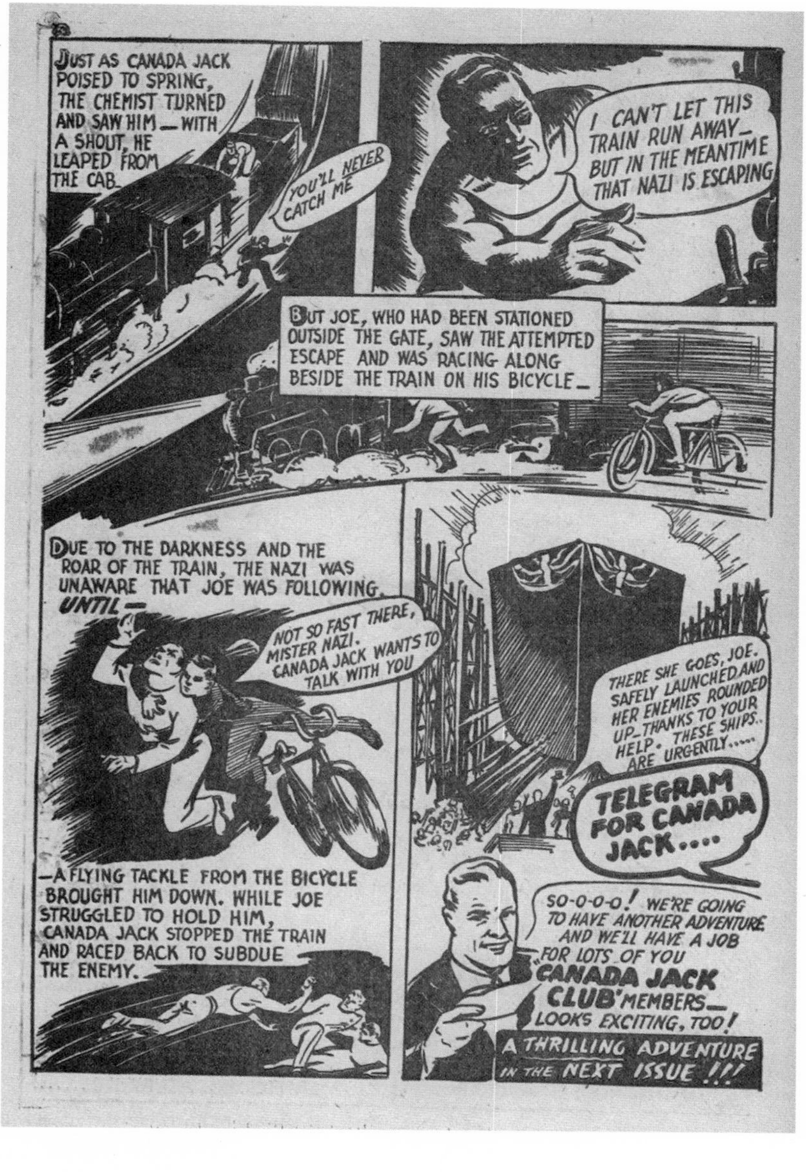
JUST AS CANADA JACK POISED TO SPRING, THE CHEMIST TURNED AND SAW HIM — WITH A SHOUT, HE LEAPED FROM THE CAB.
YOU'LL NEVER CATCH ME
I CAN'T LET THIS TRAIN RUN AWAY— BUT IN THE MEANTIME THAT NAZI IS ESCAPING
BUT JOE, WHO HAD BEEN STATIONED OUTSIDE THE GATE, SAW THE ATTEMPTED ESCAPE AND WAS RACING ALONG BESIDE THE TRAIN ON HIS BICYCLE —
DUE TO THE DARKNESS AND THE ROAR OF THE TRAIN, THE NAZI WAS UNAWARE THAT JOE WAS FOLLOWING. UNTIL—
NOT SO FAST THERE, MISTER NAZI. CANADA JACK WANTS TO TALK WITH YOU
—A FLYING TACKLE FROM THE BICYCLE BROUGHT HIM DOWN. WHILE JOE STRUGGLED TO HOLD HIM, CANADA JACK STOPPED THE TRAIN AND RACED BACK TO SUBDUE THE ENEMY.
THERE SHE GOES, JOE. SAFELY LAUNCHED AND HER ENEMIES ROUNDED UP—THANKS TO YOUR HELP. THESE SHIPS.. ARE URGENTLY.....
TELEGRAM FOR CANADA JACK....
SO-O-O-O! WE'RE GOING TO HAVE ANOTHER ADVENTURE AND WE'LL HAVE A JOB FOR LOTS OF YOU CANADA JACK CLUB' MEMBERS— LOOKS EXCITING, TOO!
A THRILLING ADVENTURE IN THE NEXT ISSUE !!!

Page 63 of Canadian Heroes *Vol. 2, No. 2 (June 1943). Art by* George Rae. *Copyright © Educational Projects.*

Spotlight

national superheroes. However, Rae, an accomplished Montreal-based graphic artist, created tight, well-paced adventures for Educational's sole superhero. Over the course of his career, from March 1943 to October 1945, Jack outwitted Nazi agents, firebugs, rumour mongers, black marketers, saboteurs, kidnappers, and enemy prisoner-of-war escapees.

Like Nelvana and Johnny Canuck, Jack did not survive the resumption of the distribution of American comics in Canada. In fact, Educational withdrew from the market in October 1945 when other companies were still determined to remain active and hoping to arrange for the shipment of their comics into the United States and/or the United Kingdom. Educational's demise was probably just as well; once the Axis menace was removed, Jack's adventures became so mundane that the villain of his last adventure was a blue jay! Like Adrian Dingle, Rae left the comics field and returned to commercial art. And again, like Dingle, he later pursued a fine-arts career. In fact, after the war, the two creators of Canadian national superheroes became friends.

As the Canadian Golden Age of Comics came to an end during the 1945–47 period, Canada's own superheroes disappeared. The appearance of Nelvana in the F.E. Howard Company's *Super Duper* No. 7 in May 1947 marked the last story of the era to feature a Canadian national superhero. Ironically,

the story was also the first adventure of a Canadian national superhero to appear in colour and thus seemed to promise a bold new future for Canada's superheroes. Instead, the next generation of Canadian kids thrilled to the adventures of foreign heroes.

Interestingly, the Canadian superheroes were not alone in their failure to survive the war's end. Even though the post-war decade witnessed an explosion in the U.S. comics industry (more than sixty million comics appeared every month), the public's appetite for superhero comics declined sharply.[10] As a result, American publishers shifted to other genres. In English Canada, the few surviving publishers reprinted and repackaged U.S. comics for the Canadian market, but even this industry collapsed in 1951 when all restrictions on the importation of American comics were lifted.

The one English Canadian publisher that remained after 1951, Superior Publishers, shut down in 1956 just as the American comics industry, reeling from the crime-comics controversy, entered a new era: the U.S. Silver Age of Comics, which began with the publication of *Showcase* No. 4 in September 1956. What distinguished this issue was the resurrection in its pages of The Flash, one of the American Golden Age superheroes. After a hiatus of more than ten years, the comic-book public — by this time consisting mostly of children — was eager for a new generation of heroes. The Flash was soon followed by a myriad of superheroes, most of them produced by two firms: DC Comics and Marvel Comics.

For Canadian kids growing up in the 1950s, comic books had been an outrageous mélange of genres: horror, crime, war, western, jungle, romance, funny-animal, *Classics Illustrated* and, to a lesser degree, superheroes. For their younger brothers and sisters who came of age in the 1960s, the medium was very different. Like the kids of the 1940s, those of the 1960s were treated to a multitude of superheroes. This was the era of great Marvel characters such as the Fantastic Four, Spider-Man, Daredevil, The Incredible Hulk, and the X-Men. However, what all Canadian comic-book readers of the 1950–1970 period had in common was a sense of alienation. For English Canadians, comics had become an American medium: the heroes were American, the settings were largely American, and even the alluring comic-book ads for toy soldiers and sea monkeys were American. Like U.S. television, comics seemed to contain an implicit message: Canada was a backwater bereft of heroes.

This situation began to change, though, in the late 1960s and early 1970s, a period that witnessed the growth of a new cultural nationalism in Canada, as well as the emergence of new underground and alternative publishers in the comics field. This period also saw the rediscovery of the lost Canadian heroes of the 1940s and the rebirth of the Canadian comics industry — what might be deemed Canada's own Silver Age of Comics.[11]

One measure of the American domination of the comics medium during the 1950s and 1960s is that when Canadian superheroes finally did return between 1969 and 1973, the first characters were buffoons. It was as if Canada's comics artists and writers recognized the absence of Canadian heroes but couldn't take such figures seriously. Nevertheless, following a spate of outrageous Captain Canadas and other intriguing satirical national superheroes, it was evident that there were creators who were determined to portray national superhero figures in a more serious fashion.[12] Contributing to this resurgence were the publication of Patrick Loubert and Michael Hirsh's *The Great Canadian Comic Books* (1971), a book-length study of the Bell Features comics of the 1940s, and the touring of *Comic Art Traditions in Canada, 1941–45*, a related exhibition mounted by the National Gallery of Canada.

The first of this new generation of national superheroes, the Northern Light, had a very unpromising start. The character's initial story, which appeared in July 1974 in the second issue of *Orb*, a Toronto-based, mostly black-and-white comics magazine, was written by American writer T. Casey Brennan and

Spotlight

had been intended for a U.S. comic character. John Allison, an *Orb* artist, learned of Brennan's unused script and offered to collaborate with Brennan on a story. James Waley, the publisher of *Orb*, welcomed the idea, and Brennan and Allison prepared a two-part story, utilizing Brennan's script but changing the character's name to the Phantom Canadian. Waley, however, was not happy with this name and pushed Brennan to find an alternative. Brennan proposed the White Light, which was altered at the suggestion of Waley's wife, Sharon, to the Northern Light.[13]

The difficulties surrounding the naming of the Northern Light, who wore red-and-white tights with a red cowl, white gloves and, for a time, a flowing cape, portended more serious problems with the original conception of the character. In his first adventure, the Northern Light travels to Mars where he becomes embroiled in a struggle between the Martian High Council and a Martian superhero, the Lone Guardian, who is responsible for protecting the Red Planet from the evils of humanity. Although the strip featured solid art by John Allison and then Jim Craig, the Northern Light did not have an auspicious debut. Not only was the script stilted and ill-conceived, but it also largely ignored the character's Canadian identity. Consequently, the initial version of the Northern Light was little more than a third-rate American superhero who

happened to have a Canadian name and costume.

However, the character was rescued by the next creative team to work on the strip — the writer James Waley and the artist Jim Craig. In the Northern Light's second, and last, adventure, a three-part story begun in 1975–76 in *Orb* Nos. 4–5 and concluded in 1977 in the fourth issue of the U.S. title *Power Comics*, Waley and Craig gave the character a new identity, transforming him into a powerful national superhero. In fact, as his name suggested, the new Northern Light was somewhat reminiscent of Adrian Dingle's Nelvana.

Originally a disillusioned architect named Ian Davis, the Northern Light becomes a superhero after he and his family are abducted by aliens who conduct terrible experiments on their captives and eventually kill Davis's wife and son. Davis himself, however, is rescued. The aliens' experiments leave Davis with a number of Nelvana-like superpowers based on the properties of light: the abilities to become one with light (and thus invisible), to burst into uncontrolled radiance, and to transport himself on light beams. He also becomes extremely strong. After his ordeal (which, for a time, he doesn't remember), Davis retreats to a secret fortress in northern Canada, becoming the leading operative of Alert, a Canadian security agency.

At the end of his final adventure the

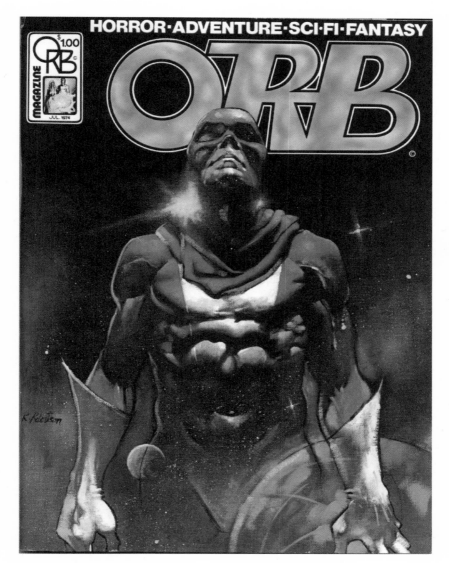

HORROR·ADVENTURE·SCI·FI·FANTASY
$1.00
ORB
MAGAZINE
JUL. 1974
ORB
R. Robertson

Cover of Orb *No. 2 (July 1974). Art by Richard Robertson. Copyright © James Waley.*

Spotlight

Northern Light confronts Conquermind, the alien responsible for all the tragedy that has befallen the Davis family. The enraged Canadian attacks and, against all odds, destroys his powerful tormentor. However, the Northern Light is not able to savour his victory, as he remains too distraught over the loss of his family. Like many of the era's heroes, Canada's new national superhero was a tormented soul. Wielding super-powers in the 1970s was a far more angst-ridden experience than smashing the Axis during World War II.

The Northern Light was the first serious national superhero to emerge after the Golden Age, but the character's impact was limited by several factors, including the fact that *Orb* folded before Craig and Waley could really hit their stride. There is, however, little doubt that the Northern Light would have grown in their hands, since Craig's later work in the U.S. superhero-comics field clearly demonstrated his affinity for the genre.

Waley and Craig's creation was also overshadowed by the publication in July 1975 of *Captain Canuck* No. 1. Although Captain Canuck appeared a full year after the Northern Light, he beat the *Orb* character to the newsstands, since the first issue of *Orb* to be distributed nationally wasn't released until November 1975. By that time, Canuck was already established as the English Canadian national superhero of the 1970s. Contributing to the success of *Captain Canuck* was the

fact that, unlike *Orb*, it was issued in colour in a regular comic-book format — the first such comic featuring a Canadian national superhero for almost thirty years.

As was the case with the Northern Light, Captain Canuck's beginnings were not all that promising. The Captain was conceived in 1971 by Ron Leishman, a Winnipeg artist who recognized the need for a staunchly Canadian superhero to personify the country's growing nationalism. The following year Leishman met fellow artist Richard Comely, and the two began to talk about Leishman's idea. Initially, the pair intended to name their national superhero Captain Canada, but copyright considerations forced them to settle on Captain Canuck. However, before Canuck could be fully developed, Leishman left Winnipeg in 1974, leaving Comely to work alone on the character. A year later, after many difficulties, Comely self-published the first issue of *Captain Canuck*. And while, because of its novelty, the comic received a great deal of media attention, the first issue left much to be desired in terms of art and script, largely as a result of Comely's inexperience with the comics medium.[14]

Comely persisted, however, and his writing and artwork improved in the next few issues. Furthermore, as a publisher, he was quick to recognize the enormous talent of two young artists, George Freeman and Jean-Claude St-Aubin, who

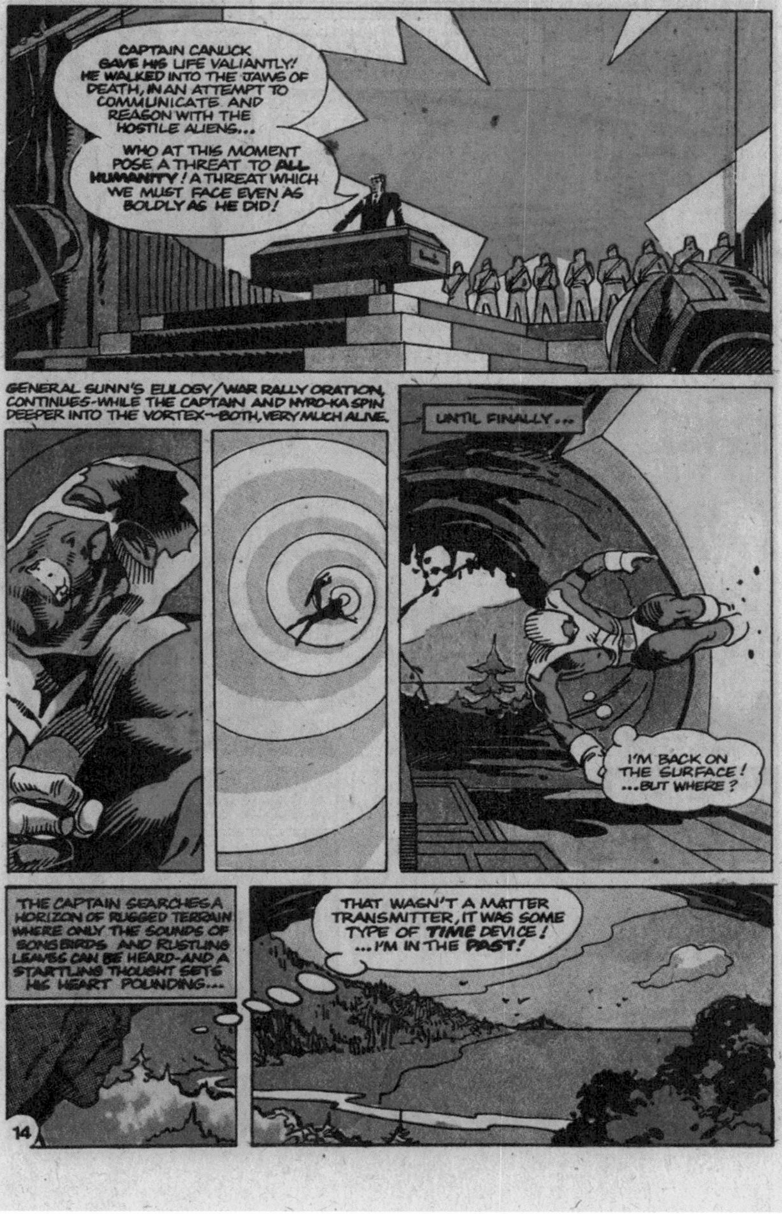
CAPTAIN CANUCK GAVE HIS LIFE VALIANTLY! HE WALKED INTO THE JAWS OF DEATH, IN AN ATTEMPT TO COMMUNICATE AND REASON WITH THE HOSTILE ALIENS...
WHO AT THIS MOMENT POSE A THREAT TO ALL HUMANITY! A THREAT WHICH WE MUST FACE EVEN AS BOLDLY AS HE DID!
GENERAL SUNN'S EULOGY/WAR RALLY ORATION, CONTINUES-WHILE THE CAPTAIN AND NYRO-KA SPIN DEEPER INTO THE VORTEX~BOTH, VERY MUCH ALIVE.
UNTIL FINALLY...
I'M BACK ON THE SURFACE! ...BUT WHERE?
THE CAPTAIN SEARCHES A HORIZON OF RUGGED TERRAIN WHERE ONLY THE SOUNDS OF SONGBIRDS AND RUSTLING LEAVES CAN BE HEARD-AND A STARTLING THOUGHT SETS HIS HEART POUNDING...
THAT WASN'T A MATTER TRANSMITTER, IT WAS SOME TYPE OF TIME DEVICE! ...I'M IN THE PAST!
14

Page 14 of Captain Canuck *No. 12 (December 1980). Art by George Freeman. Copyright © Richard Comely.*

Spotlight

approached him in 1976 and offered to work on Canuck. Increasingly, from issue No. 3 on, Freeman and St-Aubin assumed more and more of the artwork chores on *Captain Canuck*, while Comely concentrated on the scripts.

Unlike his wartime predecessors, Canuck wrapped himself in the flag, wearing a red-and-white costume that sported two maple leafs. (Of course, Canada's 1965 flag offered far more costume-related possibilities than its predecessor.) Canuck was also more conscious of the duality of Canada, and thus worked in tandem with the super-agent Kébec, the first of several French Canadian associate heroes who have appeared in Canadian comics. Furthermore, because of Comely's strong Christian beliefs and his determination to give Canuck a distinctly Canadian identity, the character eschewed violence as much as possible. In many ways, Canuck was the appropriate superhero for a middle power that was distrustful of heroism and aware of the limits of power — even though his narratives were mostly set in the 1990s when an imagined Canada had become a superpower because of its natural resources!

Like the Northern Light, Canuck acquired his powers as a result of an alien encounter. While camping with a group of Boy Scouts, Canadian International Security Organization (CISO) agent Tom Evans awakes in the middle of the night to find that the boys are missing. Evans discovers that the Scouts are being controlled by a group of aliens and then is himself seized by the extraterrestrials and exposed to Zeta rays. Neither Evans nor the boys are left with any memory of their close encounter, other than, in the case of Evans, a nagging, dream-like recollection. The boys, however, are still in the aliens' control, while Evans's exposure to Zeta rays has left him with double his normal strength and speed. CISO decides to transform the super-strong Evans into a symbol not only of its power and authority, but also of the Canadian nation.

While Canuck's first adventure did serve to introduce the character, the story, involving a Communist invasion of Canada and a mind-control device, was not very memorable. Canuck's second adventure was set partly in a lost Incan city and was decidedly more entertaining and ambitious. However, readers of the first installment, which appeared in *Captain Canuck* No. 3 in the summer of 1976, had to wait until 1979 for the remaining chapters of the story. By that time, Comely was laying the groundwork for the second half of the Captain's original run, the period that saw *Captain Canuck* become one of the finest superhero comics ever published. The search for a unique Canadian superhero that had begun in the early 1970s appeared finally to be over.

By the end of 1979, Richard Comely (then a partner in a new publishing firm,

CKR Productions) had assembled the creative team that would be responsible for the most polished work on Captain Canuck: Comely himself serving as the chief writer, George Freeman as the main artist, and Jean-Claude St-Aubin as both a co-inker and the major colourist. Probably their best effort was "Chariots of Fire," a three-part story that ran in *Captain Canuck* Nos. 11–13.

"Chariots of Fire" not only further explored Canuck's origin, but it also represented an attempt to redefine the character by bringing him backwards from the 1990s to the early 1980s. By reintroducing the aliens that had inadvertently given Canuck his super-powers, Comely was also able to unveil a time-travel device that eventually thrust Canuck back in time to the year 1040 where he ends up helping the Mi'kmaq repulse a Viking invasion. Having Canuck disappear from the year 1995 allowed Comely to portray the superhero's apparent death and thereby examine the meaning and impact of heroism. In a powerful sequence towards the end of the story, the narrative alternates between the struggles of the Earth forces of 1995 to stop an alien invasion and the efforts of Canuck and the Mi'kmaq to defeat Norse invaders (the eleventh-century portion of the story was brilliantly drawn by Freeman in a style that paid homage to Harold Foster's classic *Prince Valiant* strip). The narrative ends with Canuck helping the Earth forces of 1995 and then emerging from a time portal into the year 1980.

Unfortunately, soon thereafter, CKR Productions folded and the Captain vanished from newsstands and comic-book shops. Canuck's loss was lamented in the comics press and came at a time when his creators were bringing a new assurance and maturity to the strip. Ironically, the last published issue of the comic (No. 14, March 1981) appeared just before there were major changes in the North American comics market that would benefit alternative publishers like CKR. Nonetheless, the 1979–80 Canuck narratives will remain a benchmark for anyone committed to the portrayal of a Canadian national superhero. In fact, it is doubtful that any artist will ever surpass George Freeman's *Captain Canuck* visual storytelling for the sheer joy of its unrestrained, square-jawed heroism.

As Canuck disappeared, more national superheroes were emerging, but not characters that showed the influence of Comely, Freeman, and St-Aubin's work. The impact of *Captain Canuck* would only be felt later in the decade.

The first of these new heroes was Apache Communications' Captain Canada who, as previously noted, had been preceded by a number of satirical figures with the same name. Created by the father-and-son team of Geoffrey and Scott Stirling, two Newfoundland media executives who adopted the pseudonym Geoffrey Scott, Captain Canada first

Spotlight

77

appeared in 1980 in the St. John's *Sunday Herald*'s *Captain Newfoundland* strip. The strip, which was drawn by American artist Danny Bulanadi, was collected in 1981 in the comic-book *Captain Newfoundland*. However, it was not until the publication of a Captain Newfoundland/Captain Canada graphic novel, *Atlantis*, a few years later that the character was fully developed by the Stirlings.

Like Comely's Canuck, Captain Canada wore a red-and-white costume based on the maple-leaf flag. Captain Canada (whose alter ego was a young man named Daniel Eaton) was recruited to his superhero duties by the most powerful of the characters in the Stirlings' comics universe — Captain Atlantis. In fact, Captain Canada was joined by numerous other characters, including an aboriginal superhero, Captain Freedom, and a Québécois superheroine, Mademoiselle. While Captain Canada was, in some ways, a typical superhero — rescuing Queen Elizabeth II and Prince Charles from a giant Japanese robot in an epic battle that destroys part of downtown Ottawa — he was also very singular, distinguished by both the content of the strip and the way in which it was promoted.

In terms of content, it was apparent that the Stirlings' goal was not to produce a traditional superhero. Instead, they viewed Captain Canada as a didactic vehicle, a means to popularize certain philosophical and religious ideas. While endeavouring to produce exciting adventures designed to instill patriotism in Canadian kids, the Stirlings also sought to explore complex mystical beliefs and the nature of good and evil. As for their approach to promotion, the Stirlings did not focus on the traditional comics market. Instead, taking advantage of their media connections and experience, they sought to reach a larger audience, producing television programs and even arranging for an actor to make public appearances dressed as Captain Canada. However, despite their promotional efforts, the Stirlings' character remained decidedly unique and largely outside the national superhero tradition in Canadian comic art.

The second attempt, after Captain Canuck, to create a Canadian national superhero for the 1980s led to the emergence of a team of superheroes — John Byrne's Alpha Flight. Byrne was an accomplished Canadian artist and writer who had moved from western Canada to the United States to pursue a career in the New York comics milieu. By the late 1970s, he had become one of the most popular artists in the field. Early in his career, when still in Canada, Byrne had spoken of his strong desire to create Canadian heroes.[15] In fact, his first efforts to design such characters might even predate Ron Leishman's early conceptual work on Captain Canuck. Whatever the case, Byrne had to wait until he was an established superstar in the American comics industry before he was able to truly devote himself to Canadian superhero narratives.

When Byrne finally did turn to the invention of Canadian superheroes, he brought to the process a pent-up energy and vision that resulted in the creation of a multitude of characters, including Aurora, Northstar, Sasquatch, Shaman, Snowbird, and Vindicator (later Guardian), the character who most closely resembled a traditional national superhero.

Byrne's initial work on this Canadian superhero team appeared in the late 1970s in the U.S. title *X-Men*, but it wasn't until 1983, with the publication of a separate title, *Alpha Flight*, that he explored the characters in depth. While Byrne is a consummate professional, *Alpha Flight* belonged too much to the American superhero tradition to really answer the need for Canadian superheroes — a problem that became even more apparent once Byrne left the title after issue No. 28. Nevertheless, *Alpha Flight* remains the longest-running comic book ever to deal with Canadian national superheroes (the title's first series ended in 1994 with issue No. 130; a second twenty-issue series appeared in 1997–99 and was followed by a third series of twelve issues in 2004–05). It also has the distinction of having introduced the first openly gay superhero — Northstar.

The original Byrne Alpha Flight was not, however, without impact in the

Canadian comic-book field in the mid-1980s. Mark Shainblum, a young Montreal writer and publisher who had been an enthusiastic admirer of the later Captain Canuck narratives, saw Byrne's efforts as an object lesson in the pitfalls of conceiving distinctly Canadian superheroes within the confines of American superhero conventions. For Shainblum, a Canadian hero would have to be truly different, not just a typical U.S. superhero wrapped in the Canadian flag. The most sophisticated vision to date of a Canadian superhero was taking shape.

Part of Shainblum's success in fashioning a new approach to the national superhero derived from his awareness of the efforts that had preceded his own. Not only was he familiar with Byrne's Alpha Flight, but he also knew the Golden Age heroes. Furthermore, he was in contact with the creators of the Northern Light and Captain Canuck and was familiar with the Stirlings' Captain Canada. In his own magazine *Orion*, Shainblum had also published a Captain Canuck parody, Captain Canduck (with a script by me and art by Owen Oulton), and had produced preliminary material relating to his own national superheroes — a 1940s-style character named the Red Ensign and a contemporary hero, Northguard.

Shainblum's collaborator on the initial Red Ensign and Northguard concepts was the artist Geoff Isherwood. In 1982, following the demise of *Orion*, the two creators began to focus on Northguard. However, before their new superhero could be fleshed out, Isherwood broke into the New York comics milieu and was forced to end his involvement with the character. Not long after, Shainblum connected with Gabriel Morrissette, a Montreal-based graphic artist. Together they would redefine Northguard.

From the outset, as they developed the character, Shainblum and Morrissette strove to achieve a high degree of realism, making Northguard (whose alter ego was a young student named Philip Wise) a believable person and setting his adventures in a Montreal that was readily recognizable. While many creators rely on generic urban images, Shainblum and Morrissette photographed numerous Montreal locations so that when Northguard entered a building it was usually one that actually existed. This commitment to verisimilitude made their comics all the more convincing. However, while Northguard's adventures were more plausible than those of most superheroes, they were hardly mundane.

Shainblum and Morrissette's single Northguard narrative was a complex eight-part adventure that began in 1984–86 in five issues of *New Triumph Featuring Northguard*, published by Shainblum's Matrix Graphic Series, and was completed in 1989–90 in three issues of *Northguard* from the U.S. publisher

Caliber Press. And though the story was very much a superhero adventure, it also drew upon the thriller genre, thrusting Northguard into a murky world of intrigue involving foreign governments, multinational corporations, and a menacing right-wing organization called ManDes (Manifest Destiny).

The story opens with Wise being abducted and taken to the headquarters of Progressive Allied Canadian Technologies (PACT) in Vaudreuil, where he learns of both a threatened takeover of Canada by the mysterious ManDes organization and of PACT's development of a revolutionary cybernetic personal-weapons system called the Uniband. As a result of his brainwave patterns, Wise happens to possesses the ability to wield the device which, in effect, gives its operator the firepower of an army battalion. PACT tries to recruit Wise, urging him to operate the weapon in the coming conflict with ManDes. Wise, a comic-book fan, finally agrees to cooperate, provided that PACT will allow him to operate the Uniband as a superhero — and not just any superhero. Wise is a fan of Captain Canuck and Alpha Flight, so he wants to be a national superhero who wears a flag costume. PACT agrees and Northguard is born.

As Northguard, Wise is rapidly drawn into a vortex of violence. Eventually joining him in the struggle against ManDes is a martial-arts expert, Manon Deschamps, who also becomes a superhero, adopting

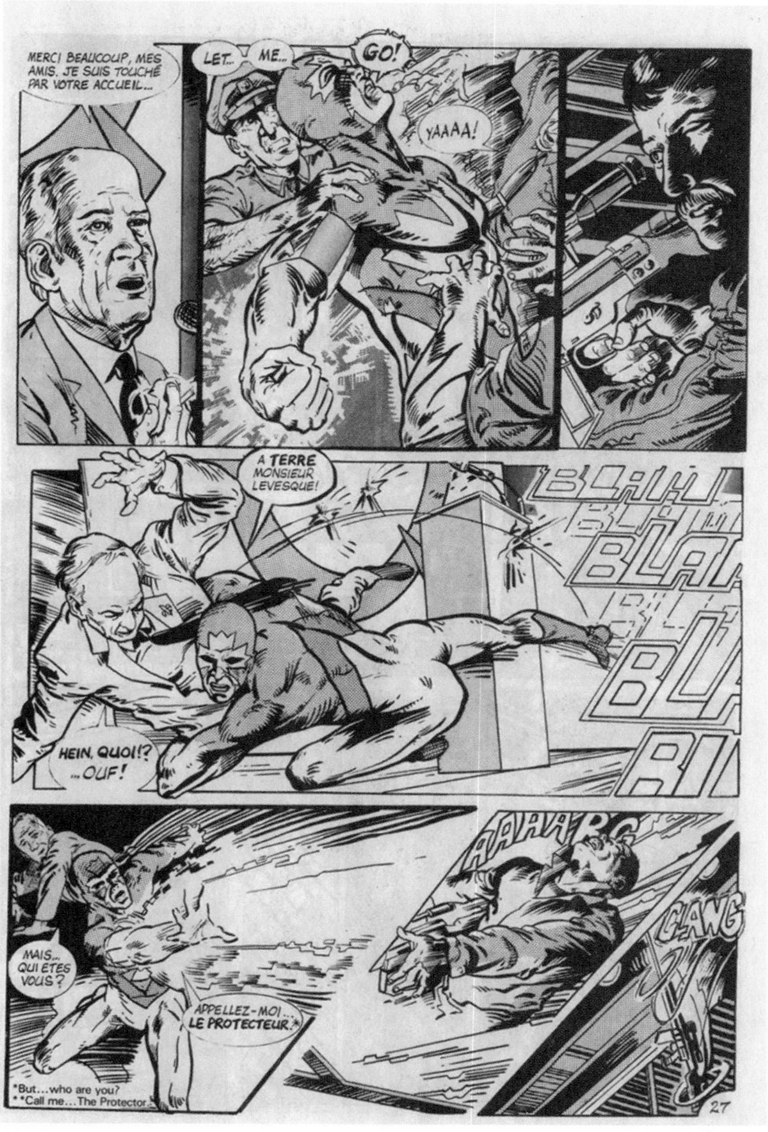

MERCI BEAUCOUP, MES AMIS. JE SUIS TOUCHÉ PAR VOTRE ACCUEIL...
LET... ME...
GO!
YAAAA!
A TERRE MONSIEUR LEVESQUE!
HEIN, QUOI!? ...OUF!
MAIS... QUI ETES VOUS?
APPELLEZ-MOI... LE PROTECTEUR.*
CLANG
*But...who are you?
**Call me...The Protector.

Page 27 of New Triumph Featuring Northguard *No. 1 (September 1984). Art by Gabriel Morrissette. Copyright © Mark Shainblum and Gabriel Morrissette.*

Spotlight

the identity of Fleur de Lys. Northguard rescues the Quebec premier from an assassin at a rally at the Montreal Forum and is then himself rescued by another PACT operative from Soviet and U.S. secret agents. Shainblum and Morrissette show that being a superhero is no easy matter. Although the bookish Wise seeks to live out his comic-book fantasies, he is soon overtaken by events and is captured by ManDes, which plans to use him and the Uniband as a weapon against PACT and Canada. The superhero-as-saviour is thus transformed into a destroyer: Wise and the Uniband will be used to trigger a massive nuclear explosion. At the last moment, though, Wise gains control of the device and destroys ManDes, becoming the hero that he was meant to be. The story ends with Wise — sobered and perplexed by his ordeal — spurning a CSIS attempt to recruit him.

By underpinning their work with realism and by examining the cost of heroism, Shainblum and Morrissette were responsible for the most mature depiction ever of a Canadian national superhero. Shainblum's writing was restrained and honest and a perfect match for Morrissette's dynamic but realistic artwork. Unfortunately, both creators ceased to work on the character in 1989.

After the demise of Northguard, Canada's national superheroes remained largely dormant until 1992 when they were the subject of my exhibition *Guardians of the North: The National Superhero in Canadian Comic-Book Art* at the Canadian Museum of Caricature in Ottawa. The first exhibition to explore a particular theme within the Canadian graphic-narrative tradition, *Guardians of the North* sparked a good deal of interest in Canada's own superheroes, even prompting Canada Post to release a special stamp issue in 1995 that commemorated Superman, Nelvana, Johnny Canuck, Captain Canuck, and Fleur de Lys.

In the year following the *Guardians* exhibition, Richard Comely relaunched Captain Canuck, giving him a new identity (Darren Oaks) and pitting him against a bizarre international conspiracy (a recurring theme for Comely). Regrettably, this new hero lacked the panache of Freeman and St-Aubin's classic version. After appearing in a few comic books published by Comely's new imprint, Semple Comics, and a short-lived newspaper strip, the new Canuck, like his much-lamented predecessor, vanished.

Then, in 1998–99, Mark Shainblum, the co-creator of Northguard and a contributor to the Captain Canuck newspaper strip, joined with the Prince Edward Island comic artist Sandy Carruthers (who had also briefly worked on the Canuck strip) in an effort to resurrect and revamp the original Captain Canuck (Tom Evans). The first chapter of their graphic narrative featuring the "New Original Captain Canuck" appeared in a small promotional

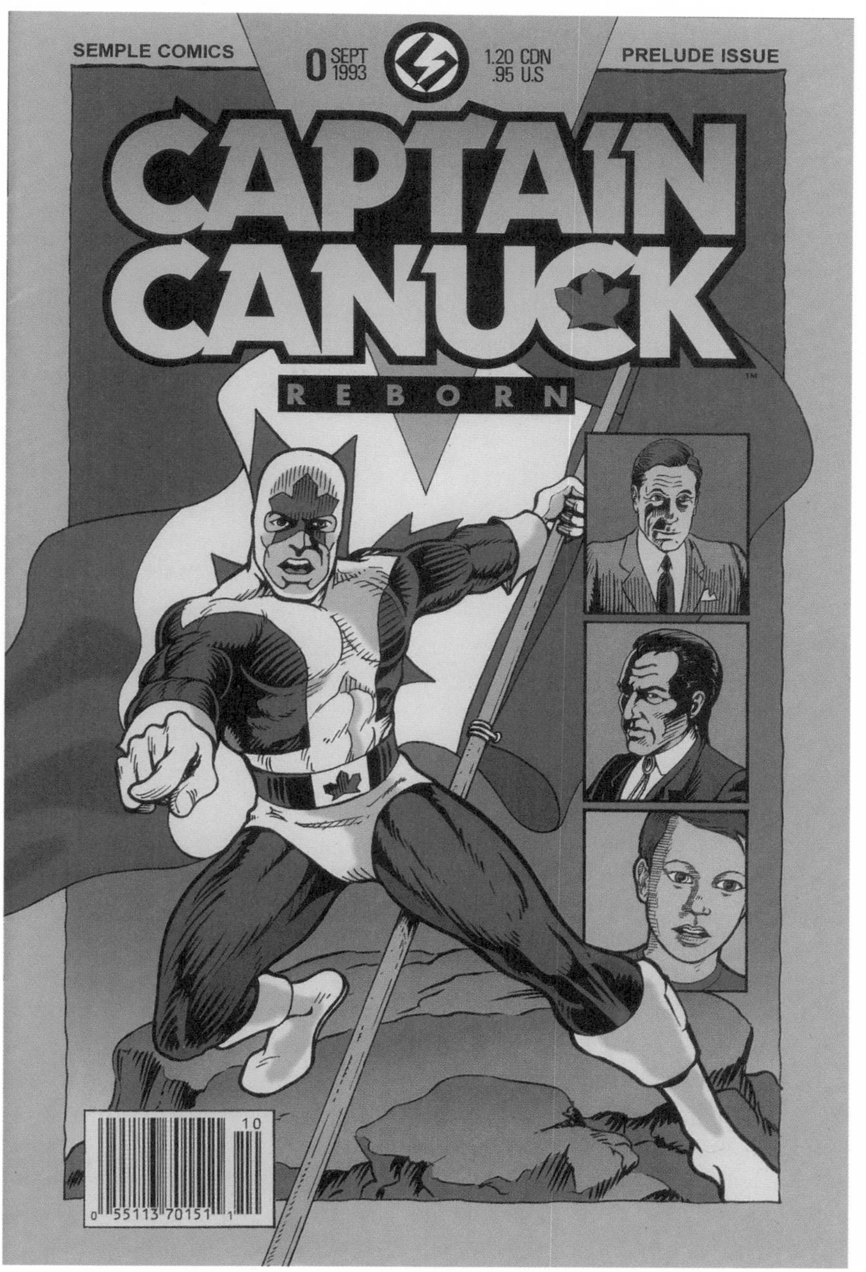
SEMPLE COMICS
0 SEPT 1993
1.20 CDN .95 U.S
PRELUDE ISSUE
CAPTAIN CANUCK
REBORN
10
0 55113 70151 1

Cover of Captain Canuck Prelude *No. 0 (September 1993). Art by Richard Comely. Copyright © Richard Comely.*

Spotlight

comic (a so-called "ashcan") with very limited distribution. Carruthers later posted portions of the story for a time on his website (*www.sandycarruthers.com*). More recently, he, Mark Shainblum, and Jeff Alward collaborated on a webcomic featuring a new Canadian national superhero, Canadiana. Her adventures are currently found on Carruthers's website. Unfortunately, these efforts have had limited impact.

Meanwhile, the irrepressible Richard Comely returned to superhero comics in 2004–05, both releasing the long-lost issue No. 15 of the original Captain Canuck series, which had been slated for publication in 1981, and collaborating with two Winnipeg artists, the brothers Riel and Drue Langlois, on the creation of a three-issue series, "Unholy War," which featured a new Captain Canuck, West Coast RCMP constable David Semple. Sadly, the latest incarnation of Canuck disappeared from comics early in 2005. However, because of the 1995 Superheroes stamp issue and Richard Comely's exceptional skills as a promoter, Canuck has become something of a nationalist icon, a curious instance of a widely recognized comic-book superhero without a regularly published comic book.

The goal of sustaining distinctly Canadian superheroes has proven to be an elusive one, even for determined creators such as Comely and Shainblum. However, the superhero genre remains a strong current within contemporary comics and among Canadian comics professionals, many of whom have contributed to the U.S. superhero field. Consequently, the dream of a national superhero is likely to persist as long as Canadians produce comic art. Superheroes and comic books now seem inextricably linked, and as long as there are superheroes, some of them will be expressly designed to personify Canada's national ideals and aspirations. Not only can we expect a new generation of national superheroes, but it is also likely that at least some of the earlier heroes will be resurrected. (Surely, we have not seen the last of Captain Canuck! In fact, just as this book goes to press, Richard Comely has relaunched the character yet again, this time in a four-part series entitled *Captain Canuck Legacy*.)

Yet, despite the persistence of Canada's engagement with superheroes, Canadians are probably too wary of the uncritical portrayal of unrestrained heroism and power for the superhero genre ever to become a mainstay of the country's indigenous comic art. In fact, one of the real fortes of Canadians during the past few decades has been satire and humour, including some very clever superhero spoofs by creators such as Dave Sim, John MacLeod, Ty Templeton, Rob Walton, Greg Hyland, Bernie Mireault, Mark Shainblum, and Gabriel Morrissette.

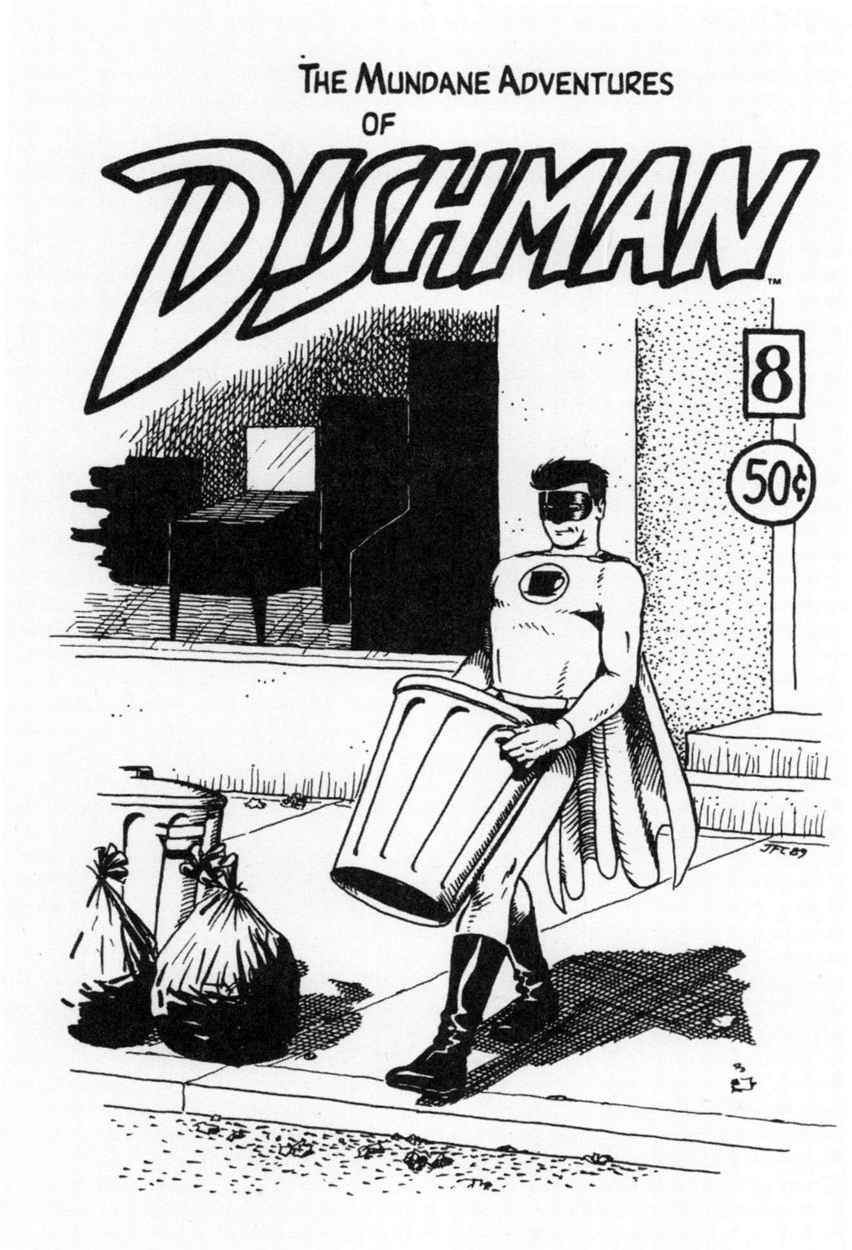
THE MUNDANE ADVENTURES
OF
DISHMAN
8
50¢
JFC89

Cover of Dishman *No. 8 (1989). Art by John MacLeod. Copyright © John MacLeod.*

Spotlight

However, while some artists are content to express their skepticism towards superheroes in satire, others have made it their mission to transcend superhero narratives completely, whether serious or humorous. Increasingly, these people view the genre as an artistic dead end and a hindrance to the development of comic art in Canada. For them superheroes represent cultural immaturity. These artists see comics as a medium that has finally outgrown its pulpish roots and which is now a serious art form, combining literature and visual art in innovative ways. Their goal is to tell adult stories, new narratives that draw on literature, autobiography, history, and other sources.

Only time will tell whether this new, presumably more mature, vision of comic art will supplant the superhero narratives that have so long been such a dominant part of the comics tradition in North America.

Crackdown on Comics:
The Lean Years,
1947–1966

4

By early 1947, Bell Features and at least one or two other reprint firms were operating in Canada. They were joined by three intrepid publishers issuing a handful of original full-colour Canadian comics: Superior Publishers, F.E. Howard Publications, and Export Publications. All of these companies were located in Toronto, and all were involved not only in comics publishing, but also in the production of pulp magazines and early paperbacks (mostly digests).

Determined to keep the Golden Age alive, F.E. Howard, which had published a small number of original and reprint comics between 1943 and 1945, obtained the rights to various Bell Features characters and published two titles, *Super Duper* and *Dizzy Don*, which were distributed in both Canada and the United States. Howard also produced a few other titles, including *Carousel Comics*, which apparently received some distribution in the United Kingdom. Export, which had been responsible for a one-shot Canadian fantasy pulp, *Eerie Tales*, issued an educational comic book, *Captain Hobby Comics*, in February 1947, and similarly arranged for distribution south of the border. However, as was the case with Howard, Export's foray into the production of original comics was short-lived. American competition, it seems, proved to be too overwhelming for both firms.

Superior Publishers, on the other hand, not only survived the difficult transitional years of 1946–47, but also began to display a particularly aggressive and innovative approach to comics publishing. Not long after releasing a single issue of *Nomad Comics* by former Maple Leaf, Bell, and Howard contributor Edward Letkeman, early in 1946, the firm published another comic book by the artist. Entitled *Zor the Mighty Comics*, it

4

featured heroes such as Zor, Dr. Justice, and Sir Guy.[1] A few months later a second issue appeared. In June 1947, it was reprinted as *Red Seal Comics* No. 19, a title that Superior had acquired from the American publisher Harry A. Chesler. (These Letkeman comics also seem to have been repackaged by Superior under the titles *Jungle Comics* and *Jungle Adventures*, both of which received distribution in the United Kingdom, as did a third issue of *Zor the Mighty* and several other Superior titles.)[2]

Apparently owned by William Zimmerman, Superior tended to dominate the Canadian comic-book scene from 1947 until 1956. In addition to using its own name, Superior (Publishing or Publishers) published under at least four other imprints: Century Publishing, Herald Printing, Duchess Printing, and Randall Publications. Although it initially eyed the post-war U.K. market, it soon shifted its attention to the larger and more accessible U.S. market.[3]

The U.S. orientation of Superior Publishers and the few other publishing houses active in 1947 was attributable, of course, to economic realities. If they no longer had the national market to themselves, and the British market ceased to be a viable long-term alternative, the country's publishers were obliged to either reprint U.S. comics for distribution in Canada and/or sell Canadian comics in the United States.

Late in 1947, though, conditions changed dramatically. As was the case in 1941, Canada's financial position vis-à-vis the United States was entering a crisis.

The Canadian economy was experiencing a post-war boom, but an alarming trade deficit with the United States rapidly developed as consumers rushed to obtain the many goods they had been denied between 1941 and 1945. Although reluctant to introduce trade barriers that ran counter to the new international trade agreement, the General Agreement on Tariffs and Trade (GATT), Prime Minister William Lyon Mackenzie King's government was forced to preserve U.S. exchange reserves by reintroducing an import ban (the Emergency Exchange Conservation Act). Once again, American publishers were excluded from the Canadian market. However, unlike 1941, the new regulations permitted publishers in Canada to purchase the rights to reprint and repackage American comics.[4]

Overnight a new comic-book industry sprang up in response to the government's actions. There was no thought, however, of resurrecting the indigenous titles that had flourished during the war years. American hegemony was a *fait accompli*. Anyway, it was much simpler — and cheaper — to acquire reprint rights than it was to establish the infrastructure needed for a distinct national industry. Moreover, publishers could not help but be aware of their vulnerability.

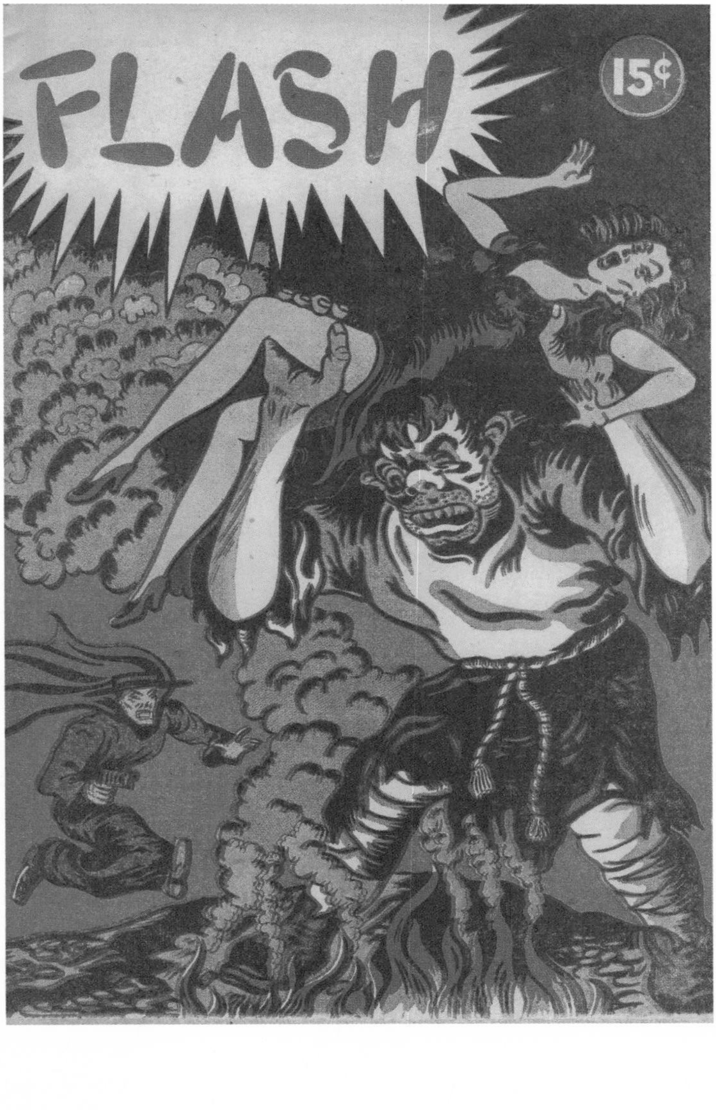
FLASH
15¢

Cover of Flash Comic Section *(September 11 1948), an example of the many oddball Canadian comics exported to the United Kingdom between 1946 and 1948. This title combines a cover reprinted from Superior's* Red Seal Comics *No. 19 (June 1947) with interior artwork from Al Rucker Publications'* Scooter *No. 1 (1945). Copyright unknown.*

Facing page: Cover of Strange Mysteries *No. 10 (March 1953). Art probably by the Iger Studio. Copyright © Superior Publishers.*

The entire reprint industry was predicated on a form of government intervention that was ultimately unacceptable to many Canadians, not to mention the country's powerful neighbour to the south.

Those firms, like Bell, which were already reprinting U.S. comics, quickly expanded their lines. Other companies arose and acquired rights from the various American publishers unrepresented in Canada. By 1948 numerous publishing houses were involved in the burgeoning new industry, including Bell, Anglo-American, Export, Superior, Wilson, Daniels, Publication Services, Derby, Gilberton Publications (which had issued some Canadian editions in 1946), and Better Publications. The last two were American subsidiaries. Many of these companies were also active in paperback publishing.[5]

While Superior was among the leading reprint firms, by the end of 1948 it was the only company also releasing original comic books. Although published in Canada, these were only nominally Canadian. In addition to continuing with *Red Seal*, the firm acquired two titles that had been previously associated with the U.S. publisher Farrell: *Aggie Mack* and *Brenda Starr*. Like all subsequent original Superior comics, these were produced by Jerry Iger's New York comic-art studio. Among the many unsigned Iger Studio artists who worked on Superior's fifteen post-1947 titles were such American luminaries as Jack Kamen, Al Feldstein, and Matt Baker (one of the few black comics artists active during this era). Another frequent contributor was Iger's partner, the writer Ruth Roche. Written and drawn by Americans artists for American readers, Superior's line was a far cry from the original Canadian comics that had preceded them.[6]

The year 1948 marked the resumption of Canada's comic-book industry, albeit in a branch-plant form, but it also witnessed events that had a profoundly negative impact on the development of North American comic art for many years to come. Across the country, parent-teacher associations, community groups, and church organizations were becoming increasingly vocal in their opposition to so-called "crime comics," which they perceived as an insidious threat to the moral development of the nation's children. According to their critics, such publications were to be blamed for everything from illiteracy to juvenile delinquency and sexual deviancy. Marshall McLuhan later attributed this linking of comics with anti-social behaviour to "naive literary logic," noting that even the "dimmest-witted convict learned to moan: 'It wuz comic books done this to me.'"[7]

Whatever the case, this concern over the possible ill effects of the images of mayhem conveyed by the medium wasn't new. In fact, opposition to comics

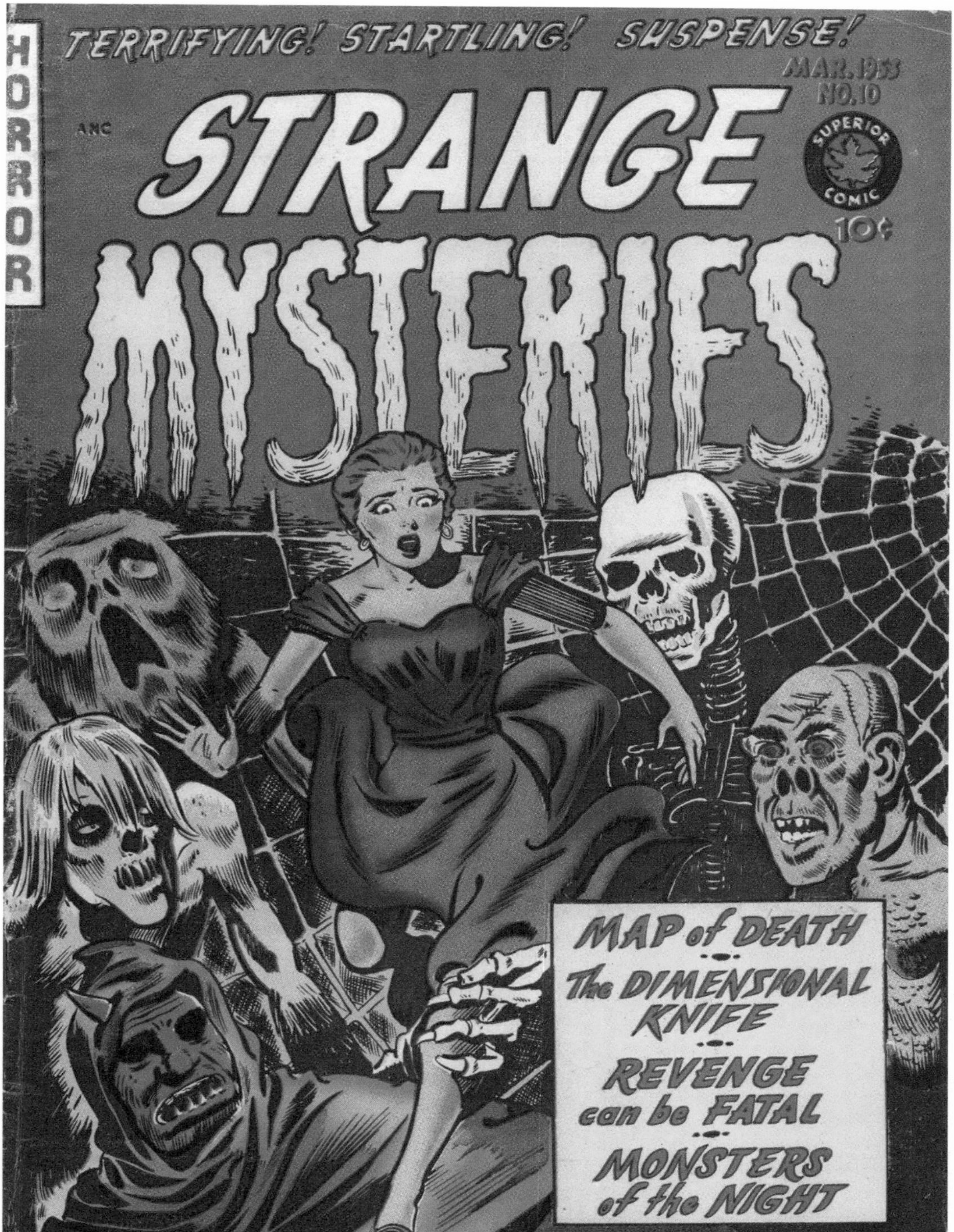
HORROR
TERRIFYING! STARTLING! SUSPENSE!
MAR. 1953
NO. 10
ANC
STRANGE
SUPERIOR COMIC
10¢
MYSTERIES
MAP of DEATH
The DIMENSIONAL KNIFE
REVENGE can be FATAL
MONSTERS of the NIGHT

portraying crime and violence had been evident in Canada as soon as the war had ended. However, by 1948 the alarm felt by a few scattered individuals had been transformed into a mass movement, one with determined and persuasive leaders such as Eleanor Gray of the Victoria and District Parent-Teacher Council and E. Davie Fulton, the Member of Parliament (MP) for Kamloops, British Columbia. Increasingly, the anti-comics crusaders came to see legislation as the only solution to the crime-comics problem. Their position was bolstered late in the year by events in northern British Columbia.[8]

In November 1948, two boys, age thirteen and eleven, stole a rifle and hid by the highway at Dawson Creek. Playing highwaymen, they eventually shot at a passing car. A passenger in the vehicle, James M. Watson, was fatally wounded. The senseless, random nature of this crime perpetrated by two young boys shocked the people of British Columbia, and the provincial Department of Health and Social Welfare launched an immediate investigation. It was soon discovered that both juveniles were avid readers of crime comic books. According to the authorities, the older boy read about fifty crime comics a week, while the younger regularly devoured thirty.[9]

The equation was obvious: crime comics engendered criminal behaviour. During the trial that followed, both the Crown prosecutor, A.W. McClellan, and the presiding judge, C.S. Kitchen, blamed comic books for the death of James Watson. Furthermore, they recommended that measures be taken to ban the periodicals. "I am satisfied," proclaimed Judge Kitchen, "that a concerted effort should be made to see that this worse-than-rubbish is abolished in some way." Needless to say, the case provided powerful ammunition to the opponents of crime comics in Canada and the United States. In fact, Chapter 11 of the most influential anti-comics tract ever published, Dr. Frederic Wertham's *Seduction of the Innocent* (1954), is entitled "Murder in Dawson Creek."[10]

In 1949 the crime-comics campaign gained substantial momentum as community groups across the country lobbied for the passage of an anti-comics law that had been drafted the year before by E. Davie Fulton. Among those who supported a legislative response to the crime-comics problem was Prime Minister Mackenzie King, who was wholeheartedly opposed to the publishing of "comics which are calculated to incline the minds of children in the way of murder and immoral acts, etc."[11] When King learned in 1948 that most members of his cabinet were initially opposed to anti-comics legislation, he was dumbfounded and confided to his diary: "It is something I cannot understand."[12]

Also caught up in the anti-comics fervour was a future prime minister, Brian

Mulroney, who, as a ten-year-old in Baie Comeau, Quebec, won a Lions Club public-speaking contest with a passionate speech about bad comics. (Mulroney later became a supporter of Fulton's leadership aspirations within the Progressive Conservative Party.)[13]

Eventually introduced as a private-member's bill, the anti-comics legislation was intended as a revision of Section 207 of the Criminal Code, which dealt with obscenity. The act, which came to be known as the Fulton Bill, made it an offence to print, publish, distribute, or sell "any magazine, periodical or book which exclusively or substantially comprises matter depicting pictorially the commission of crimes, real or fictitious."[14] For Fulton, there was no question about the perils of comic books: "the evidence shows that there is a real menace to the youth of this country in the widespread publication and circulation of crime comics."[15]

After months of intense nationwide campaigning, the bill was given first reading on September 28, 1949. The federal minister of justice, Stuart Garson, welcomed the legislation, but requested that it be submitted to various provincial attorneys general to ensure that it was enforceable. As a result of their feedback, Bill 10 was reformulated as a complete revision of Section 207, and changes were made to give it more bite. After its revision, the bill passed the House of Commons unanimously, underscoring the degree of support the crime-comics campaign enjoyed. The legislation was next sent to the Senate.[16]

By this time, the comics industry had finally awakened to the threat of censorship and asked to appear to make representations against Bill 10. The Senate obliged by referring the legislation to a standing committee. The key industry witness to appear before the Senate committee was William Zimmerman of Superior. Much like William Gaines of the noted U.S. comics firm EC who, five years later, made a famous appearance before a U.S. Senate committee, Zimmerman endeavoured to defend the crime comics, pointing to their role as a welcome outlet for children's natural impulses. Zimmerman made the fatal mistake, though, of circulating samples of what he represented as harmless entertainment for kids.[17]

As long as the debate centred on intangibles like freedom of speech and child psychology, many senators had shown some sympathy for the businessman's position. However, once they saw what was actually being peddled to impressionable children, the passage of the Fulton Bill was guaranteed. Sent back to the Senate without amendment, the bill passed by a vote of 92 to 4. As a result, on December 10, 1949, Bill 10 became law, and everyone, from the PTA to the Communist Party of Canada, breathed a

4

Facing page: Cover of Journey into Fear *No. 14 (July 1953). Art probably by the Iger Studio. Copyright © Superior Publishers.*

collective sigh of relief. The nation's young people had seemingly been rescued from the nefarious influence of foreign cultural trash.[18]

No one, though, had reckoned with the audacity of Superior Publishers. In 1949 the company launched *Bruce Gentry, Ellery Queen,* and *My Secret,* three comics that were not only often racy, but not always devoid of depictions of crime. Superior didn't inaugurate any new titles the following year, but the firm did acquire the rights to William Gaines's line of New Trend EC comics (among the most famous and most highly regarded comics ever published in the United States), a clear indication that Zimmerman wasn't particularly intimidated by the Fulton Bill. He did, however, make one small concession to his opponents: in Canada, EC's *Crime Suspense Stories* was retitled *Weird Suspense Stories.*[19]

While Zimmerman defied the ban by shifting his attention to love and horror comics, most other Canadian companies acted swiftly to reassure parents and legislators that the comics industry could behave in a responsible manner. In much the same way that their American counterparts banded together four years later, Canadian comics firms formed the Comic Magazine Industry Association of Canada (CMIAC), which promised to review all U.S. comic-book printing mats shipped into Canada to ensure that offensive material wouldn't find its way onto the nation's newsstands.[20]

Later that year, though, the CMIAC encountered a far more serious threat than censorship. The Emergency Exchange Conservation Act was relaxed sufficiently to allow certain businesses with unused import quotas to bring U.S. comics into the country. All of a sudden the spectre of an American deluge began to worry Canada's publishers. In 1951 their worst fears were realized. Stimulated by the Korean War, the Canadian economy was sufficiently strong to permit the removal of the restrictions on U.S. imports that had been imposed in 1947.[21]

Most American firms resolved, naturally, to ship directly into Canada and thereby sealed the fate of the Canadian comics industry. As was the case in 1946–47, a few companies tried to hang on by competing with the U.S. comics giants. Export, for instance, published its second original title, *Science.* By the end of 1951, however, only Superior remained, largely because it had never depended on protectionism for its survival.

In addition to continuing with his EC reprints, Superior's Zimmerman was extremely successful in penetrating the U.S. comics market with what were essentially American comic books. Thumbing his nose at Section 207, he launched two horror comics in 1951: *Journey into Fear* and *Strange Mysteries.* These were joined by *Mysteries Weird and Strange* in 1953. As well, Superior both issued more love

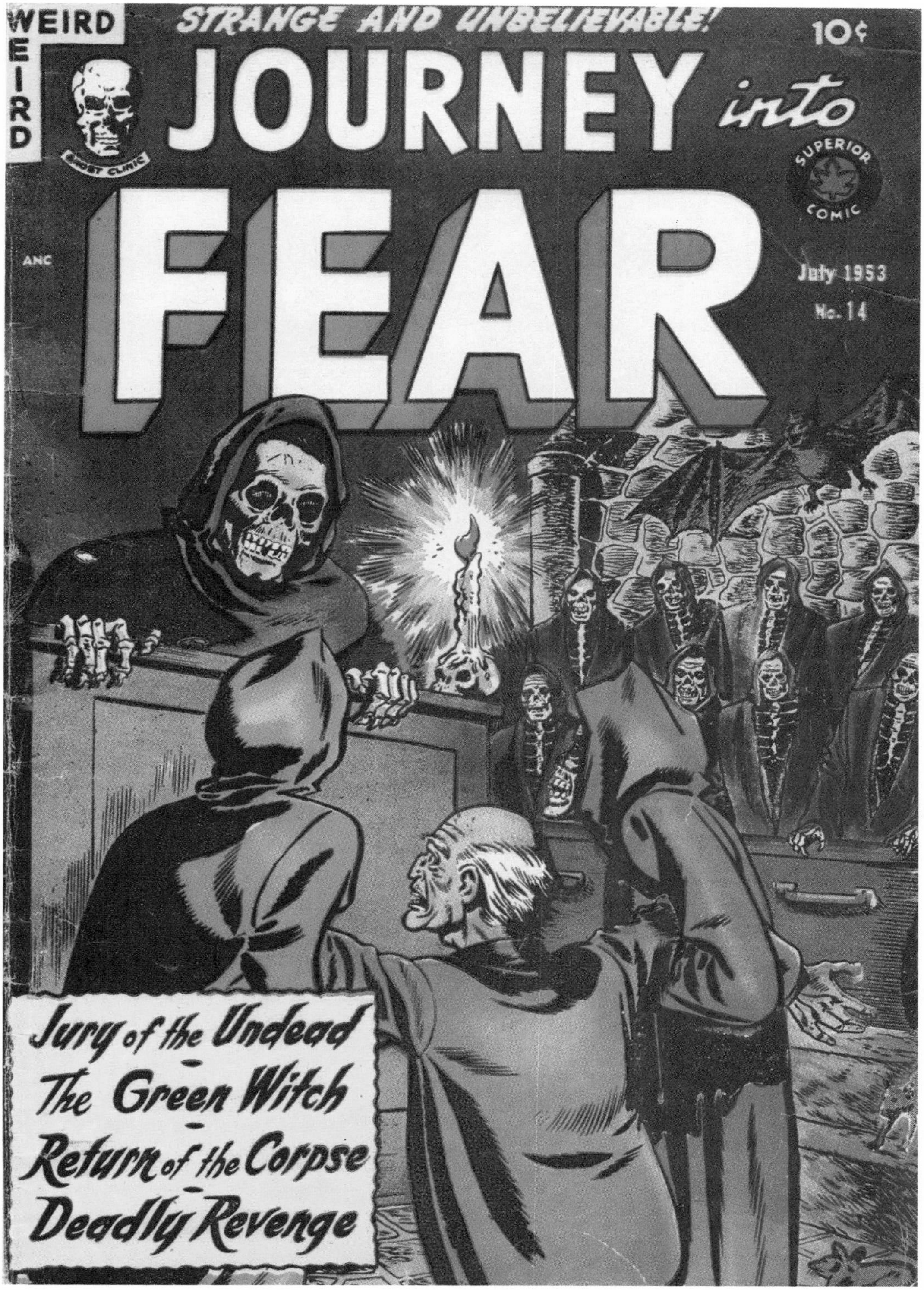
WEIRD
WEIRD
STRANGE AND UNBELIEVABLE!
10¢
JOURNEY into
FEAR
SUPERIOR COMIC
July 1953
No. 14
Jury of the Undead
The Green Witch
Return of the Corpse
Deadly Revenge

comics and diversified slightly with *Super Funnies* and *United States Fighting Air Force*.[22]

Meanwhile, as the U.S. campaign against crime and horror comics escalated, Canadian anti-comics crusaders resumed their activities. Spearheaded by E. Davie Fulton and Eleanor Gray (who were in regular contact with the most famous American anti-comics activist, Dr. Frederic Wertham), parents, educators, and religious leaders were concerned that the ban wasn't being enforced with sufficient vigour. In fact, not a single prosecution had occurred since the bill's enactment in 1949. Pressure mounted on both the political and the judicial systems to act against the publishers, distributors, and retailers who were brazenly exploiting children with lurid crime, horror, and love comics. Finally, in 1953, a conviction was obtained against a Winnipeg distributor. Later that year it was upheld on appeal.[23]

Not surprisingly, antagonism to Superior was exacerbated throughout 1954, both north and south of the border. In the spring, Wertham's *Seduction of the Innocent* (which cited some Superior titles) effectively fanned the flames of anti-comics sentiment. Furthermore, one of Zimmerman's most formidable adversaries, the MP E. Davie Fulton, appeared before the U.S. Senate Subcommittee to Investigate Juvenile Delinquency hearings in June.[24] A few months later the censorious Comics Code Authority was created in the United States in an effort to avoid government regulation of the American industry.[25] To make matters worse for Canadian comics publishers, there was another murder purportedly involving comics, this time in Westville, Nova Scotia.[26]

In 1955 the legal assault against comics intensified, with several prosecutions against Canadian distributors. Like the U.S. publisher William Gaines (EC), William Zimmerman of Superior issued his last horror comics early in 1955. By the spring he was left with only four titles: *G.I. War Brides*, *My Secret Marriage*, *Secret Romances*, and *United States Fighting Air Force*. Although the company had successfully appealed a crime-comics conviction in 1954, its days were obviously numbered.

At one school (and probably others), St. Bernadette's in Hull, Quebec, the anti-comics moral panic of the era culminated with senior students being assembled on school grounds to witness the ritualistic burning of a large pyre of comics and other objectionable publications. Apparently, no one was troubled in the least by the spectacle of a place of learning engaging in public book-burning. In Vancouver the Junior Chamber of Commerce had earlier sponsored a comic-book-burning rally where kids could exchange ten offensive comics for a single wholesome book.

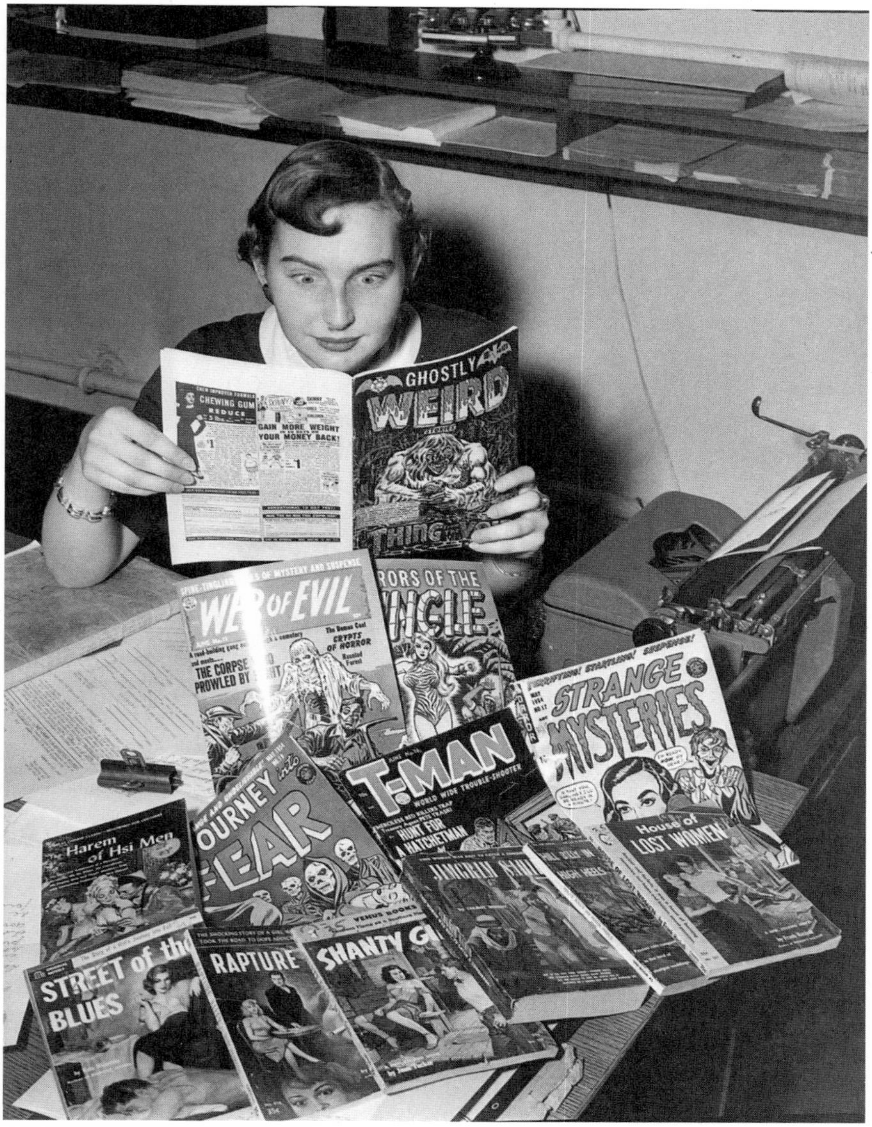

CHEWING GUM
GAIN MORE WEIGHT YOUR MONEY BACK!
GHOSTLY
WEIRD
CRYPTS OF HORROR
STRANGE MYSTERIES
T-MAN
WORLD WIDE TROUBLE-SHOOTER
HUNT FOR A HATCHETMAN
House of LOST WOMEN
Harem of Hsi Men
RAPTURE
BLUES
VENUS BOOKS

Kitchener, Ontario, police display comics and other banned publications seized from a city newsstand on April 20, 1954. Appropriately, the display includes a number of Superior Publishers titles. Negative 54-6348, Kitchener-Waterloo's Record *Photographic Negative Collection, Library, University of Waterloo. Copyright ©* *Kitchener-Waterloo* Record*/University of Waterloo.*

Another Vancouver-based organization, the Pontifical Association of the Holy Childhood, offered an even greater inducement to children. The organization formed an anti-crime-comics club in which boys and girls pledged to forfeit the reading of "bad comics" in order to preserve the purity of their immortal souls. Clearly, crime and other comics genres were no longer merely contested — they were being demonized.[27]

Because Superior was the only publisher to survive the import deluge of 1951, the firm's withdrawal from the comics field in 1956 marked the death of the Canadian comic-book industry that had been born in 1941. Ironically, but perhaps appropriately, given the American domination of the field, Canadian newsstand comics disappeared just as the so-called Silver Age of Comics began in the United States with the appearance of the resurrected wartime superhero The Flash in DC's *Showcase* No. 4. What might be deemed Canada's own Silver Age was nearly two decades away. A fascinating but somewhat ignominious chapter in Canadian publishing history had ended. Comics in North America would now be sanitized — and American.

For English Canadian kids growing up in the latter part of the 1950s and the early 1960s, the reading of U.S. comics was a major part of childhood. However, encounters with comics became a curiously alienating experience; for not only were most comic-book stories set in the United States, but even the enticing back-cover ads for various gadgets and gizmos were American, and often, much to the frustration of Canadian boys and girls, only available to residents of the United States. Comics thus served to reinforce the notion that Canada was the back of beyond. Nor was this a short-term problem. In English Canada, only U.S. comics were available on the newsstands until the 1970s. This hegemony reflected, of course, the broader American domination of Canadian culture throughout the period. With the exception of the Canadian Broadcasting Corporation's radio and television programming and a few notable magazines such as *Maclean's*, Canadian mass culture mostly originated in the United States, much to the chagrin of those who viewed a national popular culture as one pillar of a separate Canadian identity.[28]

Despite the paucity of Canadian newsstand comics, some indigenous comic books were in evidence between 1957 and 1966. Known as "giveaways," these one-shot publications harnessed the undeniable power and reach of comic art for educational and promotional purposes. Issued by various levels of government and by corporations, the giveaways were primarily created by two studios, Ganes Productions and Comic Book World.[29]

Based in Toronto, Ganes Productions was founded and operated by an advertising executive named Orville Ganes.

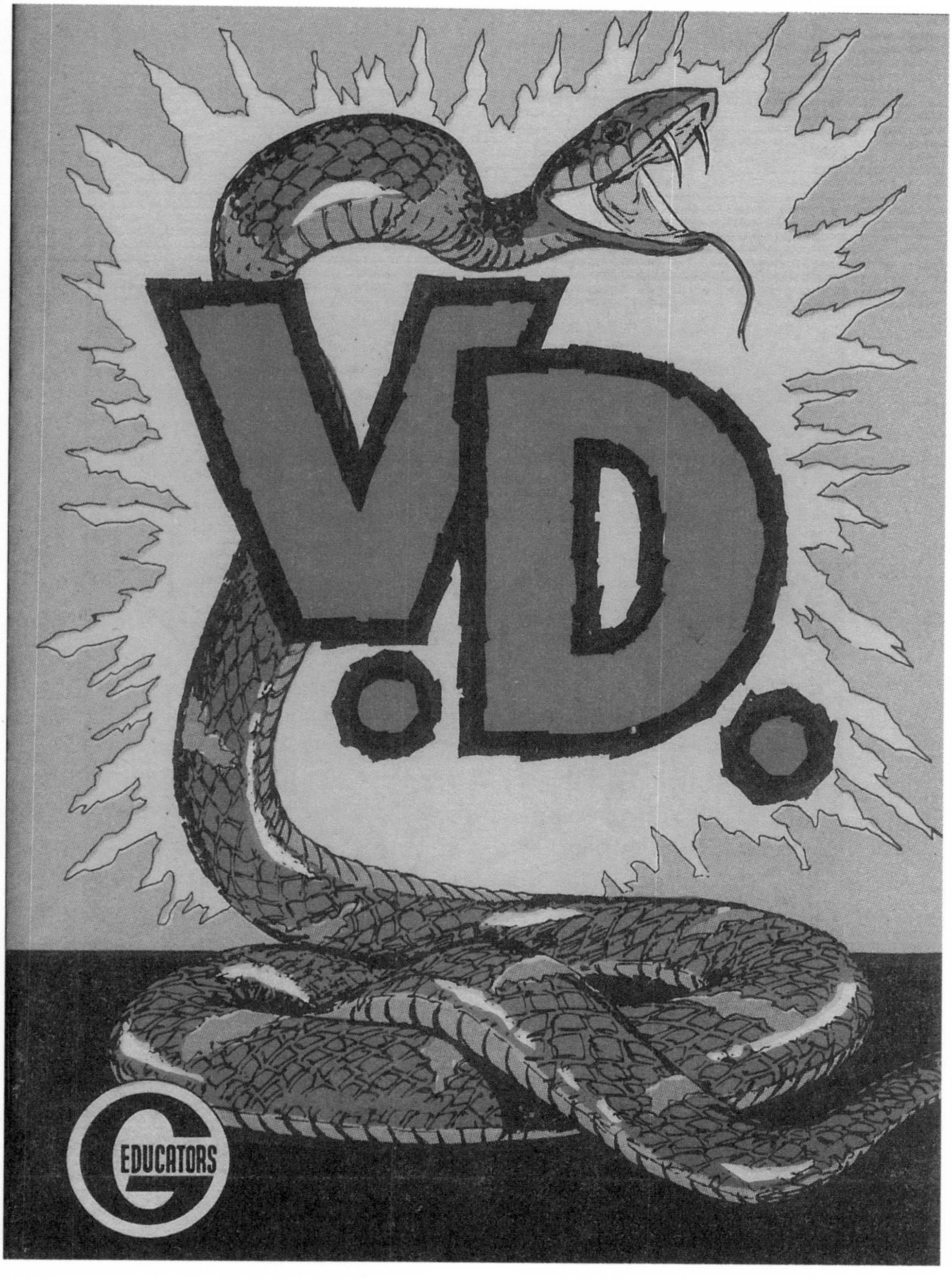
V.D.
EDUCATORS

Cover of V.D. *(1964). Art by the Ganes Studio. Copyright © estate of Orville Ganes.*

Between the late 1950s and the early 1970s, Ganes Productions produced dozens of comic books, mostly for federal and provincial government agencies. Orville Ganes, who was a skilled and innovative promoter, achieved great success in selling governments on the efficacy of the comics medium for reaching children with educational messages. Not surprisingly, the messages were often admonitions aimed at potentially wayward teens. Hundreds of thousands of Canadian adolescents were introduced to the dangers of alcohol, cigarettes, drugs, and venereal diseases in small digest-size Ganes Productions comics that were distributed free for many years in classrooms across the country.

Ganes's major competitor in the promotional-comics field was the Halifax-based studio Comic Page Features, which later became Comic Book World. The brainchild of Owen McCarron, an advertising director for Halifax's *Chronicle-Herald* newspaper who had contributed some artwork to a few comic-book titles issued by the U.S. publisher Charlton, the studio was launched in the mid-1960s and was ultimately responsible for nearly thirty different giveaway comics. Unlike Ganes's comic books, which were often smaller than regular comics and generally devoid of word balloons, McCarron's giveaways more closely resembled conventional newsstand comics. Assisting McCarron on many of his projects was

the Halifax writer Robin Edmiston. Comic Book World produced mostly full-colour comics that were distinguished by bold, engaging artwork and reasonably solid storylines. This professionalism eventually brought McCarron to the attention of Marvel Comics and Whitman Publishing in the United States.

While far from representing the resumption of the Canadian comics industry, Ganes Productions, Comic Book World, and the other smaller giveaway studios that operated during the 1950s and 1960s, helped to keep the national comic-art tradition alive during what were extremely lean years. Moreover, in the person of Owen McCarrron, the giveaway studios served as a link between the comic-art activity of the 1940s and 1950s and that of the late 1960s and early 1970s; for unlike his main rival in the giveaway market, Orville Ganes, McCarron was very much a comic-book aficionado, one who aspired to working on newsstand comics, especially superhero comics. A fan of the Canadian Golden Age, he later helped to inaugurate Canada's Silver Age of Comics.

The 1950s and early 1960s were a period of serious contraction for Canadian comic-book publishing, but it should be noted that the era did witness the publication of several new Canadian newspaper strips, including Walter Ball's *Rural Route*, Lew Saw's *One-Up*, Winslow

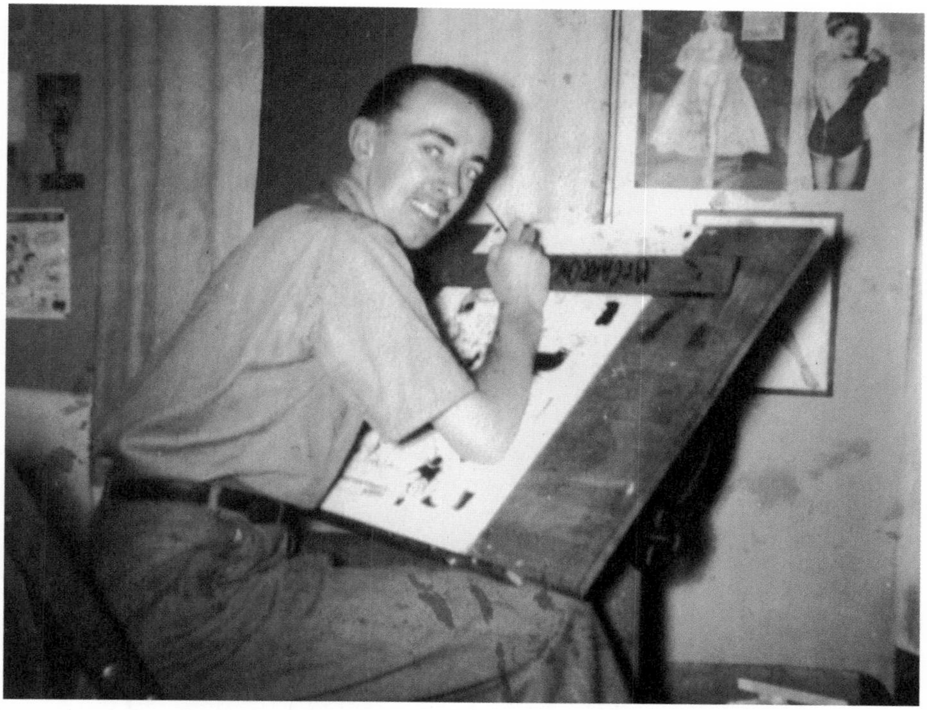

Comics fan and aspiring artist Owen McCarron at his drafting table, circa 1949. Copyright © estate of Owen McCarron.

Next page: Page 1 of "Dial 'C' for Corpse" in Strange Mysteries No. 11 (May 1953). Art probably by the Iger Studio. Copyright © Superior Publishers.

Mortimer's *Larry Brannon* (Mortimer also worked on two U.S. strips during this period, *Superman* and *David Crane*), and Doug Wright's *Nipper* (later *Doug Wright's Family*), and Al Beaton's *Ookpik*.[30]

This era also saw the publication of what could be viewed as the first English Canadian graphic novel, Lawrence Hyde's *Southern Cross: A Novel of the South Seas*, which was issued in 1951 by one of the most prestigious American small presses of the twentieth century, the Ward Ritchie Press of Los Angeles. In the book, Hyde narrates a story without words, utilizing only wood engravings. In part, the narrative deals with the effects of atomic testing in the South Pacific. Hyde's book features an introduction by the noted American artist Rockwell Kent (who had lived in a Newfoundland outport for a time during World War I), as well as a history of wordless graphic narrative (so-called "woodcut novels").[31]

Like his friend Kent, Hyde was a master of the block print and a consciously left-wing artist who sought to advance the cause of the proletariat and social justice through his artwork. However, unlike the cheap, mass-culture comics of the 1950s, Hyde's book didn't reach the masses. Instead, its impact was limited to a small group of well-heeled collectors of private-press books. Although undeniably a fine example of book-making and a work of significant artistic achievement, *Southern Cross* was too rarefied — and too far outside the aesthetic conventions of comics — to occupy an influential place within the Canadian graphic-narrative tradition. However, in his application of fine-art techniques to graphic storytelling, Hyde anticipated artistic approaches that would re-emerge in Canada in the 1990s.

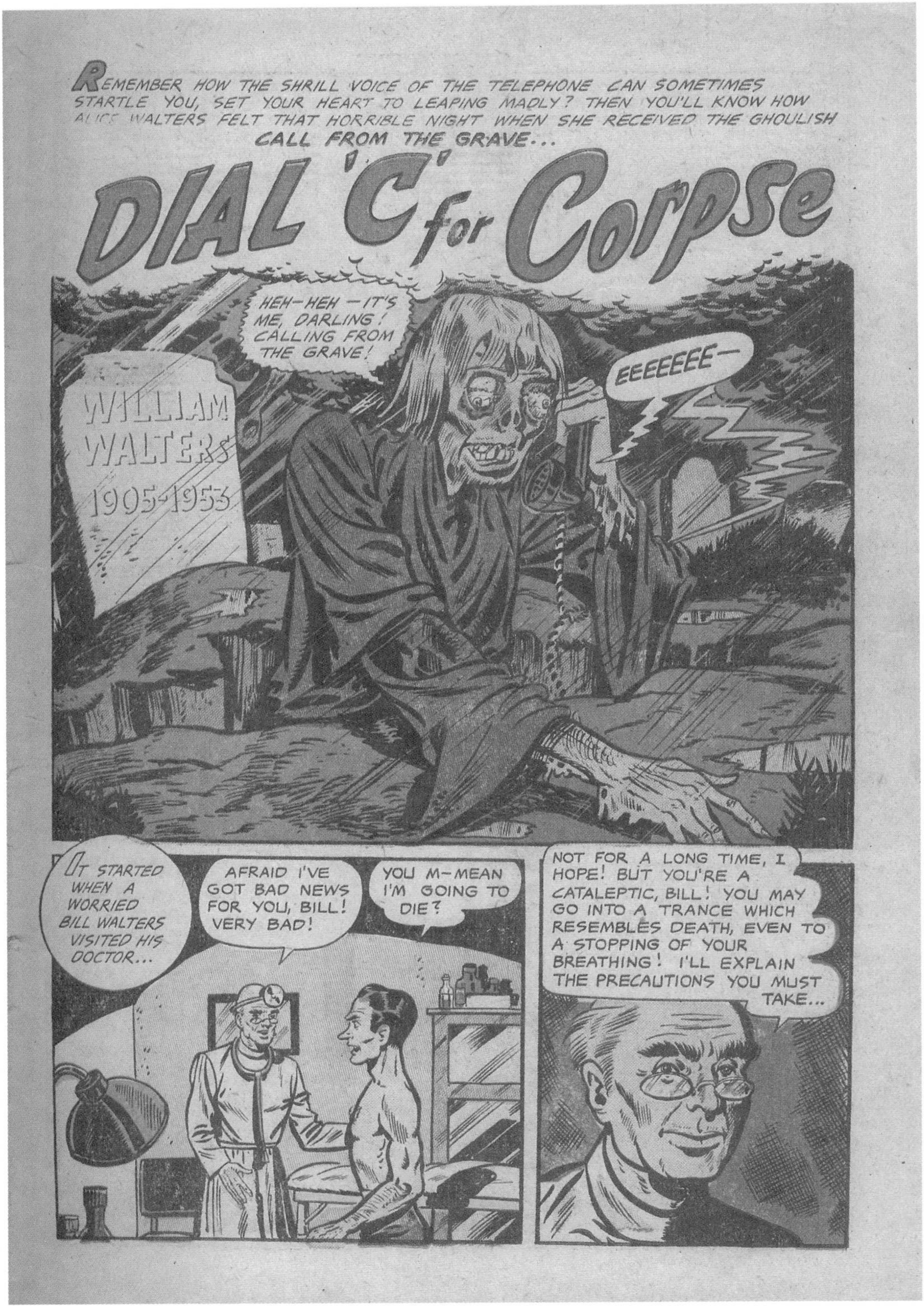
REMEMBER HOW THE SHRILL VOICE OF THE TELEPHONE CAN SOMETIMES STARTLE YOU, SET YOUR HEART TO LEAPING MADLY? THEN YOU'LL KNOW HOW ALICE WALTERS FELT THAT HORRIBLE NIGHT WHEN SHE RECEIVED THE GHOULISH CALL FROM THE GRAVE...
DIAL 'C' for Corpse
HEH-HEH —IT'S ME, DARLING! CALLING FROM THE GRAVE!
EEEEEEE—
WILLIAM WALTERS 1905-1953
IT STARTED WHEN A WORRIED BILL WALTERS VISITED HIS DOCTOR...
AFRAID I'VE GOT BAD NEWS FOR YOU, BILL! VERY BAD!
YOU M-MEAN I'M GOING TO DIE?
NOT FOR A LONG TIME, I HOPE! BUT YOU'RE A CATALEPTIC, BILL! YOU MAY GO INTO A TRANCE WHICH RESEMBLES DEATH, EVEN TO A STOPPING OF YOUR BREATHING! I'LL EXPLAIN THE PRECAUTIONS YOU MUST TAKE...

Harold Hedd and
Fuddle Duddle:
The Comix Rebellion,
1967–1974

5

WHILE THE OUTPUT OF GIVEAWAYS CONTINUED THROUGHOUT THE LATE 1960S AND EARLY 1970S, CANADIAN COMICS experienced a less tenuous but far more *outré* form of resurrection during the same period. This new expression of comic art, which differed markedly from that of the 1940s and 1950s, derived from the convergence of three developments: the widespread growth of a youth counterculture, the flourishing of the literary small-press movement, and the emergence of a national comic-book fandom. Although the comics produced by these three communities were different in many respects, they all had one key characteristic in common: they were mostly aimed at an adult (even if sometimes immature) audience.

Two important underground papers featuring comic art were launched in 1967 — Vancouver's *The Georgia Straight* and Montreal's *Logos*.[1] However, the first comic book of the period, *Scraptures,* originated not with the underground press, but rather, Toronto's literary avant-garde. Released in 1967 as a special issue of the experimental magazine *Gronk*, the title was written and drawn by bpNichol, a co-founder of Ganglia Press and a noted concrete poet who continuously experimented with various forms of graphic narrative.[2] (In retrospect, given its inexpensive production values, limited distribution, and non-commercial style of graphic narrative, *Scraptures* could be described as Canada's first new-wave or small-press comics "zine.") Late in 1967 a second new Canadian comic book appeared, Terry Edwards's *Comic Canada*. Unlike Nichol's experimental work, the mimeographed *Comic Canada* was a product of Canadian comics fandom, then in its infancy.

The next example of the new comics phenomenon to be published in English

5

Facing page: Cover of Comic Canada *No. 1 (December 1967). Art by Vincent Marchesano. Copyright © Vincent Marchesano.*

Canada was *Operation Missile*. Even though it appeared in 1968, the year that witnessed the birth of the underground-comix movement (the term *comix* served to distinguish comics produced outside the strictures of the repressive Comics Code) in the United States with Robert Crumb's *Zap* No. 1, *Operation Missile* wasn't a product of the counterculture. Nor was it, strictly speaking, a typical fan publication. Instead, given its impressive production values and content, *Operation Missile* can be viewed more as a precursor of the alternative comics that emerged a few years later. Issued by George Henderson of the Memory Lane nostalgia shop in Toronto, it was drawn by science-fiction artist Derek Carter. Henderson also launched three fanzines in 1968: *Captain George's Whizzbang*, *Captain George's Penny Dreadful*, and *Captain George's Comic Book World*.

A few more fan-produced comics appeared during 1968, including Vincent Marchesano's *The Canadian Comic* and a second issue of Terry Edwards's *Comic Canada* (now entitled *Comicanada*). These titles were followed, early in 1969, by Art Cooper's *Canada's Best Comics*. All these creators were based in Hamilton, Ontario, and all deliberately adopted titles that reflected the new nationalist spirit evident in Canadian comics fandom. Another fan publisher active in 1969 was the Sensational Comics Group of Islington, Ontario (and Marshalltown, Iowa), which issued *Sensational Display* and *Heroes and Rubber Cop*.

The year 1969 also saw the publication of Canada's first underground comic books. Probably the earliest was *SFU Komix* (with art by Bob Mercer), two issues of which were published in Burnaby, British Columbia, by supporters of the students' strike then underway at Simon Fraser University. These West Coast comix were followed by *Snore Comix*, a product of the Toronto Pop Art and Dada scene. Issued by one of the country's foremost literary presses, Coach House, it featured work by artists and writers such as Greg Curnoe, Victor Coleman, and Michael Tims. Two more issues of *Snore* appeared in 1970. Not long after, Coach House also published two graphic narratives by the surrealist Martin Vaughn-James: *The Projector* (1971) and *The Cage* (1972). His first work, a graphic novel entitled *Elephant* (1970), had been issued by New Press, another Canadian publisher.[3]

As was the case in the United States, 1970 to 1972 was the peak period of the Canadian underground-comix movement, with the publication of such titles as *Flash Theatre*, *Hierographics*, *Nature Comix*, *Bridge City Beer Comix*, *The Collected Adventures of Harold Hedd*, *Polar Funnies*, *The Time of the Clockmen*, and *White Lunch*. The key figures in this revolution were Dave Geary of Saskatoon, Saskatchewan, and Rand Holmes of

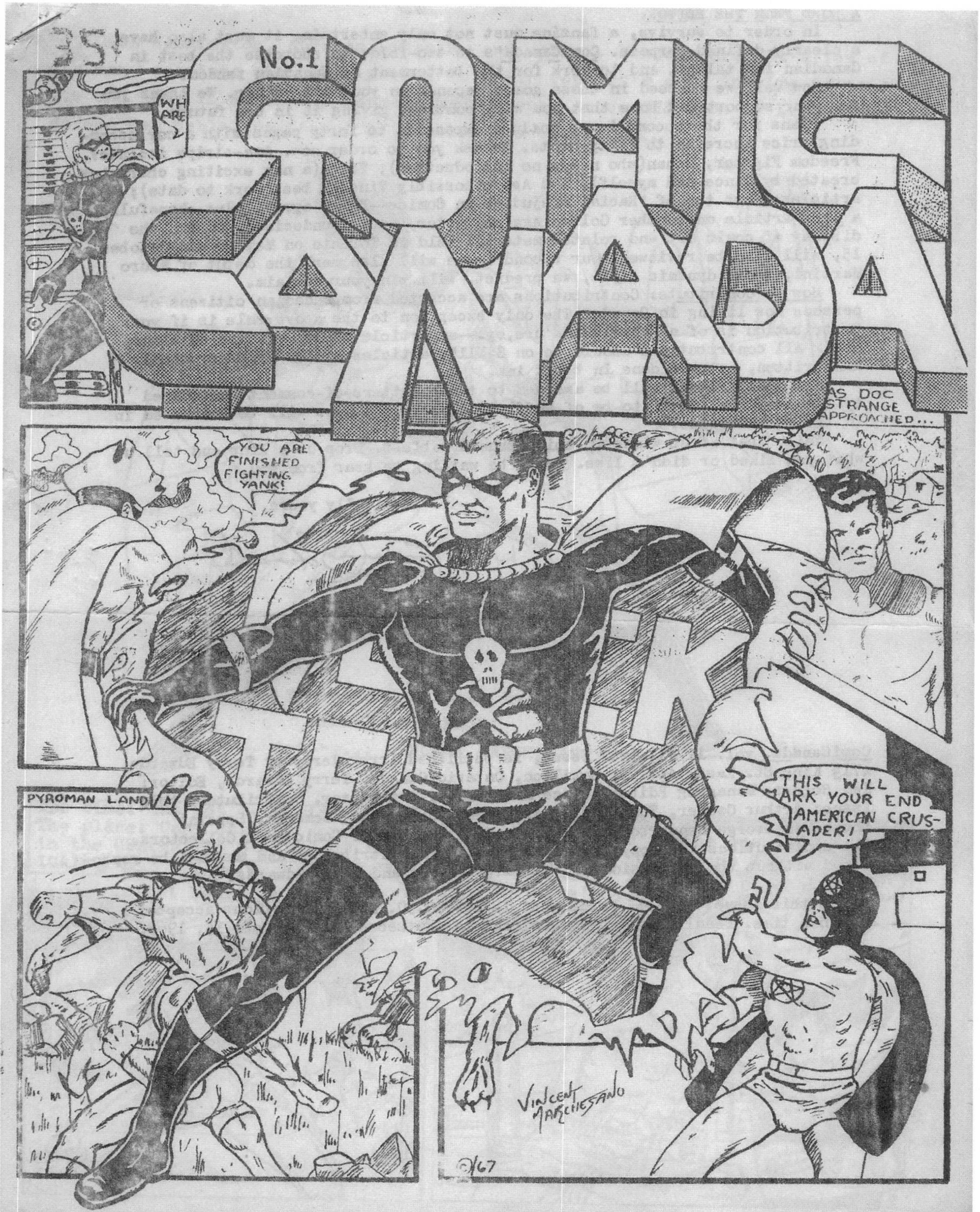
35¢
No.1
AS DOC STRANGE APPROACHED...
YOU ARE FINISHED FIGHTING YANK!
THIS WILL MARK YOUR END AMERICAN CRUSADER!
VINCENT MARCHESANO
©/67

Vancouver, both of whom remained active throughout the 1970s and 1980s. Other notable contributors to the English Canadian underground movement included Brent Boates and George Metzger. Unlike the fan and literary comics in evidence during the period, the undergrounds explored the major preoccupations of the counterculture, namely, drugs, sex, rock, and radical politics. Sold in "head" shops across the country, they openly defied not only the stringent 1950s Comics Code, but also most other mores of "straight" society.[4] Not surprisingly, like the underground press in general, they became the target of attempts at censorship.

The underground period in Canada also witnessed the publication of the first English Canadian newsstand comic since 1956. Entitled *Fuddle Duddle* (named after Prime Minister Pierre Elliott Trudeau's euphemism for a common expletive) and published by Jeffrey R. Darcey, it appeared in a magazine format and specialized in political satire. Five issues were published during 1971 and 1972, featuring work by a number of creators based in Ottawa, including Mark Lloyd, Dave Morris, Peter Evans, and Stanley Berneche. The last two, who comprised the magazine's chief creative team, were responsible for the satirical character Captain Canada, the first comic-book national superhero to appear in Canada since Nelvana's final appearance in 1947. The Captain's battle cry,

"Beavers Up!", was later immortalized in John Robert Colombo's *Colombo's Canadian Quotations* (1974).[5]

As unlikely as it might seem, at the same time they were contributing anarchic comix to *Fuddle Duddle*, Dave Morris and Stanley Berneche were freelancing for the Boy Scout magazine *Trailblazers*. Berneche's contribution was the series *True Tales of the RCMP*; Morris's was a wild strip called *The Adventures of Waldo! The Wonder Aardvark*.

Fuddle Duddle debuted the same year that the Toronto publisher Peter Martin Associates released Michael Hirsh and Patrick Loubert's *The Great Canadian Comic Books,* a book-length study of the Bell Features comics of the 1940s. (Hirsh and Loubert would later make their mark as the co-founders of Nelvana Productions, a now world-famous animation studio.) Although not entirely accurate in its depiction of the Golden Age, this groundbreaking work had a profound impact on young Canadian comic artists, encouraging the new nationalism that was evident in the fanzines that accompanied the resumption of Canadian comics publishing: Ralph Alfonso and Clifford Letovsky's *Quebec Panelogists Society Bulletin* (which was later retitled *Le Beaver*), Harry Kremer's *Now and Then Times*, John Balge's *Comic Art News and Reviews* (*CANAR*), Larry Mitchell's *The Melting Pot*, Mark B. Sigal's *Comic and the Crypt*

volume 1 number 5 50 cents
fuddle Duddle
THE HANSARD OF THE COMMON PEOPLE
CAPTAIN CANADA IN... GETTING INVOLVED
ALSO
TRICKY-DICKY INVADES CANADA
THE CANADIAN IDENTITY
LIFE IN THE 'BIG CITY'
A STONED-AGE ELECTION SATIRE
THE TRUDEAUS MEET THE DARK TIME FREAK
HANSARD LOOKS DOWN DEEP INTO INFORMATION(?) CANADA
SNAVE
MORE...

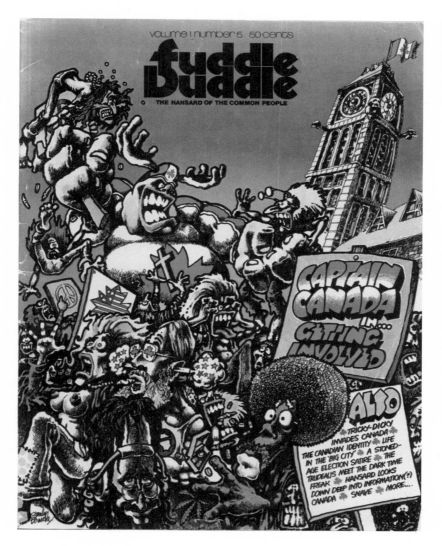

Cover of Fuddle Duddle *No. 5 (1972). Art by Stanley Berneche. Copyright © estate of Jeffrey R. Darcey.*

5

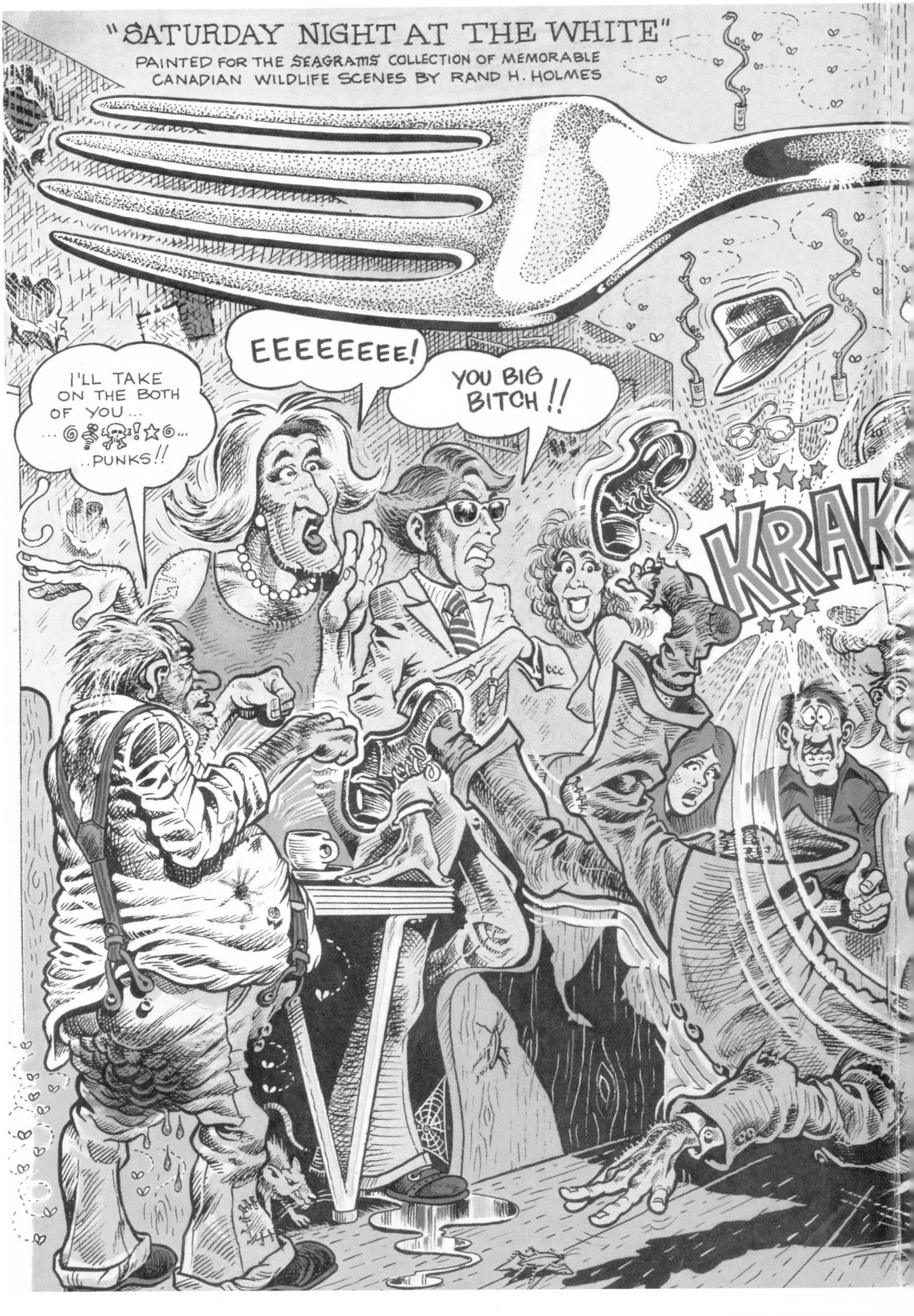
"SATURDAY NIGHT AT THE WHITE"
PAINTED FOR THE SEAGRAMS COLLECTION OF MEMORABLE CANADIAN WILDLIFE SCENES BY RAND H. HOLMES
I'LL TAKE ON THE BOTH OF YOU... ...PUNKS!!
EEEEEEEE!
YOU BIG BITCH!!
KRAK

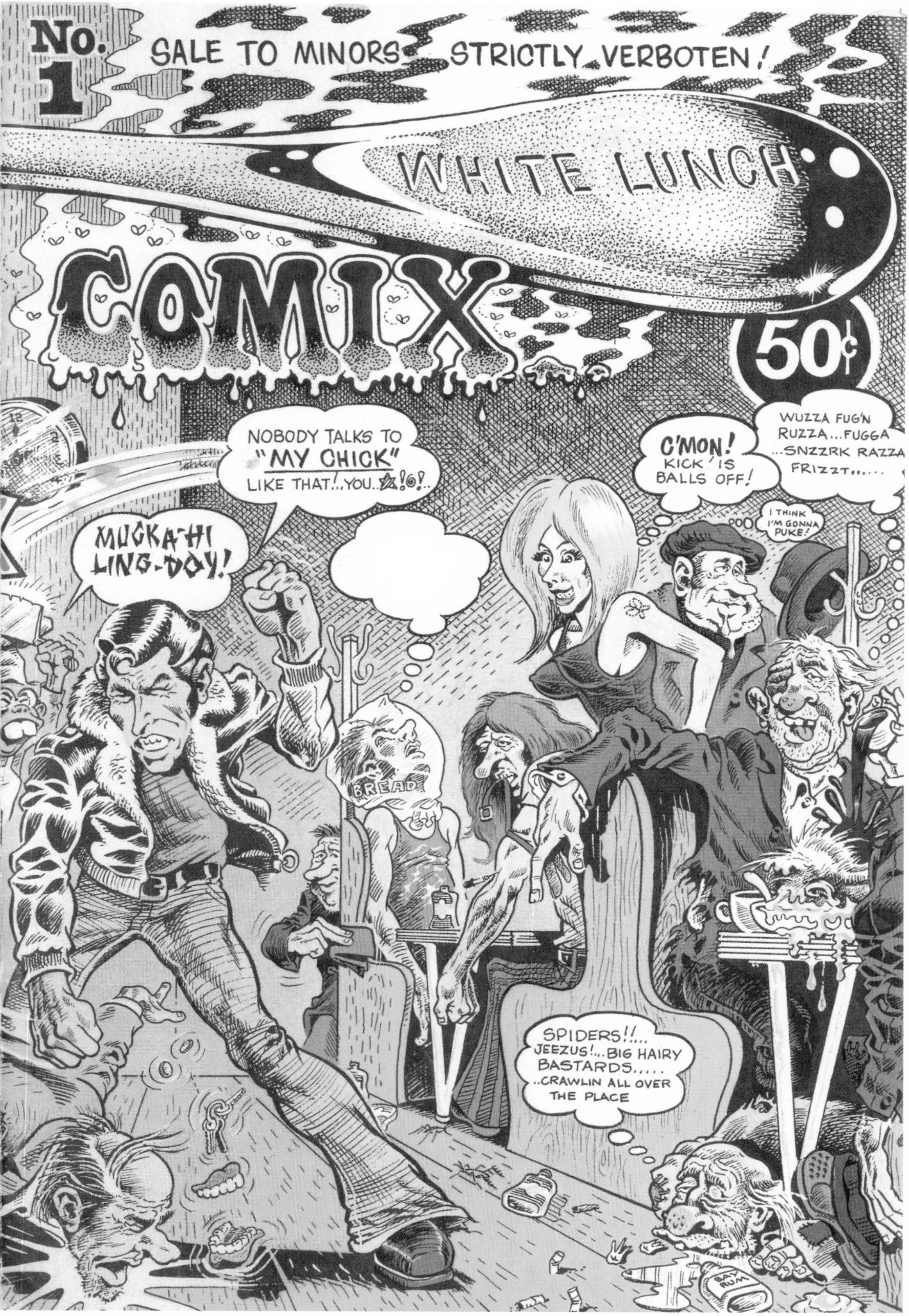
No. 1
SALE TO MINORS STRICTLY VERBOTEN!
WHITE LUNCH
COMIX
50¢
NOBODY TALKS TO "MY CHICK" LIKE THAT!..YOU..
MUCKA-HI LING-DOY!
C'MON! KICK 'IS BALLS OFF!
WUZZA FUG'N RUZZA...FUGGA ...SNZZRK RAZZA FRIZZT......
I THINK I'M GONNA PUKE!
BREAD
SPIDERS!!.... JEEZUS!...BIG HAIRY BASTARDS..... ..CRAWLIN ALL OVER THE PLACE
BAY RUM

Previous pages: Cover of White Lunch Comix *No. 1 (1972). Art by Rand Holmes. Copyright © Martha Holmes.*

(later *Comic & Crypt*), and Paul Kowtiuk's *The Journal*. These fan publications featured the work of many creators who would later emerge as major figures in Canadian comics, including Dave Sim (who first made his mark as a writer), Gene Day, and Ken Steacy.

The nationalist sentiment apparent in Canadian fandom in 1972 was furthered by a National Gallery of Canada exhibition entitled *Comic Art Traditions in Canada, 1941–45*. An outgrowth of Hirsh and Loubert's *The Great Canadian Comic Books* project, the travelling show exposed thousands of Canadians to the heroic visions of such Bell Features stalwarts as Adrian Dingle, Edmond Good, Jerry Lazare, and Edmund Legault. For those who had grown up in the 1940s, the exhibition was a nostalgic rediscovery of childhood dreams; for the generation that followed them, it was a startling revelation that comics could be Canadian.[6]

In 1973 there was a decline of underground-comix publishing both north and south of the Forty-ninth Parallel, though two notable titles were issued in British Columbia: *All Canadian Beaver Comix* and *Gearfoot Wrecks*. While these were by no means the last undergrounds published in Canada, they do mark the end of the comix movement as such. From 1974 on the focus of Canadian comic-book publishing would increasingly shift from the familiar underground concerns to more traditional genres such as science fiction and fantasy. However, these new comics would be distinguished from mainstream comic books by their more adult approach and by the large amount of artistic freedom they afforded creators, two characteristics that can be directly attributed to the influence of the underground.

At least four of these new comics debuted in 1974: Media Five's *Andromeda*, Gene Day's *Out of the Depths*, Jim Waley's *Orb*, and Terry Fletcher's *Knockout* (which had actually begun in 1973). A similar development was occurring in the United States at the same time with the release of the inaugural issue of Mike Friedrich's *Star*Reach*. Initially, the awkward term *groundlevel* was used to describe these comic books; later they would come to be called independent, then alternative comics. Among the contributors to the early semi-professional Canadian alternative comics were Gene Day, Dave Sim, Augustine Funnell, Jim Craig, Ken Steacy, Dean Motter, and Vincent Marchesano. (During this period, Day, Sim, and future star John Byrne also contributed to comics magazines issued by the U.S. firm Skywald Publishing, which was managed by Canadian Alan Hewetson.)[7] As their work clearly demonstrated, a critical mass had been achieved in the country's comics milieu. Not only was a new generation of ambitious and accomplished artists rapidly emerging, but a breakthrough had occurred in the comics-publishing

*Rand Holmes (left)
with his wife,
Martha Holmes,
and the animator
Marv Newland, at
Rand and Martha's
wedding,
Vancouver, 1982.
Photo by David
Boswell. Copyright
© David Boswell.*

field that would permit Canadians to move to the forefront of North American comic art.

From this point on Canadian comic books (with the exception of a few giveaway comics) were no longer intended for children. Not surprisingly, this shift in audience prompted considerable alarm on the part of those who narrowly equated comic art with children's narratives. Concerns about the new adult content of comics eventually culminated, especially in the late 1980s, in the familiar response of those who contest comic art — demands for censorship.

Between 1967 and 1974 there was a significant revitalization in the English

Canadian comic-book field. However, the country's English-language newspaper comic strips didn't experience a similar transformation, though there were a few new strips in evidence, most notably Norm Drew's *The Giants* and James Simpkin's *Jasper*. The former strip was subsequently drawn by Bill Payne, whose comic-strip career was brief but impressive. Both of *The Giants* artists, Drew and Payne, later contributed to comic books. (Drew also made his mark in the animation field, working on *Yellow Submarine*, *Heavy Metal*, and numerous other projects.)[8]

During this time, one of Canada's earliest comics scholars, Doug Kendig of

Facing page: Cover of Beer Comix *No. 1 (September 1971). Art by David Geary. Copyright © David Geary.*

Tappen, British Columbia, established a private comics research library and started issuing the *Comics Research Library Newsletter*. Kendig subsequently released an ambitious *Encyclopaedic Dictionary of the Comics* in serialized form.

Another significant comics-related development in this period was the involvement of the Toronto-based animation company Grantray-Lawrence Animation in the production of several Marvel Comics animated series, including *The Incredible Hulk* and *Spider-Man*. Even after the production of these Marvel cartoons shifted to New York City, Toronto's Bernard Cowan continued to serve as the series' dialogue producer and director. Among the actors recruited for voice work on the cartoons was Cowan's cousin, the noted Canadian actor and broadcaster Paul Soles, who provided the voice for Peter Parker. Although the Grantray-Lawrence cartoons were rather primitive and stilted, they did possess considerable verve and succeeded in capturing the flavour of the original Marvel superhero narratives.[9]

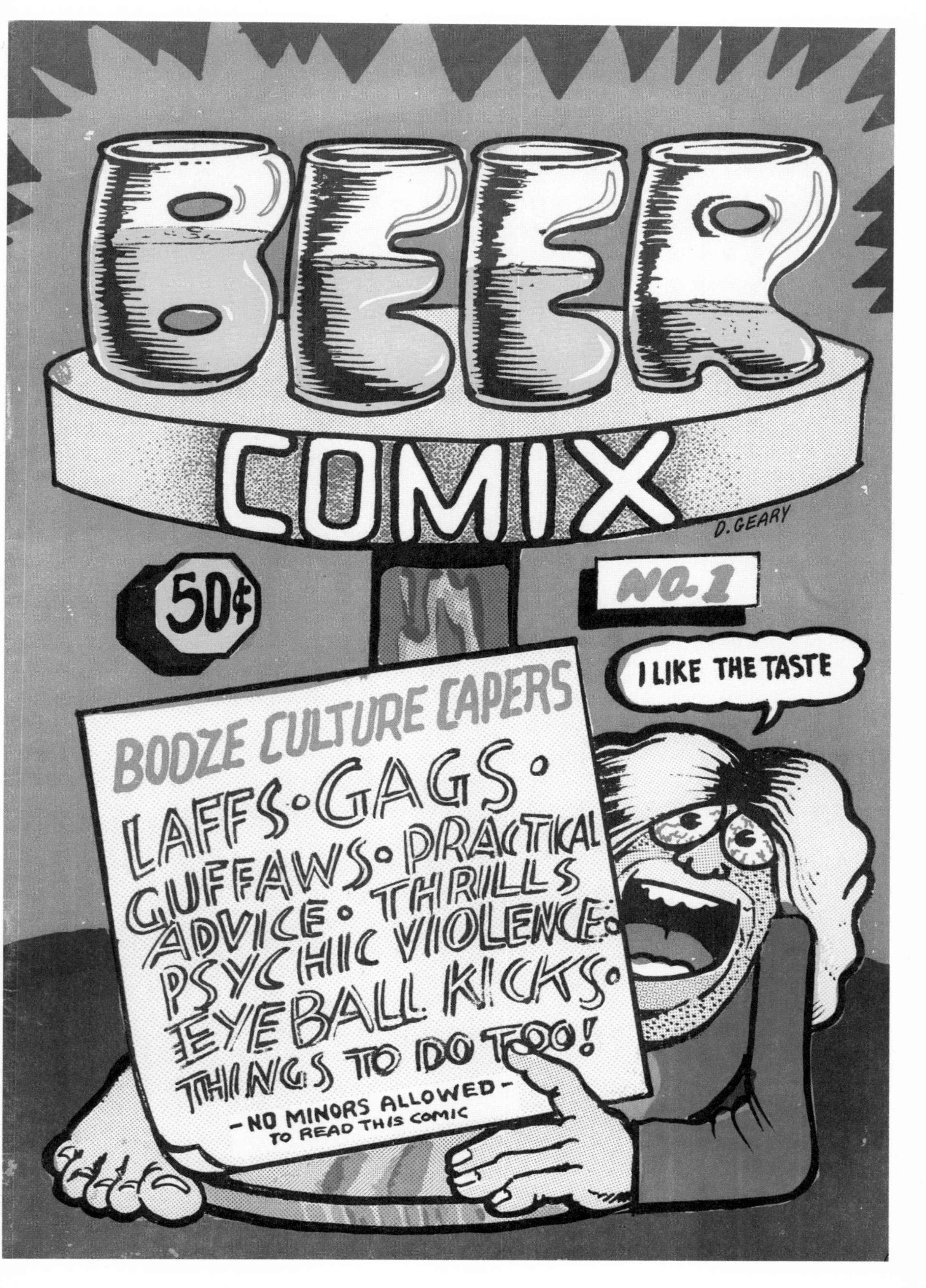
BEER
COMIX
D. GEARY
50¢
NO. 1
I LIKE THE TASTE
BOOZE CULTURE CAPERS
LAFFS • GAGS •
GUFFAWS • PRACTICAL
ADVICE • THRILLS
PSYCHIC VIOLENCE •
EYEBALL KICKS •
THINGS TO DO TOO!
- NO MINORS ALLOWED -
TO READ THIS COMIC

An Aardvark Leads the Way: Alternative Visions, 1975–1988

6

THE YEARS FROM 1975 TO 1988, WHICH MARK THE FIRST WAVE OF ENGLISH CANADIAN ALTERNATIVE COMICS, COULD be characterized as Canada's Silver Age of Comics (in contrast with the U.S. Silver Age, which dates from 1956 to 1969). Certainly, this era witnessed the publication of an extraordinary quantity of first-class Canadian comic art. In fact, more than 300 different titles appeared during the period. In addition, an extremely large number of Canadians were active in the American comics industry in the late 1970s and 1980s. Fortunately, unlike the 1940s and 1950s, such participation didn't require creators to move to the United States, though fan favourite John Byrne (*X-Men*, *Alpha Flight*, et cetera) did choose to become an expatriate.

What ushered in the new era was the nationwide release of Richard Comely's *Captain Canuck* in July 1975. (Among the contributors to the first issue of *Captain Canuck* was the giveaway-comics artist Owen McCarron, who had also appeared in several of the early Canadian comics fanzines.) While somewhat marred by wooden artwork and scripting, the full-colour comic represented the first appearance on the newsstands of a non-satirical Canadian superhero since the demise of the heroes of the 1940s. In fact, *Captain Canuck*'s very existence served to underscore the paucity of indigenous heroes that Canadian kids had experienced throughout the 1950s and 1960s. More important, the comic served to demystify the comic-book business. Suddenly, the dream of creating Canadian superhero comics became attainable.[1]

This new optimism was soon reinforced by a second development in 1975. James Waley's *Orb* magazine, which had begun life as a semi-professional alternative comic, became, in the fall, a professional,

6

nationally distributed newsstand periodical. Unlike the early issues of *Captain Canuck*, *Orb* was distinguished by first-rate artwork and scripting. (Among the most notable characters to appear in its pages was a rival national superhero, the Northern Light.) Although the magazine folded in 1976, many of its contributors soon thereafter resurfaced in U.S. and Canadian alternative comics. Waley eventually involved himself briefly with the early American independent publisher Power Comics of Detroit. Later still he was a major promoter of comic-book conventions in the Toronto area.[2]

Also in 1975–76 the publication of several more alternative comics and a number of undergrounds occurred. Among the former was an excellent magazine from Ontario's Sheridan College entitled *Gamut*. Regrettably, distribution was a serious obstacle to most of these periodicals. Denied access to the newsstands, these magazines saw their marketing and sales efforts largely restricted to advertisements in the fan press and direct contact with a handful of specialty dealers.

One of the few sources of encouragement at this time was California distributor Bud Plant, who was extremely supportive of Canadian semi-professional, underground, and alternative comics. Fortunately, a few years later Phil Seuling of New York, Plant, and other comics distributors introduced changes that

resulted in the formation of a new "direct-sales" market. Finally, small publishers were able to plug into a North American distribution network that existed independently of the newsstands. As a result, the distribution and sales of English-language comics in North America increasingly shifted away from the newsstands to comic-book shops, which began to spring up across the country, first in urban centres and then in smaller communities.[3]

Both *Captain Canuck* and *Orb* disappeared from the newsstands by early 1976, but they nonetheless inspired the efforts of several other independent publishers the following year. The first of these new ventures was an ambitious science-fiction title, *Andromeda*, published by Andromeda Publications of Toronto. Not long after, Andromeda issued a second comic book, *Arik Khan*. These Toronto-based comics were soon followed by two Vancouver publications, Jim McPherson's superhero comic *Phantacea* and Stampart's *Fog City*, a combination underground-alternative comic book.

While these new titles were impressive productions, the most significant comic to appear in 1977 was released in December by Aardvark-Vanaheim Press of Kitchener, Ontario. Entitled *Cerebus the Aardvark*, it was created by Dave Sim and published by his then partner, Deni Loubert. The title was taken from an

COMELY COMIX
FIRST FANTASTIC ISSUE!
JULY-75
No.1
35¢
CAPTAIN CANUCK
PLUS
THE OPENING SAGA OF
JONN
AND...
MUCH, MUCH, MORE!
COLLECTOR'S EDITION

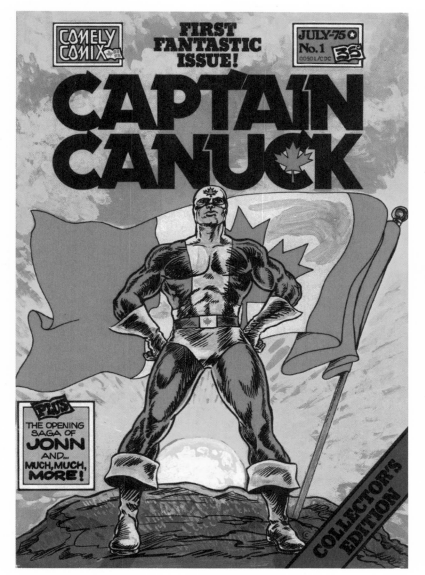

Cover of Captain Canuck *No. 1 (July 1975). Art by Richard Comely. Copyright © Richard Comely.*

6

aborted fanzine Loubert had tried to launch earlier in the year. Although it began as a clever sword-and-sorcery parody, *Cerebus* eventually evolved into a sophisticated work of art, an ambitious 300-issue graphic novel exploring not only the comics medium, but also other facets of popular culture and society at large, not to mention Sim's personal life. The longest-running original comic in Canadian history, it is truly unique and stands as one of the country's greatest achievements in comic art, one that has deservedly received international acclaim.

Cerebus ultimately became a source of much debate and friction within the comics community as readers responded to Dave Sim's increasingly controversial comics narratives and editorial ruminations. While Sim's contrarian and provocative opinions are certainly open to debate, his long-time role as an innovator, mentor, and advocate for artists' rights is not. Probably no other person has made a greater contribution to the development of Canadian comic art.

Needless to say, by early 1978, as *Cerebus* began to receive some distribution in the United States and Canada, its future success and impact weren't readily apparent. Instead, it was simply one of more than a dozen Canadian comics vying for attention during a year in which the country's comics-publishing field experienced considerable growth. A similar expansion was also evident in the fanzine milieu.

Although George Henderson's publishing activities declined in the early 1970s (when he was apparently sued for copyright infringement by the U.S. comics syndicate King Features), other publishers rose to take his place.[4] Two of the leading new figures were George Olshevsky and Tony Frutti of Toronto's G&T Enterprises, who launched the ambitious Marvel Index series in 1976 and the magazine *Collector's Dream* the next year.

Other notable comics-related fan publications of the mid to late 1970s included *The Comic Report*, *Visions*, *Fantarama*, *Borealis*, *Collector's Delight*, *Canadian Graphic Collector*, and *Strip Scene*. Also of importance was Gene Day's semi-prozine *Dark Fantasy*, a fiction periodical that brought together work by a host of contributors to the Canadian comics field such as Dave Sim, Dan Day, George Freeman, Tim Hammell, Ronn Sutton, Gordon Derry, Fabio Gasbarri, myself and, of course, Gene Day himself.[5]

This period also witnessed another major comics-related exhibition at a Canadian public gallery. Entitled *Steranko: Graphic Narrative*, the show was mounted at the Winnipeg Art Gallery in 1977. Co-curated by Philip Fry and Ted Poulos, the show focused on the innovative art of U.S. comic artist Jim Steranko, one of the most interesting and influential creators of the late 1960s and early 1970s. The exhibition was accompanied by a major book-length study of Steranko's work.[6]

As the 1970s ended, however, there was some faltering in English Canada's comics milieu. Both of Andromeda's excellent titles folded in 1979, as did *Fog City*. *Phantacea* ceased publication early in 1980. This loss of three major alternative publishers was at least partly compensated for by three developments.

First of all, by this time Aardvark-Vanaheim had become one of the true success stories of the developing direct-sales market. Second, Richard Comely, Ken Ryan, and a silent partner resumed publishing *Captain Canuck*. Their new company, CKR, which was based in Calgary, Alberta, shifted art responsibilities from Canuck's founder, Comely, to the brilliant newcomer George Freeman. In his hands, *Captain Canuck* was transformed into one of the most accomplished alternative superhero comics ever published.[7] Third, in 1979 a group of exceedingly prolific Winnipeg, Manitoba, artists (many of whom adopted pseudonyms) published their first efforts. This group eventually included Roldo, Basil Hatte, Jack D. Zastre, Frank McTruck, Bobby Starr, and Kenny Moran. A few years later, when they hit their stride, they would figure as the first "new-wave" comics coterie in the country, though stylistically and thematically they were probably more attuned to the culture of the 1960s than that of the 1980s. What distinguished their comics was the use of photocopy technology and the adoption of such non-traditional formats as mini-comics (typically four by five and a half inches) and digest-size comics (usually eight and a half by five and a half inches). Eventually, as photocopy technology improved and became even cheaper, more and more artists turned to these inexpensive formats. Such comics came to be known as "zines" or small-press comics or comix.[8]

Cerebus and *Captain Canuck* remained the most important alternative comics published in 1980–81, but there were several other significant titles in evidence. Chief among them was David Boswell's manic masterpiece *Reid Fleming, World's Toughest Milkman*. Almost as funny, and even more perverse, was Stephen Ellis and Michael Merrill's *Cows Crossing — Men Working*, a deft celebration of, well, cows. Also worthy of note was Barry Blair's *Elflord* series, which debuted in June 1980. While others utilized the new photocopy technology to produce intensely personal mini-comics, Blair created semi-professional, alternative fantasy comics.[9]

Not surprisingly, this escalation in comics publishing during the early 1980s was accompanied by increased fan activity, including conventions and publications. Among the latter were *Miriad*, *Comic Cellar*, *Gratis*, *Orion*, *Dreamline*, *Fandom Zone*, and *Plastizine*. Two fan publishers of the period, Bill Marks of *Miriad* and Mark Shainblum of *Orion*,

6

Facing page: Cover of Reid Fleming, World's Toughest Milkman *(1980). Art by David Boswell. Copyright © David Boswell.*

soon made the transition to professional comic books.

At the beginning of 1982, while a good deal of comic-art activity was underway in Canada, *Cerebus* was the only alternative comic that enjoyed any widespread distribution. *Captain Canuck*, which had once attracted an even larger readership, disappeared the previous spring. *Cerebus* was joined, however, in July by yet another Richard Comely newsstand publication, a magazine entitled *Star Rider and the Peace Machine*. An ill-conceived vehicle for its creator's conspiracy theories, the periodical folded soon after its second issue appeared in October. About the same time, Bill Marks of Toronto released *Vortex*, the first of a slick new line of alternative comics. Like *Cerebus*, it received good distribution in the United States and Canada. Marks was a major force in Canadian comics publishing throughout the 1980s, offering encouragement to some of the country's best artists.

In 1983, as the alternative market blossomed, Aardvark-Vanaheim embarked on a line of its own. Its first new title appeared in February — Arn Saba's whimsical *Neil the Horse Comics and Stories*. A Canadian, Saba (now known as Katherine Collins) had been a regular contributor to the fanzine *Fantarama*. He had also appeared in Potlatch Publications' *The 1980 Comics Annual* (edited by Ian Carr) and had contributed well-researched items on comics history to CBC Radio. The second new Aardvark-Vanaheim title, by American Bill Messner-Loebs, was *Journey*, an exceptional historical-adventure narrative. The year 1983 also saw the debut of *Quadrant*, Peter Hsu's space-fantasy comic book.

At the same time the centre of small-press activity in Canada shifted from Winnipeg to Toronto with the appearance of Chester Brown's *Yummy Fur* in July and Peter Dako's *Casual Casual Comics* in September. Another notable small-press comic, Chris Gehman's *Mind Theatre*, made its debut in London, Ontario, in December. These titles were soon followed, early in 1984, by *No Name Comix*, issued by K.G. Cruickshank of Toronto. Unlike the earlier Winnipeg mini-comics, these Ontario titles reflected a post-modern sensibility that was quite different from that of the 1960s counterculture. These artists were, in a sense, picking up where bpNichol and the Coach House comix artists of the late 1960s and early 1970s had left off, pushing comics to the limit stylistically and thematically. Chester Brown, in particular, subsequently emerged as a major figure in Canadian comic art, underscoring the important role the small press would play in the nurturing of innovative approaches to graphic narrative.

Aardvark-Vanaheim lost *Journey* to the U.S. publisher Fantagraphics in September 1984, but the Kitchener-Waterloo firm continued to grow, acquiring *Ms. Tree*,

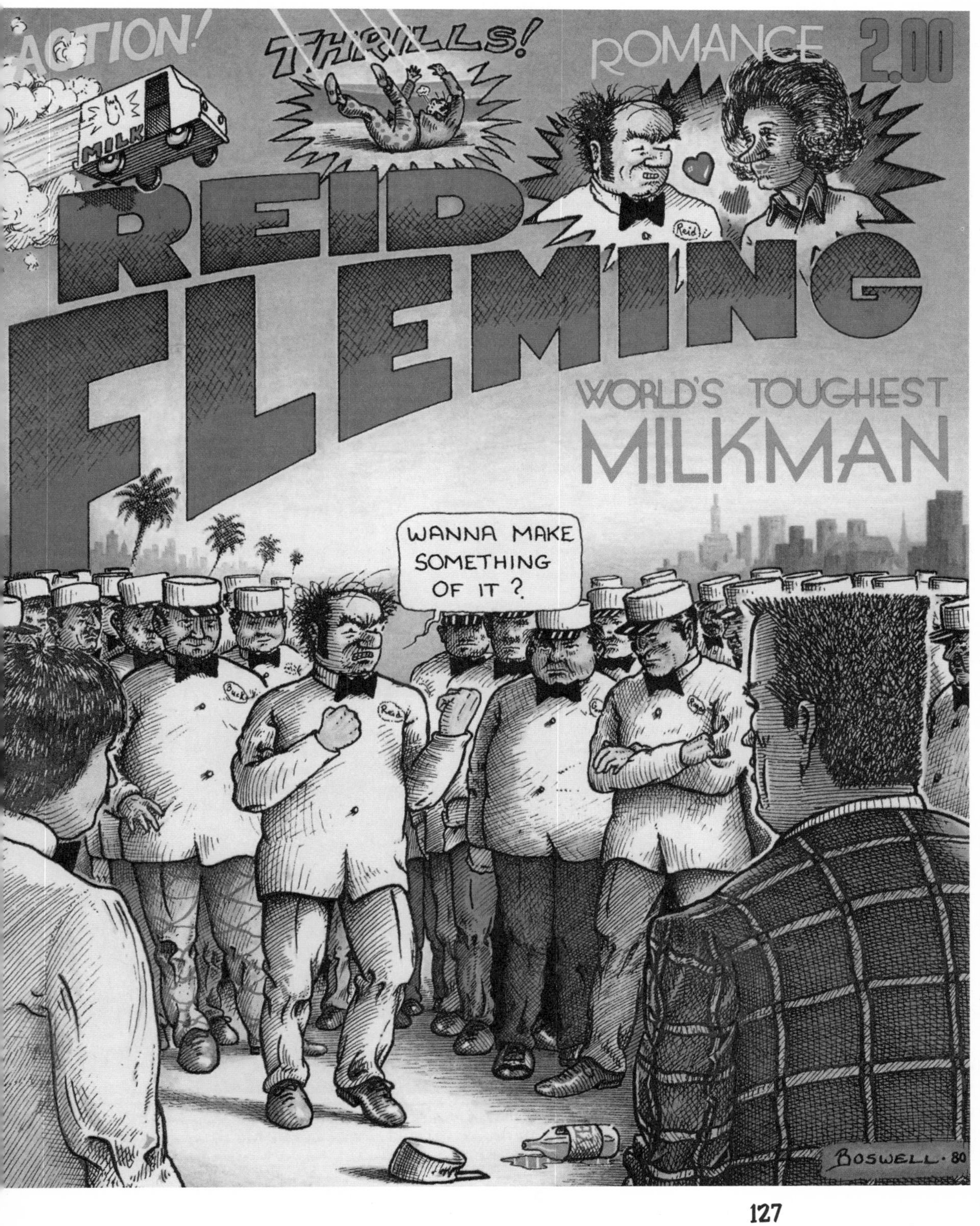
ACTION!
THRILLS!
ROMANCE
2.00
MILK
REID FLEMING
WORLD'S TOUGHEST MILKMAN
WANNA MAKE SOMETHING OF IT ?
Reid
Buck
BOSWELL · 80

Facing page: Cover of Mister X *No. 2 (August 1984). Art by Paul Rivoche. Copyright © Bill Marks.*

formerly published by the American company Eclipse; launching two bimonthly comics by American artists, *Flaming Carrot* and *Normalman*; and publishing the one-shot *A-V in 3-D*. Bill Marks's Vortex also added new titles: the much-awaited *Mister X* and Ty Templeton's *Stig's Inferno*. In addition, Mark Shainblum's Montreal-based Matrix Graphix Series unveiled a new national superhero comic, *New Triumph Featuring Northguard*. Written by Shainblum and drawn by Gabriel Morrissette, the Northguard graphic narratives represented an attempt to bring a new degree of realism and sophistication to the increasingly hackneyed superhero genre.[10]

A second Dave Boswell publication, *Heartbreak Comics*, appeared as well in 1984. In fact, as the year ended, it seemed that it would likely stand as one of the peak periods of Canadian alternative publishing, with a dozen different titles being distributed throughout North America. Even with the addition of new comic-book titles, this number fell by the spring of 1985, due primarily to major changes at Aardvark-Vanaheim, the country's leading comics publisher.

In April 1984, Deni Loubert left the firm she had co-created in 1977 and launched Renegade Press, her own imprint. At first it looked as if she would remain in Canada. However, she soon decided to leave for California. With her went four of the country's leading alternative comics: *Flaming Carrot, Ms. Tree, Neil the Horse*, and *Normalman*. Furthermore, she later inaugurated two titles that might otherwise have been published in Canada: *Black Zeppelin* and *Wordsmith*, both of which featured Canadian creators.[11]

The much-lamented departure of Loubert was partly offset by the expansion of Vortex Comics' line to include *Kelvin Mace* and *Those Annoying Post Bros.* Matrix also enlarged its output in 1985, with the launching of Bernie Mireault's *outré* limited series *Mackenzie Queen*. As well, Dave Sim added a second *Cerebus*-related title to the Aardvark-Vanaheim lineup — *Cerebus Jam*. Towards the end of the year, two more independents appeared: Aircel's *Samurai* and Strawberry Jam's *To Be Announced*, both of which demonstrated the diversification and decentralization encouraged by the new comics market. Meanwhile, John Byrne, Gene Day, Dan Day, Jim Craig, Rand Holmes, Geof Isherwood, Ken Steacy, Dean Motter, George Freeman, Dave Ross, and numerous other Canadian artists continued to contribute regularly to American comic books.

Although there were some signs towards the end of 1985 that the alternative-comics market might be faltering, in 1986 the opposite occurred: the field experienced an unprecedented expansion. In retrospect this development was predictable, given the new shape of the comics industry in North America. As the direct-sales market developed and

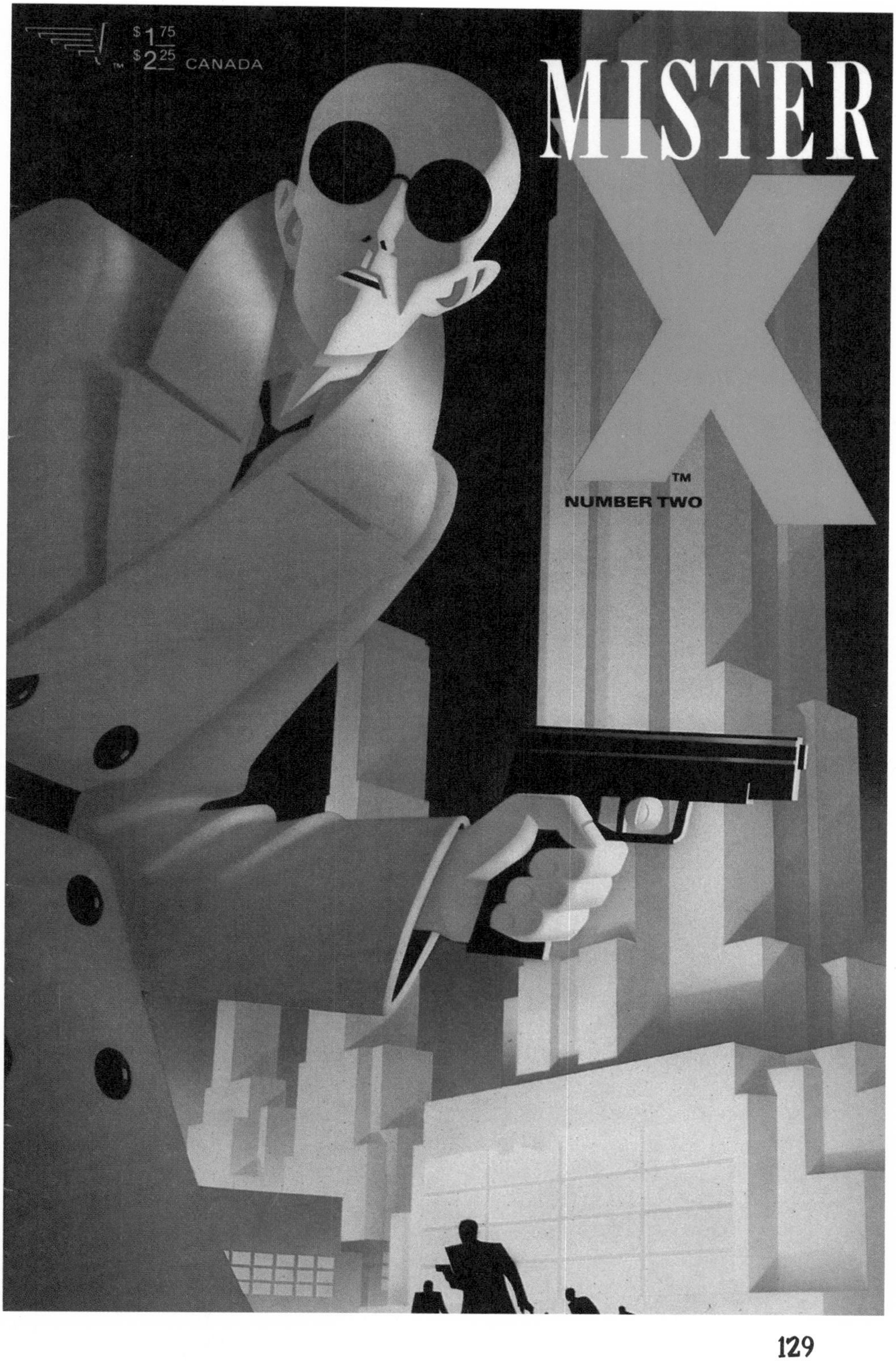
$1.75
$2.25 CANADA
MISTER
X
TM
NUMBER TWO

Mark Shainblum (left), Gabriel Morrissette (centre), and Bernie Mireault at the launch of Northguard in Toronto in 1985. Copyright © Mark Shainblum.

An Aardvark Leads the Way: Alternative Visions, 1975–1988

comic-book shops flourished, comics became increasingly fetishized as collectibles, their values carefully tracked by eager collectors in seemingly authoritative price guides. Directed less and less at children and more and more at affluent adolescents and young adults, the new alternative comics (generally produced in small press runs and, like the Canadian "whites" of the 1940s, usually featuring colour covers and black-and-white interiors) inevitably became the object of speculative frenzy.

Almost overnight virtually any alternative title, regardless of its quality, was welcomed by comics distributors as speculators rushed to invest in the next potentially hot title. For a time the message of the marketplace seemed to be: "You publish it, we will buy it." The resulting mania (fuelled, to a large degree, by the fear of missing out on the first issue of the next big thing in comics) was a boon to Canadian printing firms (which, to this day, still print many of the comics published in North America) and, at least initially, to Canadian alternative publishers.

Most publishers already active in Canada expanded their lines during 1986 and 1987 in response to the demand for new comics. This tendency was especially true of Ottawa's Aircel, which launched nearly ten new titles, including

Adventurers, Dragonring, Stark: Future, and *Warlock 5.* Among the new artists associated with the firm and its assembly-line production techniques during these boom years were Dave Cooper, Denis Beauvais, Rob Walton, Pat McEown, and Dale Keown.[12] Toronto's Vortex underwent a similar expansion, adding new titles such as *Kaptain Keen & Kompany, Savage Henry,* and *Paradax.* More significant, Vortex began publishing Chester Brown's small-press comic *Yummy Fur* in the alternative-comics format, bringing Brown's haunting, surreal narratives to a much larger audience.

The other established Canadian publishers, Matrix, Aardvark-Vanaheim, and Strawberry Jam, made somewhat more modest additions to their lines of comics, while several new publishers also became active. Among the most impressive alternative comics to appear from the newcomers were Nick Burns's *Arctic Comics,* Panic Productions' *Dan Panic Funnies,* Vanguard Graphics' *Privateers* and *Project: Hero,* Icon Text's *M the Electronaut,* and Spider Optics Comics' *Icon Devil.* In addition to comics periodicals, Aircel, Vortex, and Aardvark-Vanaheim started publishing book-length graphic novels and compilations.

The expansion of the alternative-comics market also permitted David Boswell, Michael Cherkas, Larry Hancock, Rand Holmes, Ken Steacy, Ty Templeton, Bernie Mireault, William Van Horn, Jacques Boivin, and many other leading Canadian creators to publish comics with U.S. firms.

Unfortunately, the alternative-comics market in North America was in for a rude shock. Many of the new titles that flooded the marketplace weren't especially impressive. Worse, some were plain awful. Soon the inevitable occurred: the deluge of alternative titles became a glut. As a consequence, collectors became much more wary and discriminating. Comic-book dealers, who had accumulated large quantities of alternative comics as the overheated market expanded, found they could barely give away much of their stock. When the bubble burst in the first quarter of 1987, the market for new alternative comics in North America began to decline sharply.[13]

This downturn continued throughout the latter part of 1987 and through 1988, though not all firms were equally affected by the changing market conditions. For instance, Aardvark-Vanaheim, which benefited from a loyal readership, emerged from the volatility largely unscathed. Matrix, on the other hand, ceased publishing, as did many of the new publishers who had surfaced during the boom. Strawberry Jam managed to publish one comic book in 1988. Vortex Comics, which like Matrix, had begun publishing before 1986, was able to hang on and even launched a few new titles in

6

Facing page:
Original art by
Bernie Mireault for
page 19 of
Mackenzie Queen
Vol. 1, No. 4
(1986). Copyright
© *Bernie Mireault.*

**An Aardvark
Leads the Way:
Alternative Visions,
1975–1988**

1988, including the erotic thriller *Black Kiss*, featuring artwork by the noted U.S. artist Howard Chaykin. However, by the end of the year, Vortex's publishing schedule became increasingly erratic and the firm's future seemed doubtful. Like Vortex, Aircel also continued publishing and likewise introduced a few new titles. However, in the fall of 1988 it merged with the U.S. publisher Eternity Comics/Malibu Graphics.

Between 1985 and 1988 there was a boom-and-bust cycle within the alternative-comics field, but the same pattern wasn't perceptible in the small-press milieu. Largely independent of the comics marketplace, the small presses continued to experience considerable growth. Whereas the earlier English Canadian small-press activity was centred first in Winnipeg and then in Southern Ontario, in 1985 the focus of such publishing shifted to British Columbia. Starting in 1986, however, small presses ceased to be so centralized and became a Canada-wide phenomenon.

Although much of the comic art produced in the small-press field was charming but amateurish, there were some important creators associated with the movement between 1985 and 1988. One of the most notable was Colin Upton of Vancouver who, beginning in 1985, published dozens of mini-comics, many of which portrayed his encounters with Vancouver street people and other marginal characters. Another impressive small-press creator was John MacLeod of Guelph, whose *Dishman* offered a brilliant send-up of the superhero genre. Perhaps the most significant artist of the era, though, was Julie Doucet of Montreal, who began publishing her *Dirty Plotte* comic in the fall of 1988. Like Chester Brown, Doucet utilized the freedom offered by self-publication to create unfettered explorations of her darkest dreams and desires. The resulting narratives were searing, poetic masterpieces that were eventually recognized as among the most exciting comic art in North America. According to Art Spiegelman, the author of the Pulitzer Prize–winning graphic novel *Maus*, Doucet "proved definitely that girls can be as dirty-minded as boys."[14]

Not surprisingly, Upton, MacLeod, and Doucet all eventually made the transition from the small-press movement to more widely distributed alternative comics (which can pay substantial royalties to successful creators).

Among the other outstanding small-press comics of the era were the British Columbia Cartoonist Society's *New Reality*, Don Fuller and Garrett Eng's *Masque*, Spatter Publications' *Spatter*, Roger Williamson's *Miscellaneous Stuff*, Sylvie Rancourt's *Melody*, Reactor's *Fabulous Babes*, and *The Flames of Terpsichore* by Graham Jackson and William Kimber. It should be noted, see Dick....

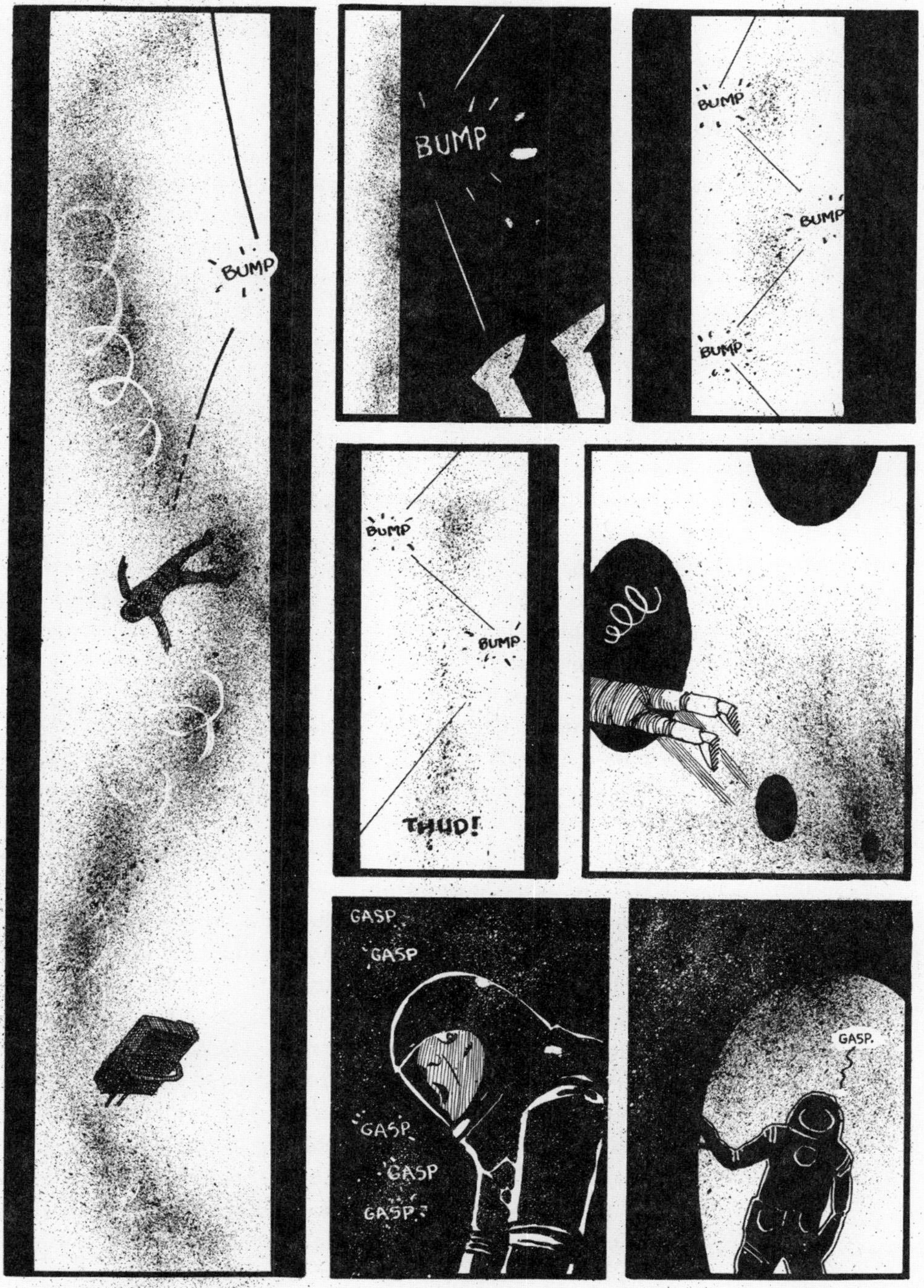
BUMP
BUMP
BUMP
BUMP
BUMP
BUMP
BUMP
THUD!
GASP.
GASP
GASP.
GASP
GASP.
GASP.

see Dick run.

*Facing page:
Winnipeg's Free
Kluck comix group
in 1981. Left to
right: Roldo (rear),
Bobby (front), Basil
Hatte, Jack D.
Zastre, and Frank
McTruck. McTruck
has captioned this
photo "Drunk
Comix."
Copyright © Frank
McTruck
(MacNichol).*

**An Aardvark
Leads the Way:
Alternative Visions,
1975–1988**

though, that none of these titles were typical small-press comics, which were usually photocopied mini-comix.

Another important development in the small-press field was the organization in 1987 by *Casual Casual Comics*' Peter Dako of *Casual Casual Cultural Exchange: A Travelling Exhibition of the Graphzine Arts*, a major exhibition of cutting-edge graphic narrative. Featuring artwork by Canadians such as Carol Moiseiwitsch and Henriette Valium, plus artists from France, Japan, England, and the United States, the show was mounted in galleries in Montreal and Toronto before travelling to Europe and Japan. It was also accompanied by a substantial catalogue that surveyed worldwide small-press comic-art activity.[15]

There were some discouraging developments in the alternative-comics field by 1988, but the preceding era did mark the welcome rebirth of English Canadian comic books. It also saw the debut of several important newspaper strips, including Fred Lucky's *The Dumplings*, Jim Unger's *Herman*, Ben Wicks's *Outcasts*, Ted Martin's *Pavlov*, Vance Rodewalt's *The Byrds*, and Lynn Johnston's *For Better or for Worse*. In 1986, Johnston became the first Canadian — and the first woman — to win the coveted Reuben Award, the highest honour in the cartooning field.[16]

Among the era's other comics-related developments were the publication in 1986 of the first serious study of English

Canadian comic books, my own *Canuck Comics* (with contributions from Robert MacMillan and Luc Pomerleau), and the establishment in 1987 of the Comic Legends Legal Defense Fund (CLLDF). Originally founded by comics creators Derek McCulloch and Paul Stockton to help a Calgary comic-book shop in its battle against an obscenity charge, the CLLDF has since offered assistance to Canadian comic-book retailers, distributors, publishers, and creators who run afoul of obscenity laws. In order to raise money for its anti-censorship cause, the CLLDF published two impressive *True North* anthologies showcasing Canadian comics creators.[17]

As comics shifted to more adult themes, there were numerous instances of censorship actions against comic-book shops and bookstores that stocked comics. In addition, Canada Customs began to pay increasing attention to shipments from U.S. alternative-comics publishers and distributors (this scrutiny continued throughout much of the 1990s). Interestingly, at a time when an increasing number of women such as Carol Moiseiwitsch, Julie Doucet, Fiona Smyth, and Sylvie Rancourt were embracing the freedom offered by alternative and small-press comics to explore taboo subjects (including sex and violence) from a woman's perspective, much of the new pressure on comics came from the feminist community, as did support

for Bill C-54, the new proposed federal anti-pornography legislation.[18]

In the fall of 1988, the renewed attacks on comics prompted the editors of the University of Ottawa's *Ottawa Law Review* to devote a special section of their journal to a reassessment of the Canadian crime-comics campaign of the 1950s.[19] Among the contributors to this issue of the *Review* was E. Davie Fulton, who was afforded an opportunity to reflect on his role as a leading anti-comics activist forty years before. Not surprisingly, Fulton remained convinced that the Canadian crime-comics legislation "was a necessary and balanced step taken in the best interests of society."[20] The year 1988 also saw the release of Toronto filmmaker Ron Mann's well-received documentary on the history of comics, *Comic Book Confidential*, which offered a very different perspective on the crime-comics moral panic of the 1940s and 1950s.

Noteworthy, too, were the activities of comics researchers Murray R. Ward of Winnipeg and Carl Horak of Alberta.

Facing page: Cover of Famous Bus Rides *No. 3 (1987). Art by Colin Upton. Copyright © Colin Upton.*

Ward carried on the groundbreaking work of Canadian indexer George Olshevsky, producing a number of impressive DC Comics indexes between 1985 and 1988. These were published by the International Comics Group. Later he oversaw the indexing of various Marvel titles. (Later still, the work of Ward and his predecessor, Olshevsky, served as the foundation for a number of on-line comics-related database indexes.) As for Horak, formerly the editor of the comic-strip fanzine *Strip Scene*, he edited a number of highly regarded publications devoted to the work of Milton Caniff, one of the great masters of the U.S. comic strip. Horak subsequently co-authored a useful book on Harold Foster's *Prince Valiant* strip.[21] (Although Horak's long-running Caniff fanzine, *Caniffites Journal*, is no longer published in Canada, he continues to serve as its editor). Among Horak's close associates was George Morley, one of Canada's leading veteran comics fans. Morley died in 2004.

All these developments, even the negative attention of censorship, pointed to a new maturity in the English Canadian comics milieu. The question was: now that comics were ostensibly an adult art form (albeit a contested one) would they be able to survive the next decade as the marketplace underwent further changes and as unforeseen threats to comic art emerged?

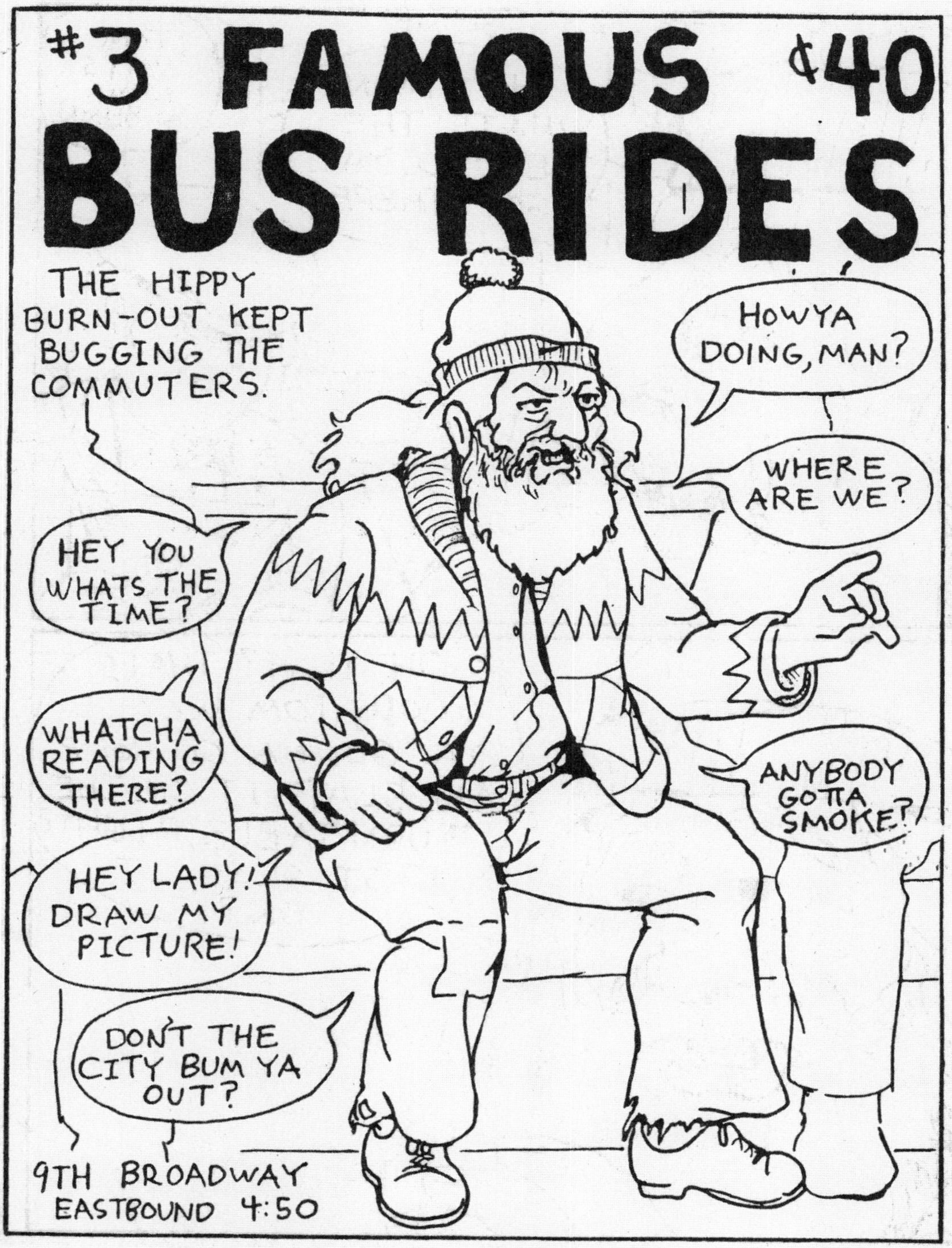
#3 FAMOUS BUS RIDES ¢40
THE HIPPY BURN-OUT KEPT BUGGING THE COMMUTERS.
HOWYA DOING, MAN?
WHERE ARE WE?
HEY YOU WHATS THE TIME?
WHATCHA READING THERE?
ANYBODY GOTTA SMOKE?
HEY LADY! DRAW MY PICTURE!
DON'T THE CITY BUM YA OUT?
9TH BROADWAY EASTBOUND 4:50

SPOTLIGHT

CHESTER BROWN AND THE SEARCH FOR NEW NARRATIVES

During the past four decades, three main subcultures have evolved within Canadian comics: mainstream, alternative, and small press. Although many artists have contributed to all three areas of graphic narrative, these currents remain largely separate, differentiated by a variety of factors,including format, aesthetic conventions, subject matter, audience, creator control, and to some degree, place of publication.

Mainstream comics are issued almost exclusively in the standard North American comic-book format (six and five-eighths by ten and one-quarter inches). They are usually in colour and are predominantly devoted to the portrayal of costumed superheroes and other fantasy figures. Whereas they were once aimed mostly at pre-pubescent boys who, especially prior to the advent of video games, couldn't resist superhero power fantasies, they are now produced for a slightly more mature audience comprising older adolescents and young adults — both male and, to a much lesser degree, female. Because the publishing of indigenous mainstream comics has proven to be a particularly elusive goal, as evidenced by the recent failure of Pat Lee's ambitious Dreamwave Productions, most of the many Canadians working in this field of comic art contribute to DC, Marvel, and other mainstream American comic-book companies on a freelance basis under a work-for-hire arrangement. While these creators endeavour to bring their own vision to superhero narratives, their contributions are subsumed within an assembly-line approach in which a group of creators, usually including an editor, writer, penciller, inker, colourist, and letterer, is brought together by the publisher. In most instances, the publishers. not the creators, own the characters and the superhero "properties." And while there is

some room for innovation within this factory system, there are definite conventions that must be respected and entrenched clichés that must be repeated ad nauseam.

Until recently alternative comics superficially resembled mainstream comics in that they were published in a similar format, though usually with black-and-white interiors. However during the past decade or so, alternative comics have increasingly appeared in other formats, including magazines (typically eight and a half by eleven inches) and a variety of digest sizes (smaller than standard comics). However, there are even more profound differences. Alternative comics are produced for an adult readership and aren't confined to a single genre or artistic style; in fact, alternative creators are contemptuous of formulaic approaches to graphic narrative and constantly push aesthetic boundaries. Moreover, alternative comics are typically produced by single creators, comics auteurs, who are responsible for all or most of the creative process, including scripts, pencils, inks, lettering, and colouring. Whereas there have only been a handful of Canadian mainstream publishers since the early 1970s, there have been many successful Canadian alternative publishers, most notably Drawn & Quarterly, now one of the leading alternative publishers in the world. Initially, the alternative comics depended almost entirely on the comic-book-store retail market. However, alternative publishers have recently begun to penetrate the regular bookstore market. In fact, many bookstores now feature special sections devoted to graphic novels.

Although some Canadian alternative publishers have published a range of titles by a variety of creators, including, in some cases, foreign creators, most alternative imprints are launched by individual creators in order to self-publish their own work. Furthermore, many of Canada's best alternative comics artists, including Bernie Mireault, Ho Che Anderson, Dean Motter, Dave Cooper, and Bryan Lee O'Malley, publish primarily with U.S. firms such as Dark Horse Comics, Fantagraphics, Image Comics, and Oni Press.

Alternative comics offer creators considerable artistic freedom, especially compared to the mainstream comics, but they are still subject to some commercial constraints and considerations — unlike the third comic-art stream, the small press. Here the dominant format is the digest (eight and a half by five and a half inches or eight and a half by seven inches) or the mini-comic (five and a half by four inches), usually produced by photocopier in black and white (though creators sometimes utilize some colour, especially in cover images, or print on colour paper stock). The small press offers little in the way of commercial reward (breaking even is an achievement for most artists), but it does provide creators with total artistic

control and freedom of expression, since the format's accessibility lends itself to the portrayal of every conceivable subject, from the most mundane, such as Colin Upton's comix-*verité* accounts of his misadventures on the Vancouver transit system in *Famous Bus Rides*, to the over-the-top surrealism and absurdism of Marc Bell's twisted Shrimpy and Paul narratives, or from Leanne Franson's humorous semi-autobiographical tales of lesbian-gay-bisexual-transgendered culture to the dark and violent heterosexual fantasies of Julie Doucet. Anything goes — and not only in terms of subject matter. The small press embraces a multitude of graphic styles, some of which test the outer limits of narrative coherence.

The first Canadian small-press comic was *Scraptures*, a digest-size exploration in visual poetry issued in Toronto in 1967 by bpNichol, a renowned Canadian poet who later produced scripts for the alternative publisher Andromeda Publications. This endeavour was soon followed by publications from several Hamilton-area comics fans: Terry Edwards's mimeographed magazine *Comic Canada* (1967–68), Vincent Marchesano's mini-comic *The Canadian Comic* (1968), and Art Cooper's magazine *Canada's Best Comics* (1969). While Nichol, Marchesano, and a handful of other creators issued more small-press comics in the early 1970s, it wasn't until later in the decade when photocopy

Facing page: Chester Brown (right) and Colin Upton during the time (1993–94) when Brown lived in Vancouver. Photo by David Boswell. Copyright © David Boswell.

Spotlight

technology radically improved that the small-press movement began in earnest. The first centre of such publishing was Winnipeg where, starting in 1979, there was an avalanche of anarchic mini-comics and digests from a group of mostly pseudonymous artists that included Roldo, Basil Hatte, Jack D. Zastre, Frank McTruck, Bobby Starr, and Kenny Moran. Not long after, small-press communities surfaced in Ontario, particularly Toronto and London, and then in British Columbia. By the late 1980s, encouraged by review journals such as *Factsheet Five* and *Comics F/X*, small-press publishing exploded, becoming a national phenomenon. Today hundreds of creators across the country issue such comics, which have become part of a broader "zine" culture, a vibrant underground current in Canadian publishing that is explored in the magazine *Broken Pencil*.

Much of the small-press output is slight and amateurish, but at its best the field has served as an important recruiting ground for alternative comics. Among the major Canadian alternative-comics creators who began their careers in the small-press movement are the previously mentioned Colin Upton, Marc Bell, and Julie Doucet, as well as the late Gene Day, Dave Sim, Greg Holfeld, John MacLeod, Pat McEown, and Dave Cooper. However, in many respects the most important comic artist to emerge from the Canadian small-press-comics

milieu has been Chester Brown. In fact, the trajectory of Brown's career, which has involved his engagement with all three currents of graphic narrative, truly reflects the evolution of Canadian comics in the modern era: the rejection of the tired and juvenile superhero adventures, the fearless search for new narratives, and the determination to establish comics as an adult art form.

Chester William David Brown's journey to widespread acclaim began with a fortuitous rejection. Born in Montreal in 1960, he grew up "in an English bubble" in the city's bedroom community of Châteauguay, where as a young teen he fell under the sway of superhero comics and resolved to become a comic-book artist.[1] After his graduation from high school in 1977, Brown went to New York to show his portfolio to editors at DC and Marvel. The response was encouraging, but he was told to further develop his skills and return the following year. That fall Brown enrolled in a commercial-art course at Dawson College in Montreal. During this period, he also contributed artwork to a few Montreal-based fanzines. After studying for a little over a year, Brown dropped out late in 1978. Not long after, he returned to New York, making the rounds at DC and Marvel. Again the response was positive, but not to the point of acceptance. Although Brown was disappointed by this second rejection, he wasn't devastated. In the interim, he had

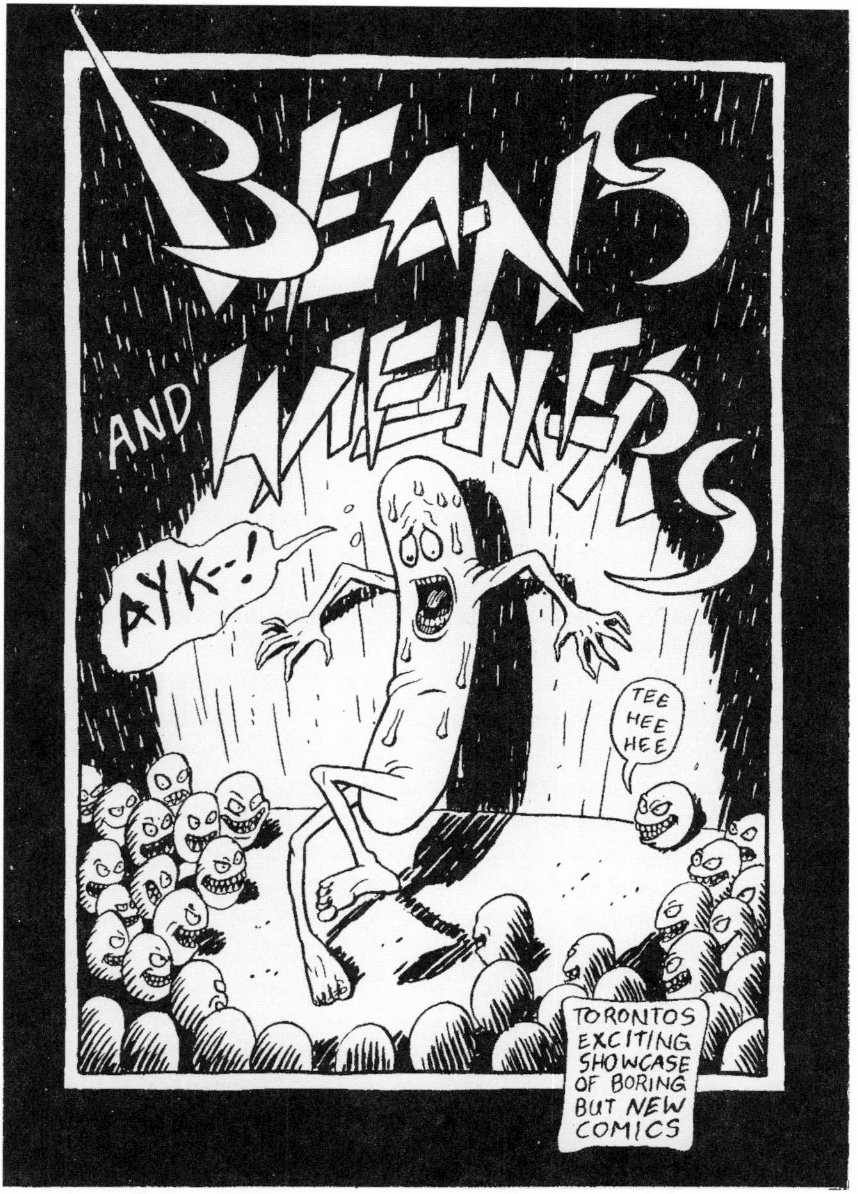
BEANS
AND WIENERS
AYK--!
TEE HEE HEE
TORONTOS EXCITING SHOWCASE OF BORING BUT NEW COMICS

Proposed cover for Beans and Wieners, *an unpublished Toronto comics anthology, 1982. Art by Chester Brown. Copyright © Chester Brown.*

Spotlight

discovered the new alternative comics and was beginning to lose interest in superhero narratives.

In fact, Brown later concluded that DC and Marvel had done him a huge favour. Musing on the shape of his probable career in superhero-comics, had he broken into the field in the late 1970s, he later speculated: "I'd either be a low-level hack or I'd have become so disgusted with the industry that I'd have to quit comics."[2] Although it wasn't obvious at the time, Brown's setbacks in New York marked a turning point in the history of Canadian comics.

In 1979, Brown moved to Toronto, joining the anglo exodus from Montreal then underway. About this time he began submitting work to a variety of underground and alternative comics publishers. Here, too, he met with rejection. Nonetheless, he remained committed to his art and lived a frugal lifestyle that permitted him to continue drawing strips. In 1981 he submitted a two-page narrative, *City Swine*, to Art Spiegelman's groundbreaking *Raw Magazine* — the *New Yorker* of comix. The strip was ultimately turned down, but the rejection note indicated that the work had come very close to being accepted. For Brown, living and working in anonymity on the cultural margins, this was crucial encouragement and confirmation that he was on the right track.[3]

In 1982, Brown and the well-known film archivist and collector Reg Hartt worked on an anthology comic entitled *Beans and Wieners*, which was intended to showcase some of the artists active in the new Toronto comics scene.[4] This project eventually fell through, but Brown wasn't concerned, since he had by then realized that the best way to get his work into print was to self-publish. Brown's main inspiration for this decision was the poet and innovative small-press publisher John W. Curry (jwcurry), a close associate of sometime comics creator bpNichol. Curry and Brown had been introduced to each other by Brown's girlfriend of the time, Kris (now Akami) Nakamura, who also encouraged Brown to publish his own work.

Brown finally took the plunge in July 1983, publishing (under the Tortured Canoe imprint) the first issue of an eight-page digest with the vaguely obscene title of *Yummy Fur*. Not long after, he found himself at the centre of Toronto's burgeoning small-press-comics milieu. Among the other significant creators active during this early period were Peter Dako, whose digest *Casual Casual Comics* commenced publishing in December 1983, and K.G. "Kat" Cruickshank (Lateral Drift Publications), whose *No Name Comix* first appeared in January 1984.

Once Brown began publishing his own work he was confronted with new challenges. "The hard part," he recalled, "was trying to convince stores to sell those zines."[5] However, slowly but surely, Brown was able to find a growing number of comic-book shops, independent bookstores, and various counterculture retailers that were willing to stock his comics. Later he also plugged into the loose network of zine publishers that was then evolving in North America. Between July 1983 and the end of 1984, Brown published six issues of his *Yummy Fur* digest (the earliest issues featured work from 1981–82, including the *City Swine* strip that had been rejected by *Raw*). As the title started to garner more attention, he was obliged to issue reprints in 1984. In fact, demand for back issues prompted Brown, in February 1985, to release a digest-size compilation, *Yummy Fur 1–6*, which also included a new one-page strip, *Fire with Fire*.

Brown's comics were now attracting a great deal of interest as evidenced by the fact that early in 1984 he, Dako, Cruickshank, Barbara Klunder, and other comix artists were featured in a cutting-edge show called *Kromalaffing* at Toronto's Grunwald Gallery. The Toronto small-press-comics artists were now part of the city's avant-garde, mingling with musicians, writers, painters, and other members of the vibrant counterculture then centred in the Queen Street West neighbourhood.

By the time Brown published a seventh — and final — issue of his digest comic in September 1985, it was obvious he had already outgrown the small-press milieu he had helped to create. Not only was he contributing illustrations and strips to an increasing number of other small-press publications, but the quality and originality of his work was beginning to be recognized by publishers and editors outside the world of zine culture, most notably Bill Marks, then the Toronto-based publisher of an ambitious line of Canadian alternative comics issued under the Vortex imprint.

Although Bill Marks's role in Canadian comics has been obscured by the achievements of Chris Oliveros and Drawn & Quarterly, from 1982 to 1990, Marks was a key player in the volatile and challenging alternative-publishing field and must be credited with advancing the careers of some of Canada's leading comics creators, including Seth, Paul Rivoche, Ty Templeton, Maurice Vellekoop, Ken Steacy, Dean Motter, Rob Walton, and the late Klaus Schonefeld. He also furthered the development in Canada of the graphic novel, the format that permitted alternative comics to reach a more mainstream readership and thus become more economically viable. Moreover, Marks (who was satirized in a less-than-subtle fashion in *Cerebus* as Bill Mox) represented a crucial link between the early alternative publishers, such as Orb and Andromeda, and the major publishers of the 1990s, particularly Black Eye Productions and Drawn & Quarterly. However, his greatest

Spotlight

147

Facing page: Cover of Yummy Fur *No. 28 (May 1992). Art by Chester Brown. Copyright © Chester Brown and Drawn & Quarterly.*

achievement was probably his decision in 1986 to turn *Yummy Fur* into an alternative comic, thereby bringing Chester Brown's disturbing, singular visions to a whole new audience.

The first issue of Vortex's *Yummy Fur* was delayed for several months but finally appeared in December 1986. It, together with issue Nos. 2 and 3 (1987), consisted of reprints from the first seven installments of Brown's original digest comics. Subsequent issues featured new material. Initially, Brown continued the shocking surrealist narratives found in the digest comics. However, he later surprised his readers by shifting to unsettling autobiographical stories.

The transformation of *Yummy Fur* into an alternative title changed financial realities for Brown. A major boom was then underway in the black-and-white alternative-comics field, and he soon found himself receiving sufficient earnings from *Yummy Fur* so that he could quit his day job and, provided he lived resourcefully, devote himself full-time to comic art. Unfortunately, the boom ended quite abruptly in 1988, and Vortex and other Canadian alternative publishers experienced serious financial setbacks. In fact, most ceased publishing. Vortex managed to hang on, but this disruption in the marketplace forced Brown to return to work in 1988 for a year or so. Since that time he has lived exclusively off his comics — no mean achievement and one that few Canadian artists can match.[6]

Another impact of the new *Yummy Fur* was that it brought Brown's work to a much larger readership and sparked demand for his art. As a result, he was soon contributing covers, strips, and illustrations to a variety of periodicals both inside and outside the comics milieu. Furthermore, his work was now widely reviewed in the comics and alternative presses. He was also sought out for interviews by periodicals such as *The Comics Journal* and *Comics Interview*. In short, Brown was becoming an alternative-comics star.

Meanwhile, in Brown's hometown, the centre of the comics universe began shifting in 1987 from Queen Street West to the Annex neighbourhood. Not far from the one-time Markham Street location of George Henderson's Memory Lane, the first comic-book store in Canada, Steve Solomos and Sean Scoffield opened The Beguiling, one of the most important comic-book shops in North America. What distinguished The Beguiling was its orientation towards alternative and small-press comics. It was, as subsequent owner Peter Birkemoe noted, "a store with an agenda."[7] Soon Brown and his friends and fellow artists Seth (Gregory Gallant) and Joe Matt became closely associated with the store and its defiant championing of comics as a serious art form.

In 1989, as the alternative-comics market finally began to recover, Vortex

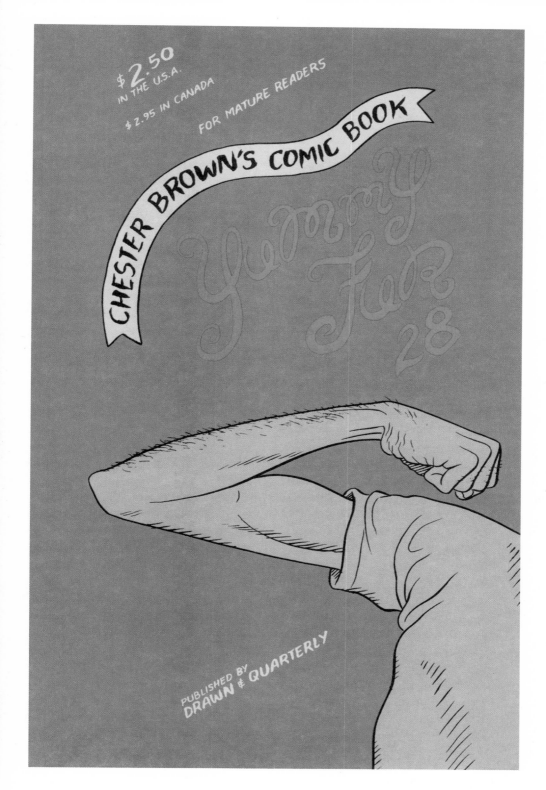

$2.50
IN THE U.S.A.
$2.95 IN CANADA

FOR MATURE READERS

CHESTER BROWN'S COMIC BOOK

Yummy Fur 28

PUBLISHED BY
DRAWN & QUARTERLY

Facing page: Cover
of Louis Riel No. 3
(December 1999).
Art by Chester
Brown. Copyright
© Chester Brown
and Drawn &
Quarterly.

issued Brown's first graphic novel, *Ed the Happy Clown*, which brought together material originally published in *Yummy Fur* Nos. 1–18. For Brown the book represented a major breakthrough. Within the comics field, the collection resulted in his winning two prestigious 1990 Harvey Awards (Best Cartoonist and Best Graphic Album) as well as the 1990 U.K. Comic Art Award (Best Graphic Novel/Collection). More important perhaps, the book prompted critical attention outside the comics field, including praise from *The Rolling Stone* and *The Village Voice*. According to the latter, Brown's book contained "the most extreme art you'll ever encounter."[8]

Although Vortex issued a second, revised edition of the *Ed* book in 1992, Brown's relationship with the publisher came to an end. Starting with issue No. 25 of *Yummy Fur* (July 1991), Brown associated himself with a new publisher, Chris Oliveros's Drawn & Quarterly, based in Montreal. Oliveros, who had recruited Julie Doucet from the small press in 1990 (in much the same fashion that Bill Marks had done with Brown several years before), also published Brown's comic-art confreres Seth (*Palooka-Ville*) and Joe Matt (*Peepshow*). Canadian comics were soon revolutionized, and Chester Brown was at the forefront of the new comics.

Brown published seven more issues of *Yummy Fur* (1991–94) with Drawn & Quarterly before embarking in 1994 on *Underwater*, a new and radically different comics series. For a variety of reasons he stopped working on the *Underwater* narratives in 1997, following the appearance of the eleventh issue. Then, after a hiatus of nearly two years, Brown launched a third series, the historical narrative *Louis Riel*, which appeared in ten issues from 1999 to 2003. Next, starting in 2005, he returned to his original *Ed* narratives from the early issues of *Yummy Fur* and began reworking these, with additional commentary, in a new comic-book series, *Ed the Happy Clown*, which is expected to comprise nine issues. (The *Ed* narratives were optioned many years ago by the Canadian filmmaker Bruce McDonald and may yet appear in a feature film, as improbable as that might sound.)

While these four series of comic books have solidified Brown's reputation within the comics field, their periodical format didn't allow him to break out of that milieu which, frankly, remains something of a cultural ghetto. What really transformed Brown's career, enabling him to reach out far beyond the comics subculture, was Drawn & Quarterly's championing of the graphic-novel format. Since Brown became associated with the firm in 1991, it has released three of his graphic novels, *The Playboy* (1992), *I Never Liked You* (1994, 2002), and *Louis Riel* (2003), as well as *The Little Man: Short Strips, 1980–1995* (1998), a compilation of short

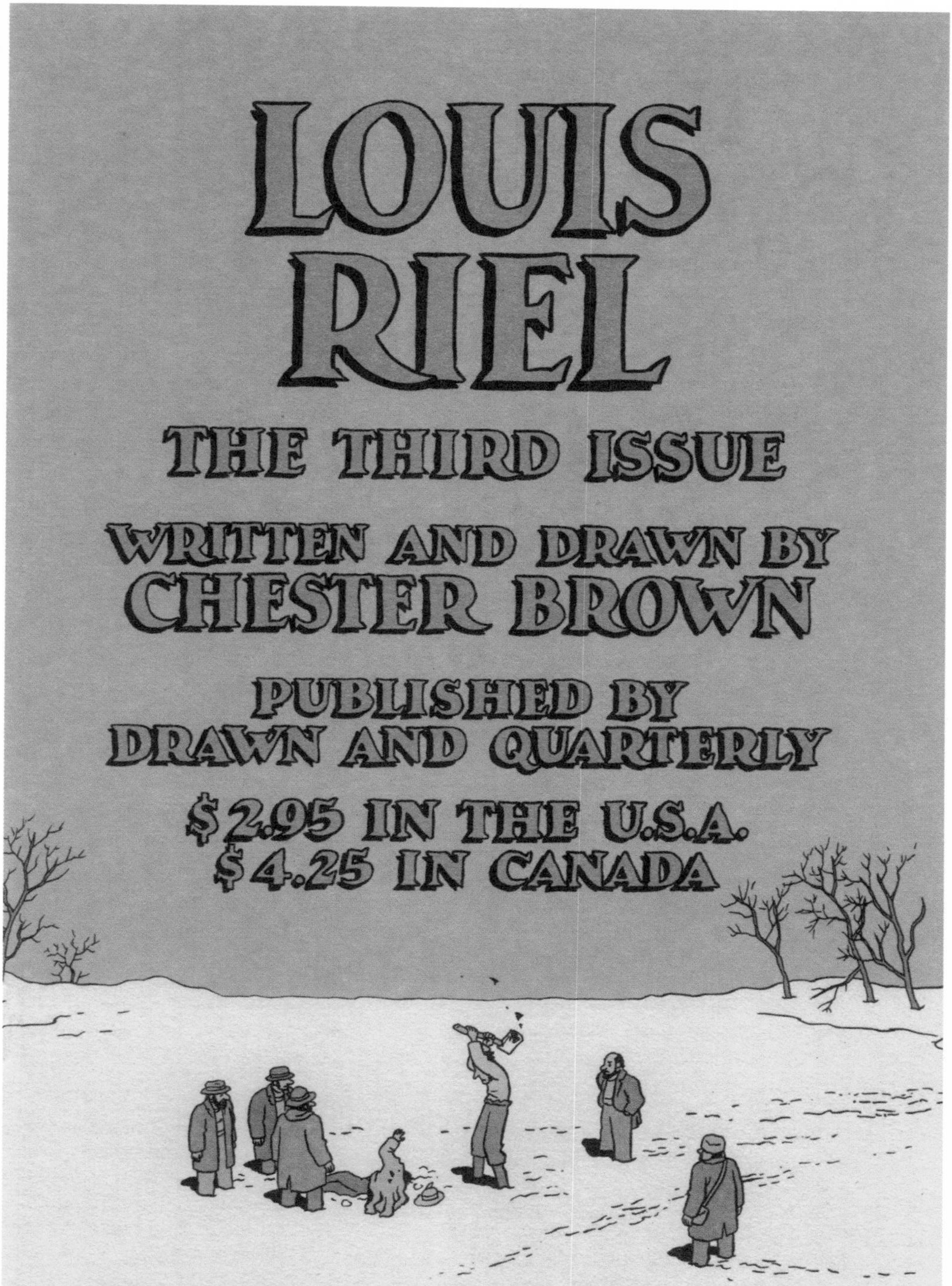
LOUIS RIEL
THE THIRD ISSUE
WRITTEN AND DRAWN BY
CHESTER BROWN
PUBLISHED BY
DRAWN AND QUARTERLY
$2.95 IN THE U.S.A.
$4.25 IN CANADA

Facing page: Cover of Ed the Happy Clown *No. 7 (2006). Art by Chester Brown. Copyright © Chester Brown and Drawn & Quarterly.*

narratives and fugitive pieces from *Yummy Fur* and other sources. While all of these books have won Brown new converts and considerable critical acclaim, the real breakthrough volume, especially in Canada, has been his most recent book, *Louis Riel*, which has received attention and praise from such mainstream publications as *The New York Times Magazine* (the July 11, 2004, issue featured a cover by Brown), *Time*, *Maclean's*, the *Globe and Mail*, *Le Devoir*, and *Canadian Art*. It also won Brown two more Harvey Awards — for Best Writer and Best Graphic Album. The book even prompted a visit to Brown by curators from the National Gallery of Canada.

Louis Riel is a remarkable work of sustained visual narrative, but its historical underpinnings and accessibility to mainstream readers might be misleading to some newcomers to comics, since it represents only one part of an extraordinary oeuvre that, taken as a whole, isn't for the faint-hearted. Readers who see Brown as primarily a graphic historical novelist may not appreciate that he is an artist who has been compelled for more than two decades to explore dark and disturbing truths — about himself and his society. Like the great American artist R. Crumb, he is less a typical comic-book artist and more an artist who has chosen to express himself in comics (though Brown would probably prefer to be known simply as a cartoonist). To really understand Brown's achievement, it is necessary to closely examine his narrative strategies and his willingness to push comics to the limit, even if it means accepting false starts and outright failures.

Brown has published a variety of short strips and other narratives, but his main body of work consists of six graphic storylines: *Ed the Happy Clown*, *The Playboy*, *I Never Liked You*, *The Gospels*, *Underwater*, and *Louis Riel*. Taken together these narratives represent a breadth unmatched by any other comic artist in Canada. (Only Dave Sim, with whom Brown has collaborated, comes close.)[9]

When, early in his career, Brown rejected superheroes, dismissing them as "a dead end genre," he didn't turn, like some of his contemporaries, to familiar alternative-comics genres such as science fiction, fantasy, or *noir* detective narratives.[10] Instead, in one of the most daring acts in comic-art history, he plunged headlong into his subconscious, embarking on a strip that he drew panel by panel without a script — and without any sense of where it would go or where it would end, embracing, in his own words, "surrealistic spontaneous creation."[11] Brown ventured wherever his characters took him, however dark and disturbing the consequences, all the while resisting any urge to censor himself. As he later recalled, "I never set boundaries for myself."[12]

The result, serialized in *Yummy Fur*

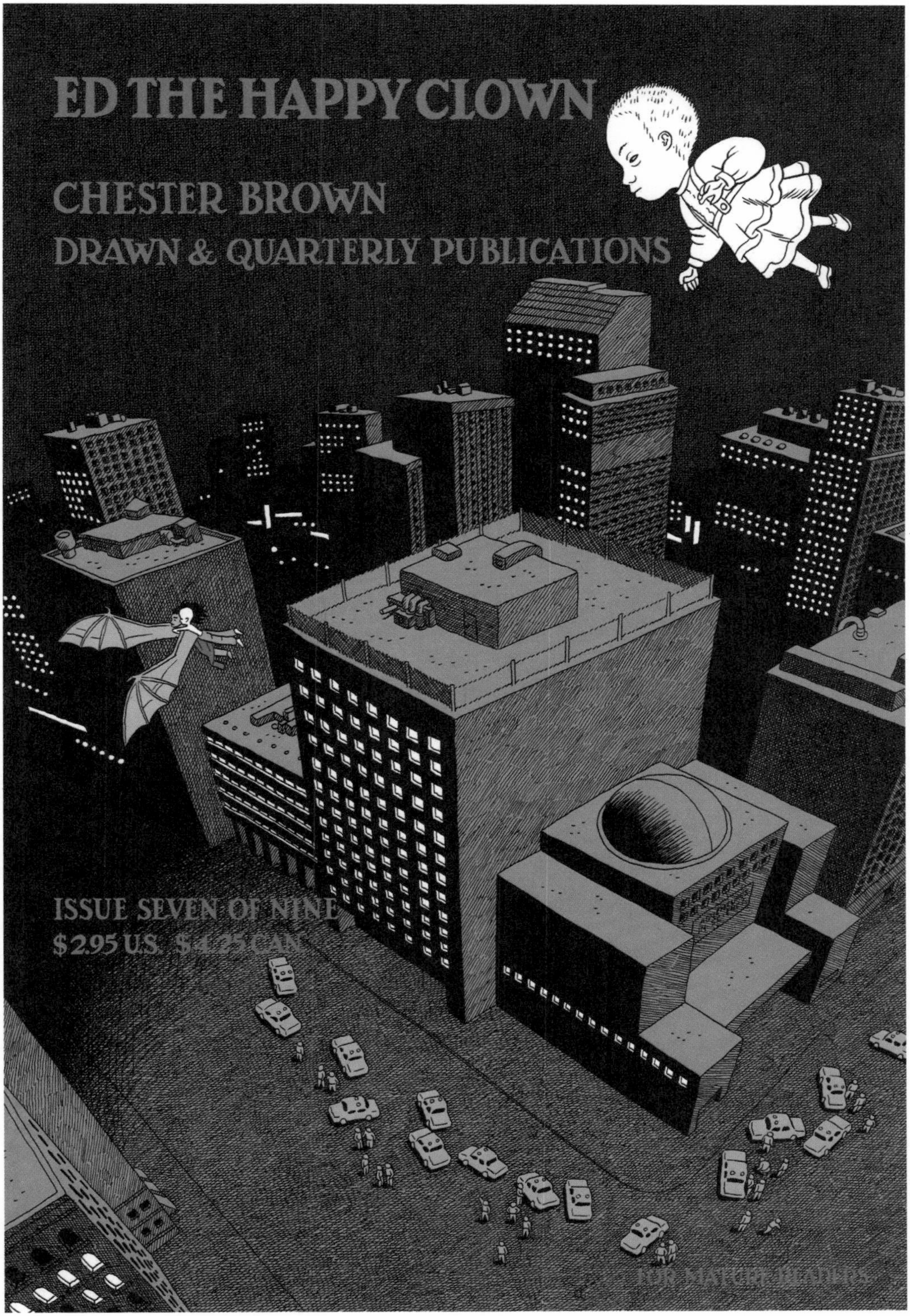
ED THE HAPPY CLOWN
CHESTER BROWN
DRAWN & QUARTERLY PUBLICATIONS
ISSUE SEVEN OF NINE
$2.95 U.S. $4.25 CAN

between 1983 and 1988, was *Ed the Happy Clown*, an audacious and complex dream-like narrative weaving together several story strands that draw on a variety of sources, including pulp science fiction, schlock horror, religious literature, and television clichés. Transitions within the absurdist storyline are often abrupt and unexpected, resulting in deliciously bizarre juxtapositions as well as clever overlapping narratives in which Brown revisits events from another point of view. The narrative is not only scatological, blasphemous, grotesque, and violent in the extreme, but also deeply funny — not so much black humour as pitch-black humour. The main storyline, which defies easy summation, focuses on a hapless clown named Ed and the series of ludicrous and disturbing calamities that befall not just him, but also a guilt-ridden misfit named Chet Doodley and Doodley's beautiful girlfriend, Josie, who sheds her life and her clothes early in the strip and ends up becoming a vampiric wraith.

Among the other dramatis personae in this twisted dramatic comedy about sex, death, religion, and alternate realities are rat-eating, penis-god-worshipping pygmies who have taken refuge in the sewers; a succession of mad scientists; an alternate-world President Ronald Reagan, whose head ends up on Ed's penis; a man who can't stop defecating and whose anus becomes a portal to Dimension X;

Brown's version of Saint Justin; pygmy killers; vampire hunters; an alternate world Prime Minister Brian Mulroney; and the Mounties. Brown accomplishes the nearly impossible feat of tying all this dangerous, charged material together in a coherent narrative (he has offered different endings to the story and will likely continue to do so).

The *Ed* narratives, which *The Village Voice* characterized as "jaw-droppingly uncensored," are distinguished not just by their content, but also by the improbable maturity of Chester Brown's art.[13] Brown arrived in print almost fully formed as an artist, with a compelling style that was quite unlike anything that had preceded it, though there were subtle hints pointing to the likely influence of comic-art masters such as Harold Gray, R. Crumb, and Jack Kirby. That doesn't mean Brown hasn't grown as an artist, because he has, but he was very good from the very start — an accomplished draftsman who drew with surety and emotional depth.

This emotional resonance was even more evident in Brown's next narrative, *The Playboy*, which was originally serialized in *Yummy Fur* issues 21–23 (1990) before it was collected in a graphic novel in 1992. Here Brown turns from improvisational experiments in surrealist narration to a far more conscious and deliberate act of remembrance in which he dredges up his adolescent experiences with soft-core pornography in the form

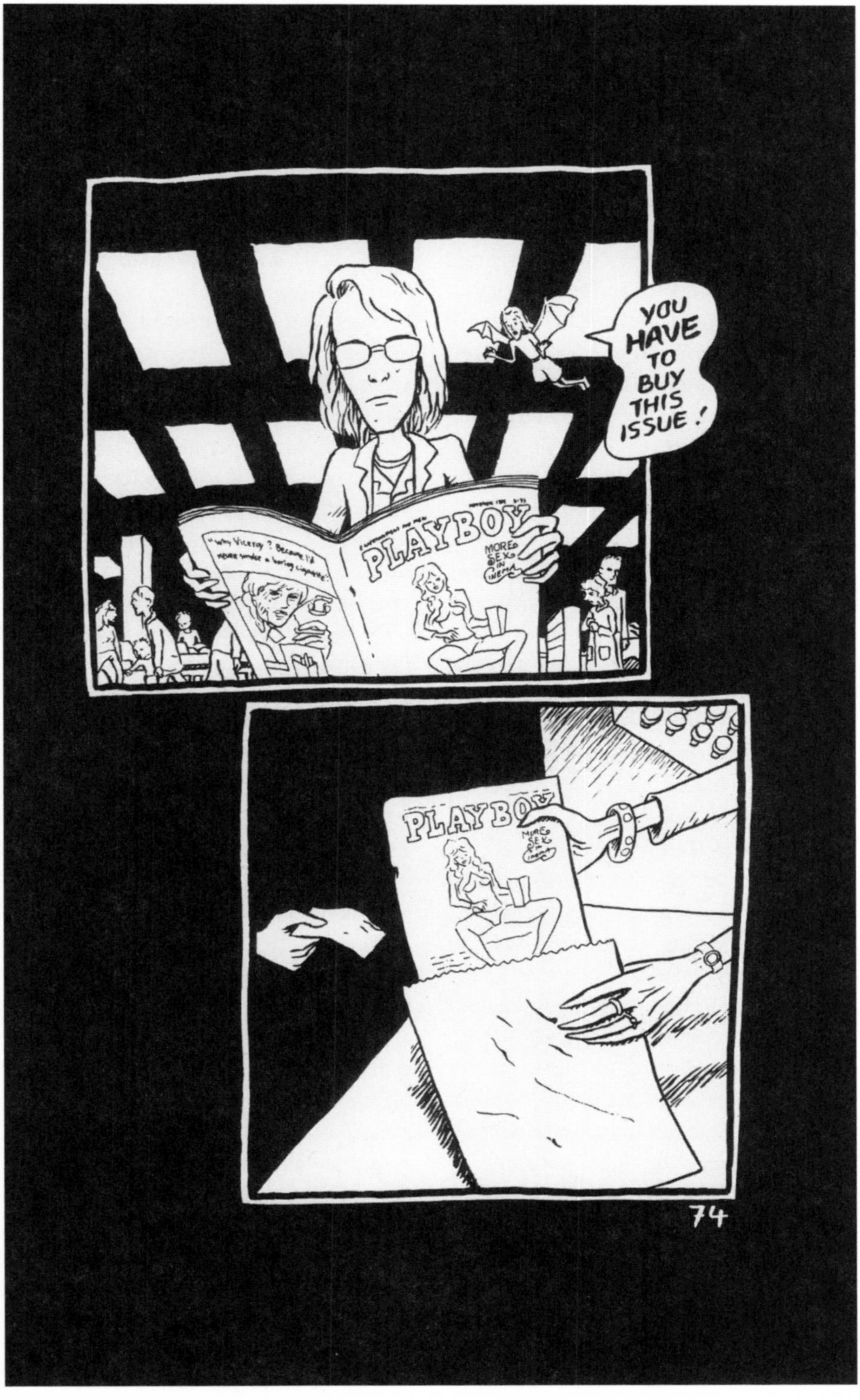
YOU HAVE TO BUY THIS ISSUE!
PLAYBOY
PLAYBOY
74

Page 74 of The Playboy *(1992). Art by Chester Brown. Copyright © Chester Brown and Drawn & Quarterly.*

Spotlight

of *Playboy* magazine. The story is set in a specific place and time, Châteauguay in the mid to late 1970s, and is portrayed visually with a more understated and realistic style than was evident with the *Ed* narratives. Brown's haunting verisimilitude extends not only to his suburban milieu, but also to the specific issues of *Playboy* that had an impact on his young life.

According to Brown, his work draws on two main emotions: outrage and guilt.[14] It is the latter that pervades *The Playboy* as Brown depicts the extreme self-loathing that attends his younger self's obsessive encounters with the masturbatory fantasy world of *Playboy* magazine. This is autobiography at its most painfully honest but told with an almost matter-of-fact detachment that only serves to enhance the emotional impact.

Brown describes a recurring cycle of desire and disgust as he is enticed by the latest issue of *Playboy*, tries to purchase it without being noticed, smuggles it (or the Playmate section torn from the magazine) into his house, masturbates (in a less-than-typical fashion, draped over a chair and using two hands, almost in an act of supplication), and then tries to dispose of the magazine through a variety of means: hiding, burial, and burning. Frequently, he is lured back to the discarded magazines. He is like a character out of Edgar Allan Poe or Fyodor Dostoyevsky, a pathetic high-school Raskolnikov haunted by his transgressions.

Later in the narrative he describes his growing interest in the magazine's interviews and other features. He then details his discovery of used bookstores in Montreal, which permit him to accumulate a collection of back issues until 1978 when the threat of discovery forces him to dispose of the magazines in heavy bundles that he lugs to Montreal in his art portfolio and throws out in garbage bins. As the narrative comes to a close, he muses on his continuing, obsessive relationship with the magazine and its effect on his confused relationships with women during his twenties.

Some readers have viewed the narrative as an indictment of pornography, but Brown's intentions are more complicated — and less predictable. For him the story is an act not just of confession but catharsis. It allows him to expose the shame he felt as a teen and underscores the fact that his engagement with pornography didn't encourage aggression or hostility towards women, but rather a withdrawal into his private world. "I wanted to explain how my experience led me to do the opposite — go into a room by myself and shut the door."[15] In fact, Brown contends that the adolescent shame and disgust that he felt about his Playmate fantasies were the products of a repressive culture. To his mind, the problem is not *Playboy*, but rather a sick society that equates natural desire with sin.[16] Thus, while *The Playboy* represents a departure for Brown, it shares two overriding characteristics with his earlier work: a willingness to expose painful truths about himself and a contempt for political correctness and liberal pieties.

For all its power, however, *The Playboy* is, in a sense, merely a prologue to a more ambitious autobiographical narrative, *I Never Liked You*, which was originally serialized in *Yummy Fur* Nos. 26–30 (1991–93) and subsequently collected in a graphic novel published by Drawn & Quarterly. Whereas *The Playboy* is about teen lust and guilt, *I Never Liked You* is more about the agonies of unrequited love. Curiously, the art in this strip is sketchier than Brown's previous work (perhaps the unfinished look is deliberate, given the strip's subject matter), but the scripting is much tighter. *The Playboy* is disjointed in places, but not this work, which is very much structured like a novel, intertwining several storylines and making effective use of page layout to shift the mood and alter the pace. (Brown's tendency to create panels separately and then assemble them as he sees fit on the page allows for a great deal of layout flexibility; it also facilitates any subsequent revisions or alterations.)[17] Some of the strip's most touching and haunting moments are interludes of silence captured in pure pictorial storytelling.

In the strip, Brown returns to his high-school years in Châteauguay and explores his confused relationships with three neighbourhood girls: Connie; her younger sister, Carrie; and Sky. At the same time he portrays two other ongoing sources of turmoil and pain during his teen years: bullying by a group of kids intent on forcing him to swear (the strip's original title was *Fuck*) and the tragedy of his mother's gradual mental breakdown and then death. (Brown later explored his mother's mental illness in a powerful short strip entitled *My Mom Was a Schizophrenic*, which serves as a kind of coda to *I Never Liked You*.)[18]

Above all, *I Never Liked You* is a book about adolescent angst and the tentative and awkward groping towards adulthood, including the defences young people erect in an effort to shield themselves from pain and the mounting pressure of more adult responsibilities. In the midst of an expanding emotional vortex, a gangly and petulant young Chester eventually shuts down. Unable to give or receive love, he retreats into his art. In some respects, Brown's portrayal of his younger self corresponds very much with his confrere Seth's description of his own adolescence: "A typical comic book kid, over-sensitive, not good at sports, without many friends."[19]

Brown regards *I Never Liked You* as his best and most successful work before *Louis Riel*.[20] It is certainly a poignant narrative, one that captures not only the particular tragedies that befell his family, but also the commonalities of teen life, including the

Spotlight

Facing page: Cover of the second edition of I Never Liked You *(2002). Art by Chester Brown. Copyright © Chester Brown and Drawn & Quarterly.*

unavoidable cruelties that punctuate the lives of inarticulate, hormone-driven adolescents. The book has no false notes, and together with *The Playboy*, it rightly confirms Brown's position as one of the true masters of the graphic memoir. Among those who have praised this aspect of Brown's oeuvre is the British artist Eddie Campbell, who claimed that Brown's "autobiographical comics are the most sensitive comics ever made." Another admirer, the American artist Gilbert Hernandez, observed that "*The Playboy* and *I Never Liked You* are probably the best graphic novels next to *Maus* and Jason's *Hey, Wait ...*"[21] However, at the same time that Brown was producing these two masterpieces and pushing the boundaries of comics even farther beyond superheroes, he was experimenting with other narratives radically different from either the surrealism of *Ed* or the confessional accounts of his troubled adolescence.

From the beginning of Brown's comics career, it was apparent that religion had probably played a prominent part in his early life. For instance, there are references to religion in the *Ed* narratives as well as sequences that draw on religious iconography, particularly the Saint Justin storyline. Furthermore, Brown's autobiographical narratives contain numerous overt references to his family's strict religious values, including the prohibition against swearing that figures so prominently in *I Never Liked You*. Even more telling perhaps are the normal staples of teen life that are absent from his memoir: sex (other than masturbation), drugs, alcohol, and smoking. It is not surprising then that Brown's search for new narrative sources led him to a text that had so obviously dominated and shaped his young life, namely, the Christian Bible.

For those who only know Brown's work from his published graphic novels, it might come as a surprise to learn that from 1987 to 1997 he contributed comics adaptations of the Gospels to most issues of his *Yummy Fur* and *Underwater* comics. To date, Brown has completed the Gospel of Mark (*Yummy Fur* Nos. 4–14) and published more than twenty installments of the Gospel of Matthew, starting in *Yummy Fur* No. 15. Mostly, these figured as so-called backup stories. However, one entire issue of *Yummy Fur* (No. 32, January 1994) was devoted to a Gospel adaptation. Brown also published interesting notes on the stories in *Yummy Fur* No. 16 (June 1989) and *Underwater* No. 7 (August 1996).

Although the Gospels adaptations remain unfinished, they represent Brown's longest-running narrative and his most sustained strip prior to *Louis Riel*. They also contain some of his best comic art. Initially, Brown's adaptations were more or less straightforward visualizations of the Biblical texts. Increasingly, though, with the Matthew adaptation, he brought more improvisation and interpretation to the

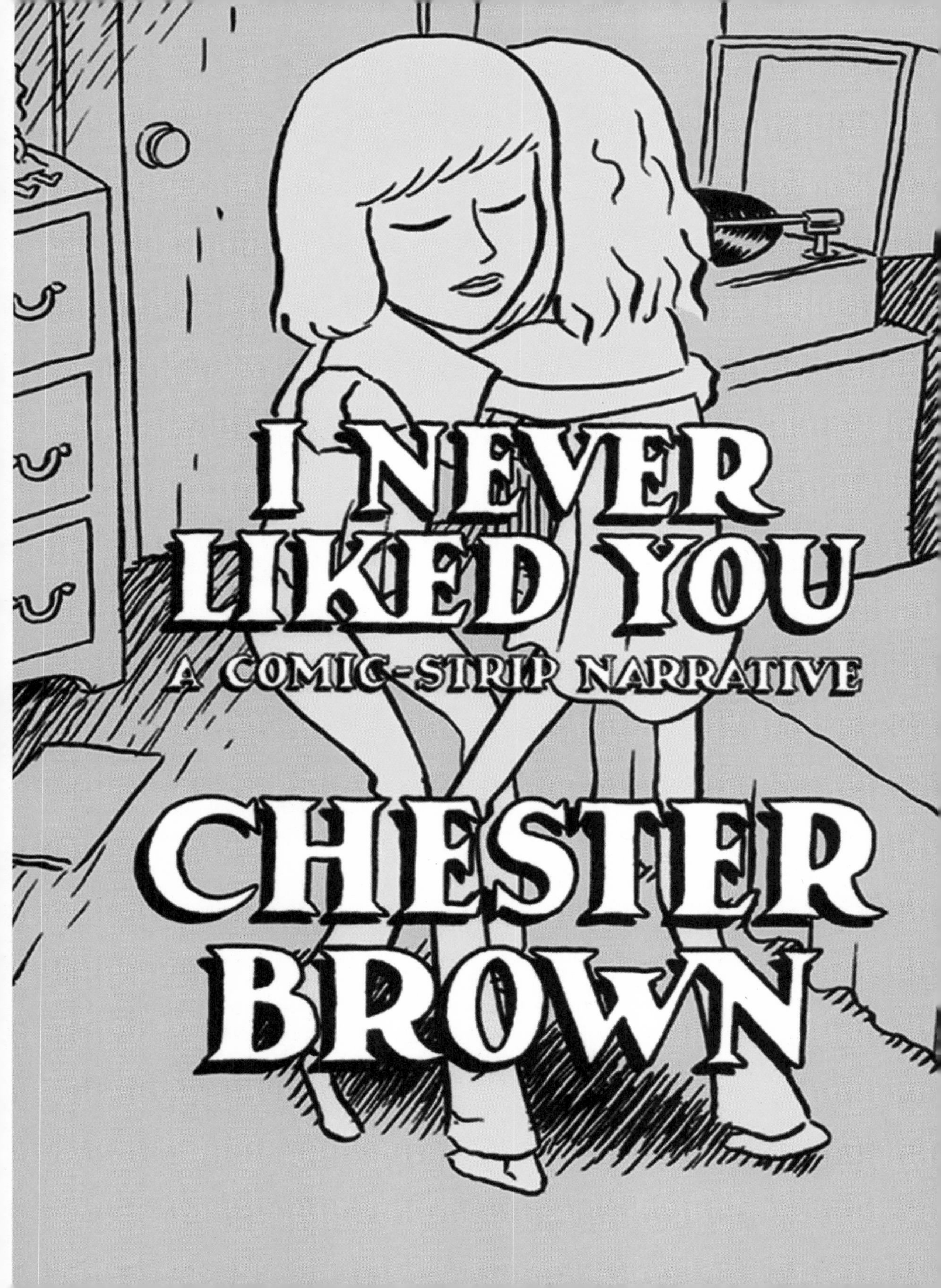
I NEVER LIKED YOU
A COMIC-STRIP NARRATIVE
CHESTER BROWN

narrative, offering a startlingly fresh take on the Gospels. But it isn't a pretty picture. His Holy Land is a place of pestilence and brutality. The Apostles are loutish and uncomprehending. As for Jesus, he is portrayed as a bony, balding figure who towers above his followers and delivers his parables and sermons in a driven, frequently angry manner. He is an obsessive outsider, almost like a character out of a Flannery O'Connor novel, with, in her words, a burning faith "hidden in his head like a stinger."[22]

However, all this darkness, all these Gothic elements, serve a useful narrative purpose, alienating the reader — in a Brechtian sense — and thereby forcing us to re-interpret familiar stories and to hear afresh the words of Christ. The result is that we end up more or less in the same position as Jesus's confused disciples, struggling to understand the meaning of Jesus's words and the validity of his claims of divinity. Like them, we are left asking, "Who is this man?" To his credit, Brown focuses on this question and not the answer. As he explained in 1991: "I can't know what kind of man Jesus was. He must have been impressive in some way to inspire such devotion in his followers. How? I don't know."[23]

Brown has indicated numerous times that he will resume work on his idiosyncratic versions of the Gospels at some point in the future. He also intends to collect them eventually in book form.

Meanwhile, they remain the most important uncollected work in his published oeuvre. However, they aren't the only unfinished body of work put aside by Brown. From 1994 to 1997 he worked on a strip, *Underwater*, in which his inventiveness and ambitious experimentation with narrative strategies seemed to hit a brick wall.

It is clear that *Underwater* marks a radical departure for Brown. For one thing, his artwork is far more stylized, reminiscent in some ways of his earlier non-autobiographical narratives (according to Brown, Frank King and Harold Gray are the main influences on the look of the strip).[24] As for subject matter and narrative structure, it is apparent from the outset that Brown is intent on challenging his readers in a new way, deliberately eschewing the accessible storytelling that characterize not only his preceding work but also the Gospel adaptations that accompany most chapters of *Underwater*. Instead, this story is conceived as a narrative puzzle, one that is complicated to the point of obscurantism. The challenge for readers is significantly exacerbated by Brown's use of an invented language that over time incorporates an increasing number of English words.

The storyline, which Brown steadfastly refuses to explain, centres on the birth and early childhood of two twins, one of whom — the girl Kupifam — becomes the narrative's main protagonist. Although the

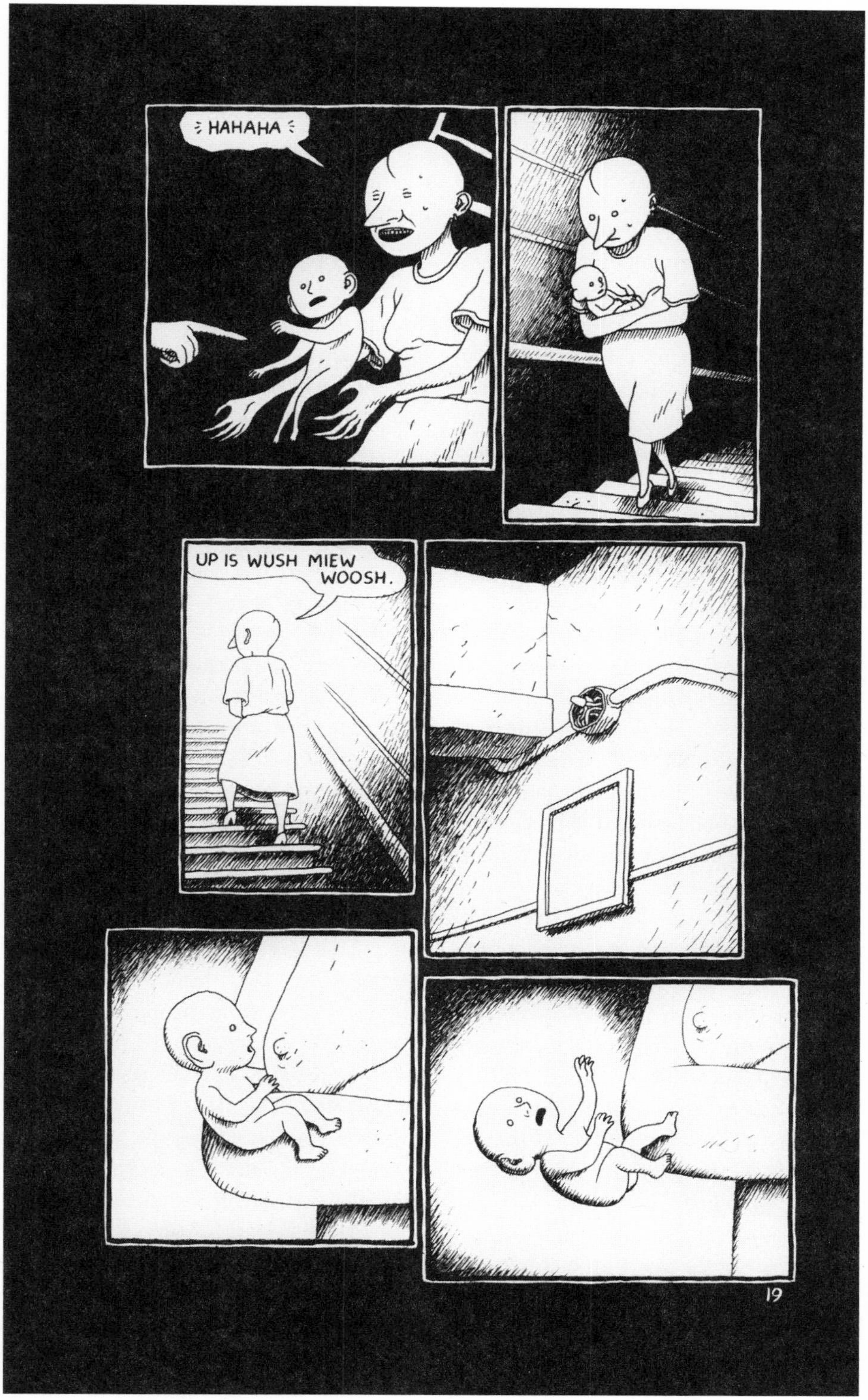
HAHAHA
UP IS WUSH MIEW WOOSH.
19

Page 19 of Underwater *No. 1 (August 1994). Art by Chester Brown. Copyright © Chester Brown and Drawn & Quarterly.*

Spotlight

Facing page: Page 17 of Underwater *No. 7 (August 1996). Art by Chester Brown. Copyright © Chester Brown and Drawn & Quarterly.*

story seems to weave together dreams and interiority with events occurring in the external world, nothing in the narrative is truly realistic. Virtually every panel exudes a dream-like quality. The twins are less like real children and more like little adults fumbling towards comprehension of their surroundings, their family, and their lives. Although Brown offers scant guidance to readers in the pages of the *Underwater* comic book, he did indicate in a 1997 interview that the strip "was about more than just childhood." He also noted that the classic Chinese novel *Dream of the Red Chamber* was a major influence on the strip, which probably accounts for its complexity and the centrality of dreams.[25]

In any event, the letter columns of *Underwater* soon reflected the bewilderment experienced by most of Brown's readers. Nonetheless, many gave Brown the benefit of the doubt and gamely attempted to interpret the strip's events, teasing out meaning and trying to decipher what Brown himself later called "*Underwater* gibberish."[26] Others, however, strongly resented the strip's hermeneutic demands. The noted American cartoonist Bill Wray, a long-time admirer of Brown's work, probably spoke for many readers when he lamented: "I feel like I'm drowned."[27]

Brown's loyal readership had followed the many twists and turns of his artistic evolution for one simple reason: the rewards were substantial — and often sublime. Readers learned to trust him. With *Underwater*, however, Brown's instincts seemed to fail him. The narrative was a bold experiment, but one that ultimately didn't work. The strip's meaning was too elusive, readers drifted away, and sales dropped. Brown himself began to have second thoughts about the strip. One major problem, he later revealed, concerned the pacing of the narrative, for as the strip developed, he realized it would take more than 300 issues to finish the story.[28]

After the completion of issue No. 11 of *Underwater* in 1997, Brown put the strip aside in order to work on the *Little Man* book project. However, in February 1998, when he was slated to resume work on *Underwater*, he came to the realization that he couldn't go on. Later he recalled: "I had lost my way."[29] The recent death of his father also contributed to his decision. (Apparently, Brown plans to return to the strip in the future, with the intention of restructuring the narrative.)[30]

Underwater, as originally conceived, must be regarded as a failure, but it is an admirable one in that it exhibits two of Brown's chief strengths as an artist: his willingness to take risks and his abiding desire to experiment with new narratives, not to mention his formidable drawing skills. Perhaps because *Underwater* was focused so much on subjective realities, Brown began to look at more objective sources for his next major narrative. He

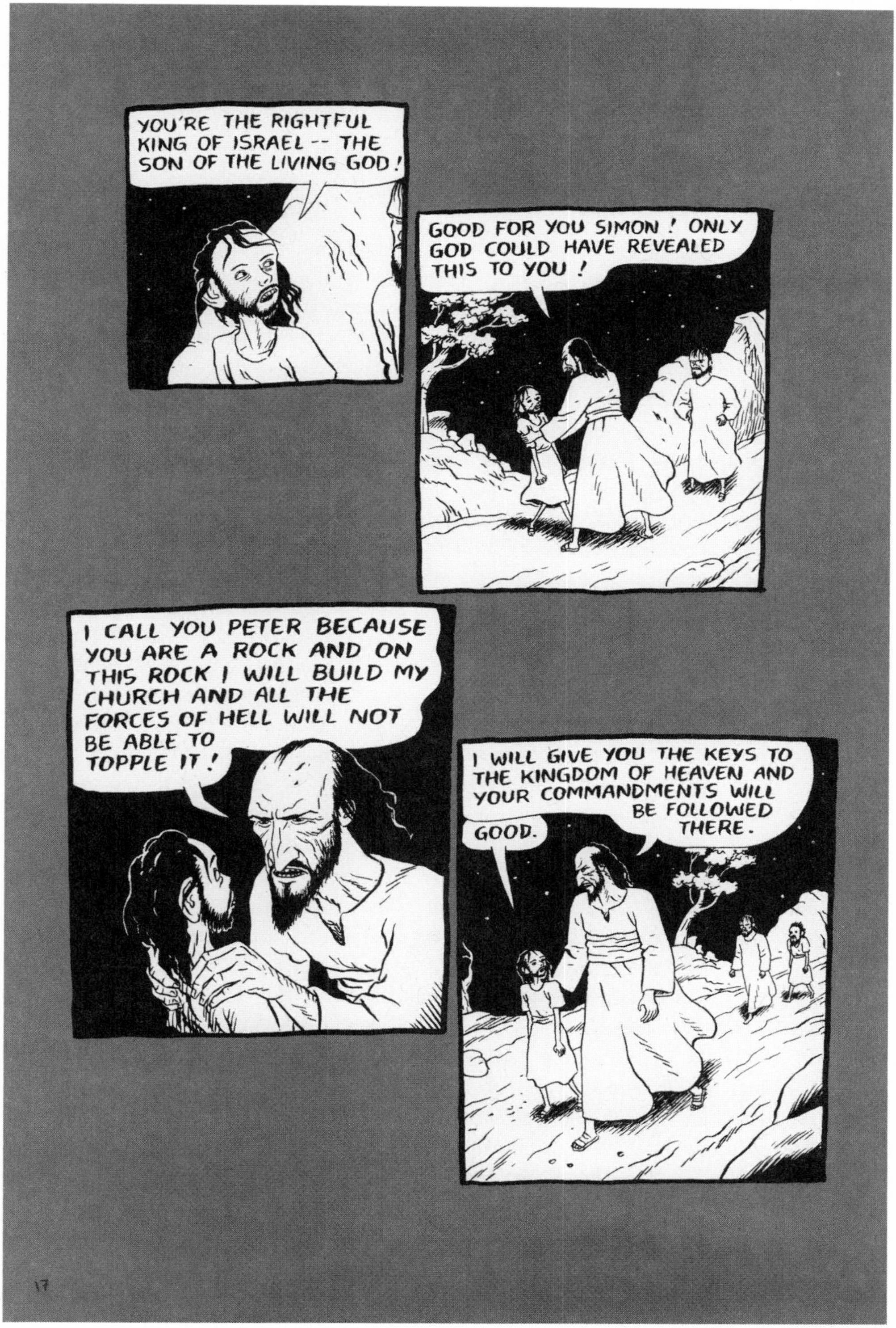
YOU'RE THE RIGHTFUL KING OF ISRAEL -- THE SON OF THE LIVING GOD!
GOOD FOR YOU SIMON! ONLY GOD COULD HAVE REVEALED THIS TO YOU!
I CALL YOU PETER BECAUSE YOU ARE A ROCK AND ON THIS ROCK I WILL BUILD MY CHURCH AND ALL THE FORCES OF HELL WILL NOT BE ABLE TO TOPPLE IT!
I WILL GIVE YOU THE KEYS TO THE KINGDOM OF HEAVEN AND YOUR COMMANDMENTS WILL BE FOLLOWED THERE.
GOOD.

had also come to appreciate, during his work on the *My Mom Was a Schizophrenic* short strip (which had originally appeared in *Underwater* No. 4), that he enjoyed the process and demands of research. As he later commented: "After finishing the schizophrenia strip, I thought, 'I'd like to do something like this again, something where you … try to cram a lot of research into a comic strip.'"[31] This newfound appetite was certainly satisfied by Brown's next project, which required months of serious historical — and related visual — research and resulted in his longest and most ambitious narrative to date.

In 1995, while still working on *Underwater*, Brown read *Riel: A Life of Revolution* (1994), Maggie Siggins's popular biography of the Métis leader Louis Riel. At the time Brown was fascinated by the book and noted that Riel's dramatic life would lend itself to a comic-strip adaptation.[32] Early in 1998 he decided that Riel would be the subject of his next comics project. The attraction was obvious: the leader of two rebellions against central Canadian authority, Riel was one of the most controversial figures in Canadian history, someone who straddled major divides, most of which still impact the country today: French-English, Native-White, Protestant-Catholic, and East-West. Moreover, as Riel was a deeply religious man with messianic tendencies and a history of apparent mental illness, his story also highlighted two themes that

have long preoccupied Brown: religion and madness. Furthermore, as a libertarian with anarchist tendencies, Brown was fascinated by two other themes pivotal to the rebellions led by Riel: the role of property rights and the intrusion of the state in people's lives.[33]

It should be noted that Brown comes by his interest in Canadian history honestly. His grandfather — and namesake — was the noted McMaster University historian Chester William New, who is probably best remembered for his award-winning biographical study *Lord Durham* (1929).

As Brown embarked on his new project (with some assistance from the Canada Council), he threw himself into an intensive study of the historiography relating to Louis Riel, first rereading Siggins and then reviewing other biographies of Riel and the major histories of the Red River Rebellion of 1869–70 and the North-West Rebellion of 1885. Of particular interest were two somewhat revisionist books by Thomas Flanagan, *Louis "David" Riel: "Prophet of the New World"* (revised edition, 1996) and *Louis Riel and the Rebellion: 1885 Reconsidered* (revised edition, 2000). Brown was especially intrigued by the former in which Flanagan not only explicates Riel's religious ideas, but also rejects the simplistic diagnoses of Riel's supposed mental illness. Although Siggins and Flanagan appear to be the major influences on Brown's interpretation of Riel, he also

Chester Brown
and the Search
for New Narratives

read a large body of other historical literature, including the conspiracy theories advanced by D.N. Sprague and Don McLean. (According to these authors, Prime Minister John A. Macdonald deliberately provoked the 1885 rebellion in order to garner support for the completion of a transcontinental railway.)[34]

In addition to historical research and interpretation, Brown was obliged to make a number of crucial aesthetic decisions about his narrative. His major influence in this regard was Harold Gray, the late creator of *Little Orphan Annie*, one of the true masterpieces of the American comic strip in the twentieth century. Not only did Brown emulate Gray's deceptively simple drawing style, including his tendency to portray huge bodies and small heads, but he also opted for simple square panels arranged in a six-panel grid. Most important perhaps, he adopted Gray's "emotional restraint," eschewing extreme close-ups and opting for a minimalist approach that saw him "focus on imagery and … try to have silent panels as much as possible."[35] As for writing, Brown decided that *Louis Riel* would be his most tightly scripted narrative. In fact, his script, which also served as a very rough storyboard, ran to more than 200 pages and was revised several times before he began drawing.[36]

Brown originally conceived of *Louis Riel* as a book, but his publisher, Chris Oliveros, argued for serialization in a comic-book series before publication in book form. The artist agreed to this approach but insisted on certain format concessions. He wanted the comic book, which began publication in 1999, to have a "warm" feel, so he demanded that it be smaller than regular comic-book size and that it be printed on yellow newsprint.[37] This strategy proved to be a brilliant design choice, since the resulting comics had a nineteenth-century feel, resembling the pulpish Victorian dime novels. The *Louis Riel* comic book ran for ten issues (1999–2003). The narrative was then revised and collected in a hardcover graphic novel.

Although Riel's life had been the subject of other sustained graphic narratives, including a twenty-four-page story by Mark Zigler, Jon Fraser, John Heard, and Dana Wodkiewicz in issue No. 2 of the early Canadian alternative comic *Canadian History Comic Book* (1972), and a French-language young adult graphic novel, *Louis Riel, le pere du Manitoba* (1996), by Zoran Vanjaka and Toufik El Hadj-Moussa, it was apparent from the outset that Brown's *Louis Riel* was not only far superior to any other comic-strip version of Riel's life that had preceded it, but that it was a masterpiece of modern Canadian comic art and a major breakthrough in terms of the scope of comics. As Brown had demonstrated throughout his career, comics could, and should, be about anything.

Facing page: Page 107 of Louis Riel: A Comic-Strip Biography *(2003). Art by Chester Brown. Copyright © Chester Brown and Drawn & Quarterly.*

In its final graphic-novel form, *Louis Riel* is a remarkable achievement. Divided into four main parts, it covers Riel's role in the Red River Rebellion, his exile in the United States, his incarceration in a mental asylum in Montreal, his complex religious convictions, his leadership of the North-West Rebellion, and his trial and execution. In addition to the main narrative, the book is augmented by twenty-three pages of endnotes, a bibliography, and an index. Brown's notes are fascinating. In addition to identifying sources, they reveal his creative process and the difficult decisions he had to make in relation not only to interpretation but also storytelling. Like a filmmaker or a historical novelist, he was constantly confronted by the challenge of how best to portray events and advance his narrative, something that required a deft approach to artistic licence.

Brown very much succeeds in his goal of telling the Riel story with pictorial and editorial restraint. He manages to portray Riel in all his complexity and yet avoid simple conclusions regarding issues such as the legitimacy of Riel's sense of mission, his true motives, and his achievements. Furthermore, at many critical junctures Brown offers, in his notes, alternative perspectives on events. Although Brown, like his mentor Gray, distrusts big government and thus buys into the conspiracy theories relating to the role of Prime Minister Macdonald in the 1885 rebellion, he doesn't demonize Sir John A. In fact, by the end of his narrative, he comes to the conclusion that he "would rather have lived in a state run by John A. Macdonald than one run by Louis Riel."[38] Such a statement seems to indicate that Brown's political views evolved over the course of the five-year Riel project. However, even if he is somewhat less anarchistic in his outlook, he very much remains a libertarian.

The excellence of Brown's work was quickly and widely recognized. *Louis Riel* was not only a major critical success, but also a commercial one. In fact, it became the first Canadian graphic novel to feature on bestseller lists. In 2004 it also appeared in translation in France (Casterman) and Italy (Coconino).

Since the completion of his groundbreaking magnum opus, Brown has been poised to plunge into another major project. According to his wide-ranging, Riel-related discussions with Dave Sim in *Cerebus* Nos. 295–97 (available on the Web at *www.cerebusfangirl.com*), Brown intends to return to autobiography and further explore his relationships with women, including his encounters with prostitutes. Meanwhile, he is currently reworking his *Ed* narratives in a new Drawn & Quarterly comic-book series.

Wherever his artistic explorations take him next, it is virtually certain that Chester Brown will continue to do what

< RISE, LOUIS DAVID RIEL -- YOU HAVE A MISSION TO ACCOMPLISH FOR THE BENEFIT OF HUMANITY. >
< WHY DO YOU CALL ME DAVID ? I DON'T HAVE A MIDDLE NAME. >
< DAVID IS THE NAME I GIVE YOU AS MY PROPHET OF THE NEW WORLD. >
< WHERE ARE YOU TAKING ME ? >
< I AM TRANSPORTING YOU TO THE FOURTH HEAVEN TO EXPLAIN THE NATIONS OF THE EARTH TO YOU. >
IN EARLY MARCH 1876, ONE OF RIEL'S FRIENDS VISITS L'HOSPICE St JEAN DE DIEU (A LUNATIC ASYLUM NEAR MONTREAL).
<-- AND HE STARTS CRYING IN PUBLIC FOR NO APPARENT REASON. EITHER THAT OR HE STARTS BELLOWING LIKE A BULL. >
< HE ACTUALLY THINKS HE IS A BULL. OR SOMETIMES HE THINKS HE'S THE BIBLICAL KING DAVID. AND HE LOCKS HIMSELF IN HIS ROOM AND TAKES OFF ALL HIS CLOTHES AND TEARS THEM UP. >
< YOU CERTAINLY NEED TO COMMIT HIM. >

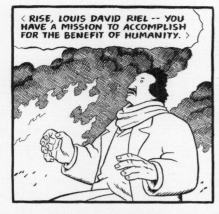

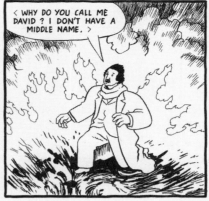

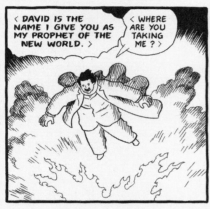

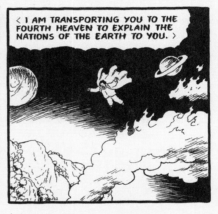

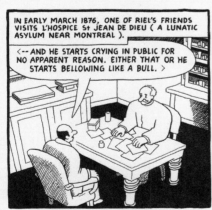

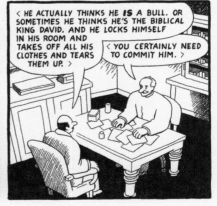

he has done for more than twenty years: push comics in new directions, searching for new narrative subjects and new ways to depict those narratives. Like Dave Sim, Seth, Dave Cooper, and a handful of other Canadian comics artists, he has managed to live his life as an alternative comics artists without compromising his vision — even if it meant, at times, living as a cultural outsider, unrecognized beyond a small coterie of comics fans.

Although his cultural exile has ended and Brown is now being celebrated, like R. Crumb, as an important artist, it is doubtful that such mainstream recognition will result in any compromises from Brown. His approach to his art has always been fearless and searingly honest. For this reason he will never be a safe artist. Graphic narrative is obviously a compulsion for Brown, one that has constantly led him to difficult and disturbing subjects and themes. His long-time readers know this and are willing to follow wherever he leads for the simple reason that his daring, finely crafted stories consistently have the resonance and depth of the best literature and film. He is a master of his art form and one who, fortunately for his readers, is uncomfortable with limits. The reinvention of Canadian comic art during the past twenty years owes much to his restlessness and daring.

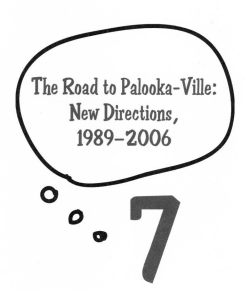

The Road to Palooka-Ville:
New Directions,
1989–2006

7

SINCE 1989 THE NORTH AMERICAN COMICS INDUSTRY HAS UNDERGONE SEVERAL PAINFUL RESTRUCTURINGS AS PUBLISHERS, distributors, and creators have been forced to adjust, especially since the mid-1990s, to significant economic, technological, and cultural changes, including the advent of the new media and the erosion of the mass audience for comics. These developments have encouraged the evolution in Canada of three somewhat separate subcultures: mainstream (mostly superhero) comics, alternative comics, and small-press zines.

To a large degree, this growing divide within the comics community has centred on the role of the creator in comics and on the nature of the appropriate target audience for graphic narrative. Chester Brown, one of Canada's leading alternative and small-press creators, probably spoke for many of his confreres when he argued in 1991 for a new direction in comic art: "For comics to progress as an art form we have to forget superheroes altogether. It's a dead-end genre. We have to start drawing comics that will appeal to adults and the only adults who enjoy superhero comics are adults with stunted intellects and adolescent tastes."[1]

However, not all Canadian creators shared Brown's absolute disdain for the superhero genre. Between 1989 and 1995 numerous Canadians were active in the U.S. superhero field, including Ken Steacy, George Freeman, Gabriel Morrissette, Neil Hansen, Kent Burles, Stuart Immonen, Dale Keown, Denis Rodier, Tom Grummett, Ty Templeton, Richard Pace, Dave Ross, Peter Grau, Jason Armstrong, Max Douglas, Jean-Claude St. Aubin, Mark Shainblum, and Lovern Kindzierski, whose Winnipeg-based graphic-arts firm significantly advanced comic-book colouring.

By far the most important superhero creator of the era, though, was Alberta

7

artist Todd McFarlane, who first achieved recognition in the late 1980s while working for Marvel Comics. In 1991, after a bitter dispute over creators' rights — a crucial issue that had simmered throughout the 1980s, thanks to the efforts of Dave Sim and other activists — McFarlane left Marvel, stunning his legions of fans. Early the following year he defiantly rallied other creators and co-founded Image Comics, a major new American comic-book company. Not long after, Image began publishing McFarlane's comic book *Spawn* which, for a time, was one of the world's best-selling comics. The phenomenal commercial success of *Spawn* led, in turn, to a host of spinoffs, including a feature movie, a line of toys, and an animation series. Previously frustrated by his lack of creative control at Marvel, McFarlane (now based in Arizona) heads a multimedia empire that rivals that of his former employer. Somewhat ironically perhaps, McFarlane found himself on the other side of a creators'-rights dispute in 2002 when he, as a publisher, was sued by the writer Neil Gaiman.[2] (McFarlane was also at the centre of a free-speech-protection case involving the former National Hockey League tough guy Tony Twist.)[3]

The early success of Image accelerated profound changes then underway in the superhero genre. Throughout the 1990s the portrayal of superheroes became supposedly more "adult." This development didn't always mean that such comics increased in sophistication and depth, featuring more complex and believable characters. Instead, it often resulted in darker, more violent, and more explicit narratives that involved a bewildering multitude of excessively brawny heroes and anti-heroes. Despite its shortcomings, this new approach initially seemed to promise a brighter commercial future. Ultimately, however, these graphic narratives were aesthetically bankrupt as scripting and characterization were sacrificed to flashy presentation.

Not surprisingly, since the mid-1990s, the audience for such narratives has been shrinking. In addition to a general decline in the quality of scripting and a stultifying homogeneity, the superhero genre has been beset by other, perhaps more fatal, problems, including the loss of young readers (apart from the ubiquitous Archie comics, which remain exceedingly popular in Canada, there are very few accessible entry points into comic books for children), competition from video games (which increasingly incorporate complex narratives) and other media (superhero movies, role-playing games, et cetera), and the closed nature of the superhero universes, which have become progressively inaccessible to the uninitiated. Due to these factors, the unthinkable occurred during the 1990s: mainstream comics ceased to be a truly mass medium.

One effect of this decline has been that many of the Canadian creators who were

The Road to
Palooka-Ville:
New Directions,
1989–2006

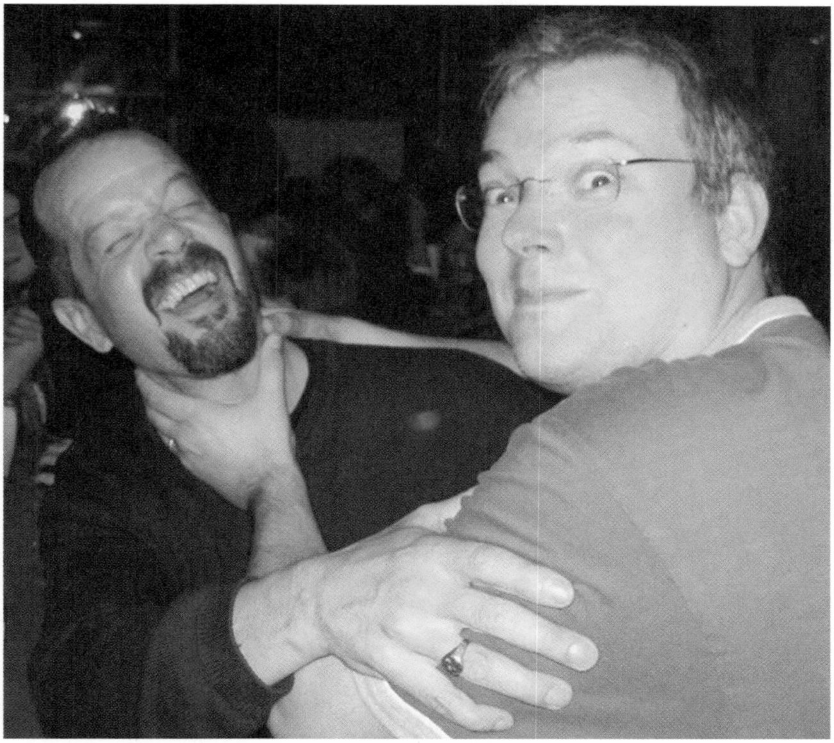

Darwyn Cooke (left) and Steve McNiven discuss comics at a Halifax restaurant in 2004. Photo by Calum Johnston. Copyright © Calum Johnston.

7

active in the U.S. superhero comics in the 1980s and early 1990s have left the field (more than a few now work as storyboard artists in Canadian animation, television, and films). It should be noted, though, that some of the leading Canadian artists who contributed to superhero comics between 1980 and 1995 still work in the genre, including John Byrne, Todd McFarlane, Ken Steacy, George Freeman, Ty Templeton, Dave Ross, Denis Rodier, Tom Grummett, and Dale Keown (Full Bleed Studios). In addition, since the mid-1990s they have been joined by impressive newcomers such as Neil Vokes, Yanick Paquette, Tim Levins, Cary Nord, Chris Bachalo, Darwyn Cooke, Cameron Stewart, and Steve McNiven. In fact, prompted in part by a number of successful Marvel-related blockbuster movies, superhero comics have finally begun to recover. The contributions of the new generation of superhero artists have also probably been a key factor.[4]

As for mainstream comics publishing in Canada, it has continued to be a particularly elusive goal as exemplified by Richard Comely's failed attempt to resurrect Captain Canuck under the Semple Comics imprint.[5] (Undeterred by earlier setbacks, Comely launched yet another new Captain Canuck series late in 2004, and in 2006 he tried again.) From 2002 to 2004 one of the few bright spots in this area was Pat Lee's Dreamwave Productions. A former Image contributor, Lee and the numerous artists associated with his Toronto-based studio initiated a line of successful comics, including a series of titles featuring Hasbro's popular Transformers toys. The various products of the Dreamwave studio

The Road to
Palooka-Ville:
New Directions,
1989–2006

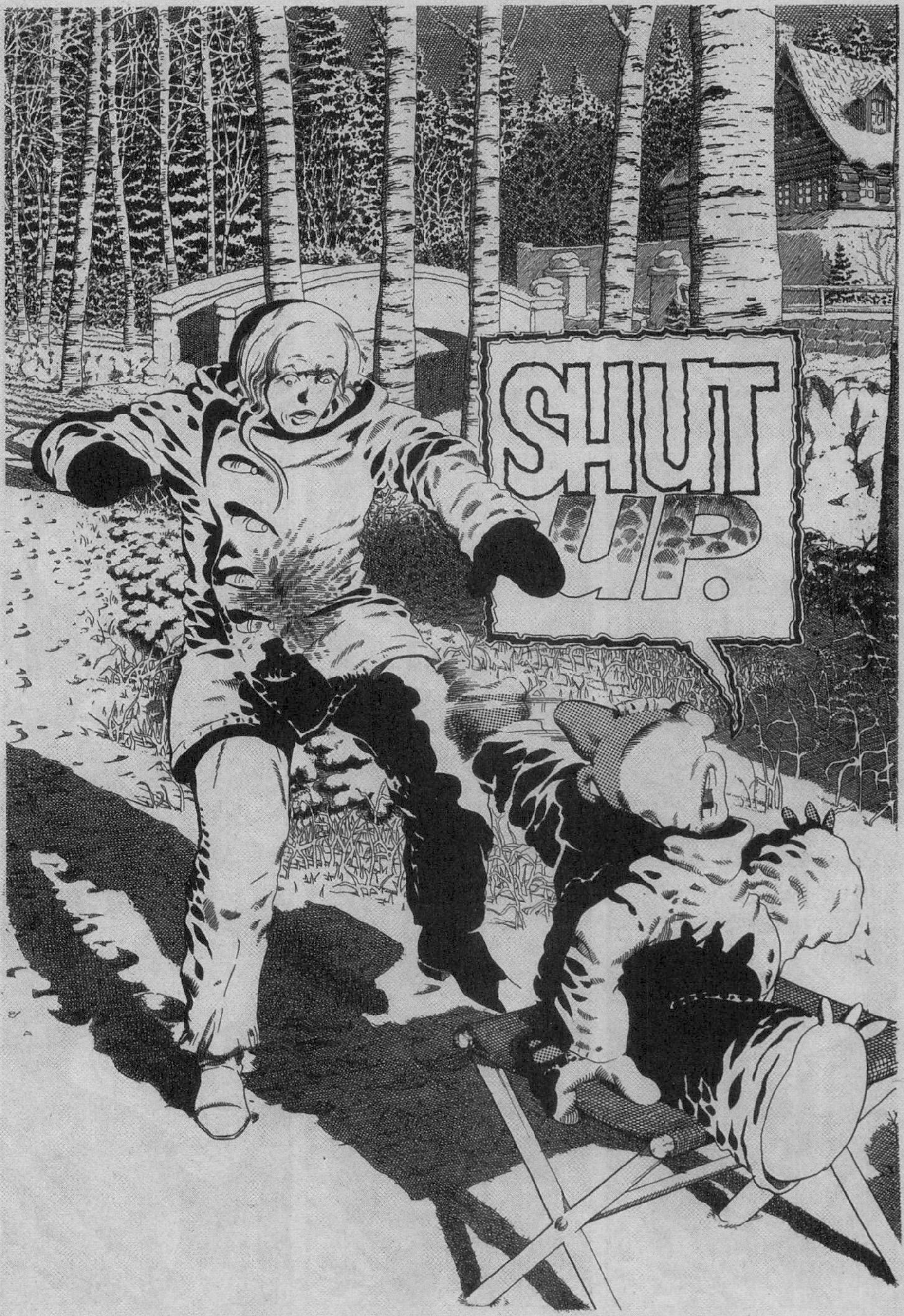
SHUT UP.

478

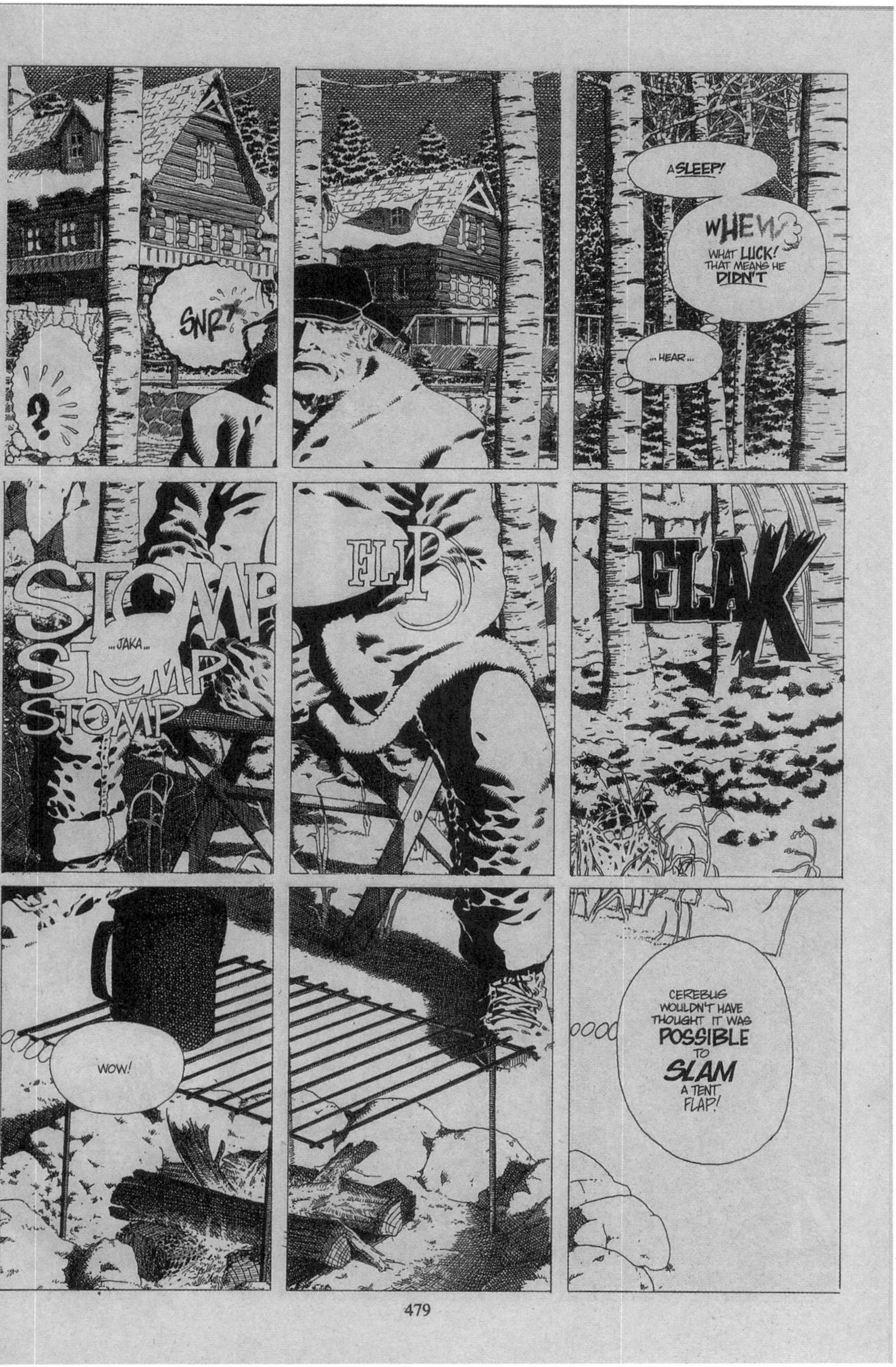
SNR?
?
A SLEEP!
WHEW WHAT LUCK! THAT MEANS HE DIDN'T
...HEAR...
STOMP
...JAKA...
STOMP
STOMP
FLIP
FLAK
WOW!
CEREBUS WOULDN'T HAVE THOUGHT IT WAS POSSIBLE TO SLAM A TENT FLAP!
479

Pages 478–79 of Cerebus No. 255 (June 2000). Art by Dave Sim and Gerhard. Copyright © Aardvark-Vanaheim.

7

Facing page:
Cover of Dirty
Plotte *No. 6*
(January 1993). Art
by Julie Doucet.
Copyright © Julie
Doucet and Drawn
& Quarterly.

The Road to Palooka-Ville: New Directions, 1989–2006

weren't especially sophisticated graphic narratives, but they were distinguished by strong design and very polished artwork. However, early in 2005, Dreamwave folded, another casualty of the vicissitudes of comics publishing.

While superhero comic books faltered to some degree during the past decade or so, alternative comics proved, from an aesthetic point of view, to be far more resilient, nurturing North America's most exciting and creative comic art. However, the business side of alternative publishing remained volatile. In fact, by the end of 1989, virtually all the significant publishers that had been active in Canada during the first wave of alternative-comics publishing had disappeared or were on the verge of folding, with the exception of Dave Sim's Aardvark-Vanaheim, which throughout the 1990s continued to produce impressive (few can match the striking sense of design displayed by Sim and his talented collaborator Gerhard), even if sometimes controversial, *Cerebus* narratives.[6]

Today many await with great anticipation Sim's future evolution as an artist following the conclusion of his ambitious *Cerebus* saga, which ended early in 2004 with the publication of issue No. 300. Reflecting on his more than twenty-six-year commitment to *Cerebus*, Sim noted that his "very, very long and intricate story" concluded more or less as he had anticipated it would. He also admitted he had paid a huge price for his single-minded devotion to the *Cerebus* project, observing that "the cumulative weight of that kind of ambition is daunting. The longer you go on … the more enemies you make and the more important it becomes to persevere."[7]

Dave Sim's defiance and perseverance as an independent creator certainly served as an important inspiration to other Canadian comics creators, for despite the many obstacles confronted by Sim and other alternative publishers, numerous aspiring Canadian publishers have boldly entered the field since the early 1990s. Among their number were Special Studio, Drawn & Quarterly, Tragedy Strikes Press, Black Eye Productions, Highland Comics, Mad Monkey Press, Semple Comics, Predawn Productions, Davan and Associates, Egesta Comics, Blind Bat Press, Exclaim! Brand Comics, Planet Lucy Press, Subterranean Comics, High Impact Studios, I Box, Crash Communications, Ironlungfish Press, Deep-Sea Comics, Fractal Comics, Belmont Publishing, Helikon Comics, Victory Comics, Dreamer Comics, Catfish Comics, Aporia Press, Too Hip Gotta Go Graphics, Arcana Studio, and Speakeasy Comics.

For the most part these new publishers issued a handful of comics and then folded, usually after a year or two. Two major exceptions to this rule were Black Eye Productions, which was active

176

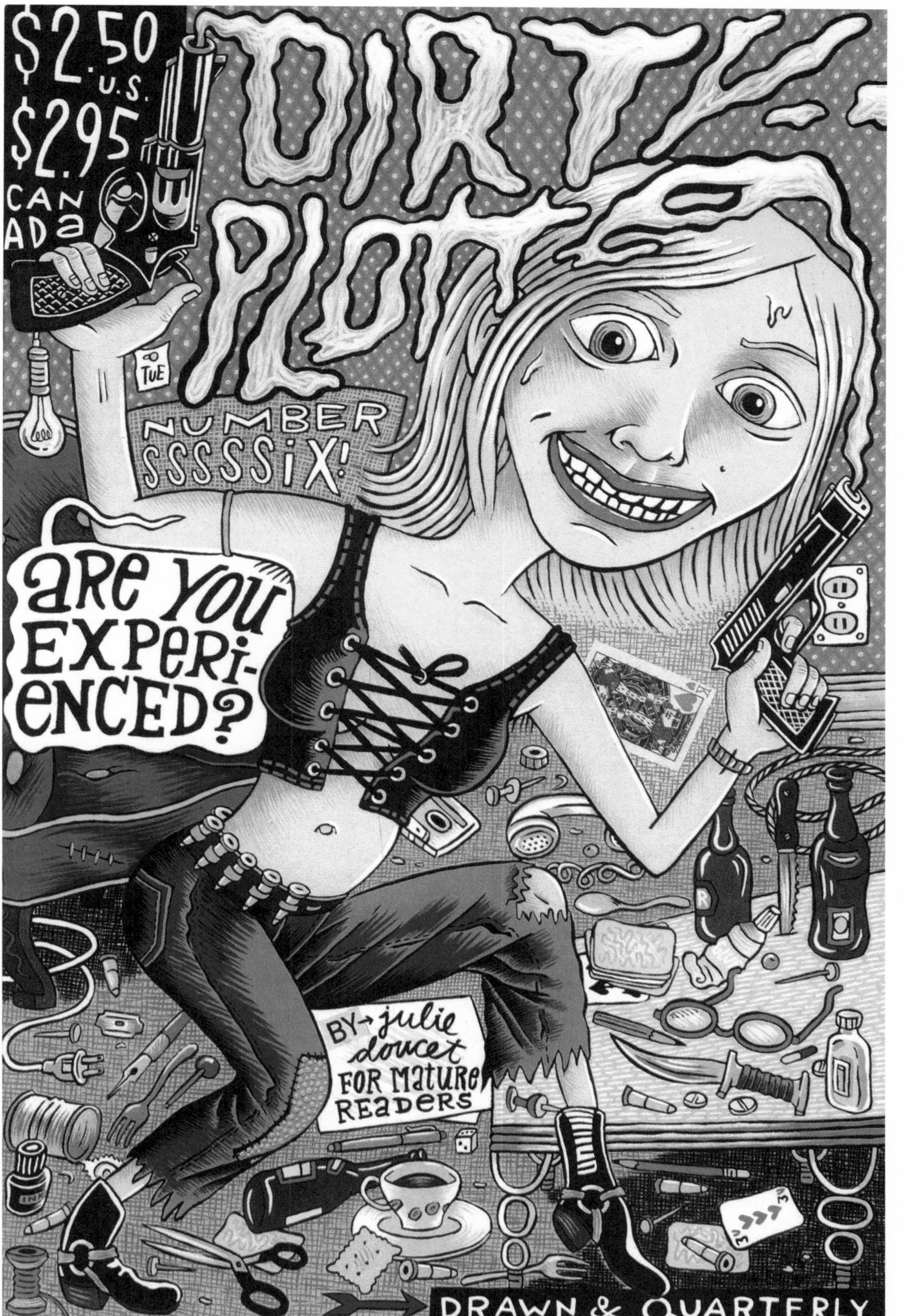

$2.50 U.S.
$2.95 CANADA
DIRTY PLOTTE
NUMBER SSSSSIX!
TUE
are you EXPERI-ENCED?
BY→ julie doucet
FOR Mature READERS
DRAWN & QUARTERLY

Facing page: Seth's Dominion cityscape (created from recycled FedEx boxes) from his Art Gallery of Ontario exhibition in 2005. Photo by David Briggs Photography. Copyright © David Briggs Photography.

for much of the 1990s, and Drawn & Quarterly, which was launched in 1990 and still has a major presence today. Both firms shared a commitment to publishing the best comics possible, whether by Canadian or foreign creators, and both viewed graphic narrative not merely as a form of popular entertainment, but rather as a serious art form. Furthermore, the two publishers embraced non-traditional comics, encouraging innovation in terms of technique and genre. In the case of Drawn & Quarterly in particular, this commitment to excellence and experimentation, combined with sound business instincts, soon thrust the firm into the forefront of Canadian — and then international — comic art. As the 1990s progressed, it became increasingly clear that English Canadian comics had found a belated and much-needed champion in the person of Chris Oliveros, Drawn & Quarterly's founder.

It was probably no accident that Chris Oliveros's publishing firm emerged in Montreal, a hothouse of comic art where creators and readers have long been exposed not only to the comic art of Europe and America, but also that of English Canada and Quebec. In fact, no other city in North America can boast such a rich co-mingling of traditions. From such a vantage point Oliveros clearly saw that comics in North America were trapped in a superhero ghetto. He also realized that this preoccupation with a genre designed primarily for adolescent boys represented a serious obstacle to the maturation of comic art in North America.[8]

Determined to steer comics in another direction, Drawn & Quarterly made its debut in April 1990 with *Drawn & Quarterly*, the first issue of an alternative-comics anthology magazine. Not long after, Oliveros convinced Julie Doucet to transform her brilliant *Dirty Plotte* from a self-published zine into a professionally produced alternative comic book. Drawn & Quarterly then recruited a coterie of exceptional Toronto artists: Seth (*Palooka-Ville*), Joe Matt (*Peepshow*), and Chester Brown (*Yummy Fur*, *Underwater*, and *Louis Riel*). Since joining Drawn & Quarterly, all four artists have achieved international recognition, figuring among the leading practitioners of modern comic art. Initially, they were known for their autobiographical narratives. However, Seth and Chester Brown have since shifted to the exploration of historical subjects.

In 2002, Seth collaborated with the U.S. singer and songwriter Aimee Mann, contributing strips and illustrations to the booklet that accompanied her CD *Lost in Space* (SuperEgo Records). Seth's evocative artwork provided an effective counterpoint to Mann's haunting lyrics. He also achieved a long-held ambition in 2002 by becoming a regular contributor to *The New Yorker*.[9] Earlier Seth had explored his fascination with the magazine in a

powerful, wistful narrative, *It's a Good Life, If You Don't Weaken*, which was first serialized in *Palooka-Ville* before being issued by Drawn & Quarterly as a graphic novel. In the narrative, he embarks on a search for a fictional Canadian contributor to *The New Yorker*, the cartoonist Kalo.

Seth's signal contributions to modern comic art were recognized in 2005 in an impressive exhibition, *Present Tense: Seth*, at Toronto's Art Gallery of Ontario. In addition to featuring artwork from his ambitious *Clyde Fans* graphic narrative and the strip *Hush*, the show included a remarkable sculptural representation of a streetscape from Dominion, the fictional city featured in *Clyde Fans*, the first part of which was collected in a graphic novel by Drawn & Quarterly in 2004.

During the past decade, Drawn & Quarterly promoted the work of many other Canadian alternative-comics creators, including Maurice Vellekoop, Luc Giard, Carol Moiseiwitsch, Fiona Smyth, Bernie Mireault, and David Collier. Oliveros has also published numerous important international artists such as Mary Fleener, Adrian Tomine, Jacques Tardi, Peter Bagge, Jason Lutes, Richard Sala, and David Mazzuchelli. Today Drawn & Quarterly is deservedly recognized as one of the leading comics publishers in the world. In the North American context, it is doubtful that any other publisher has done more to encourage alternative approaches to graphic narrative.

In addition to the creators associated with Drawn & Quarterly and with Aardvark-Vanaheim, there were a number of other important Canadians active in alternative comics at various times during the 1990s. Among the most notable were Ho Che Anderson (*King, Pop Life*, and *El Ogro*), Greg Hyland (*Lethargic Comics*), Rob Walton (*Ragmop*), Bernie Mireault (*The Jam*), Diana Schutz, Jacques Boivin (*Melody*), Dean Motter (*Mister X* and *Terminal City*), Jay Stephens (*Atomic City Tales*), Dave Cooper (*Suckle, Weasel*, and *Crumple*), David Boswell (*Reid Fleming*), Mike Cherkas (*Silent Invasion* and *Suburban Nightmares*), Larry Hancock (*Silent Invasion* and *Suburban Nightmares*), Ken Steacy, Tara Jenkins (*Galaxion*), Greg Beettam and Stephen

7

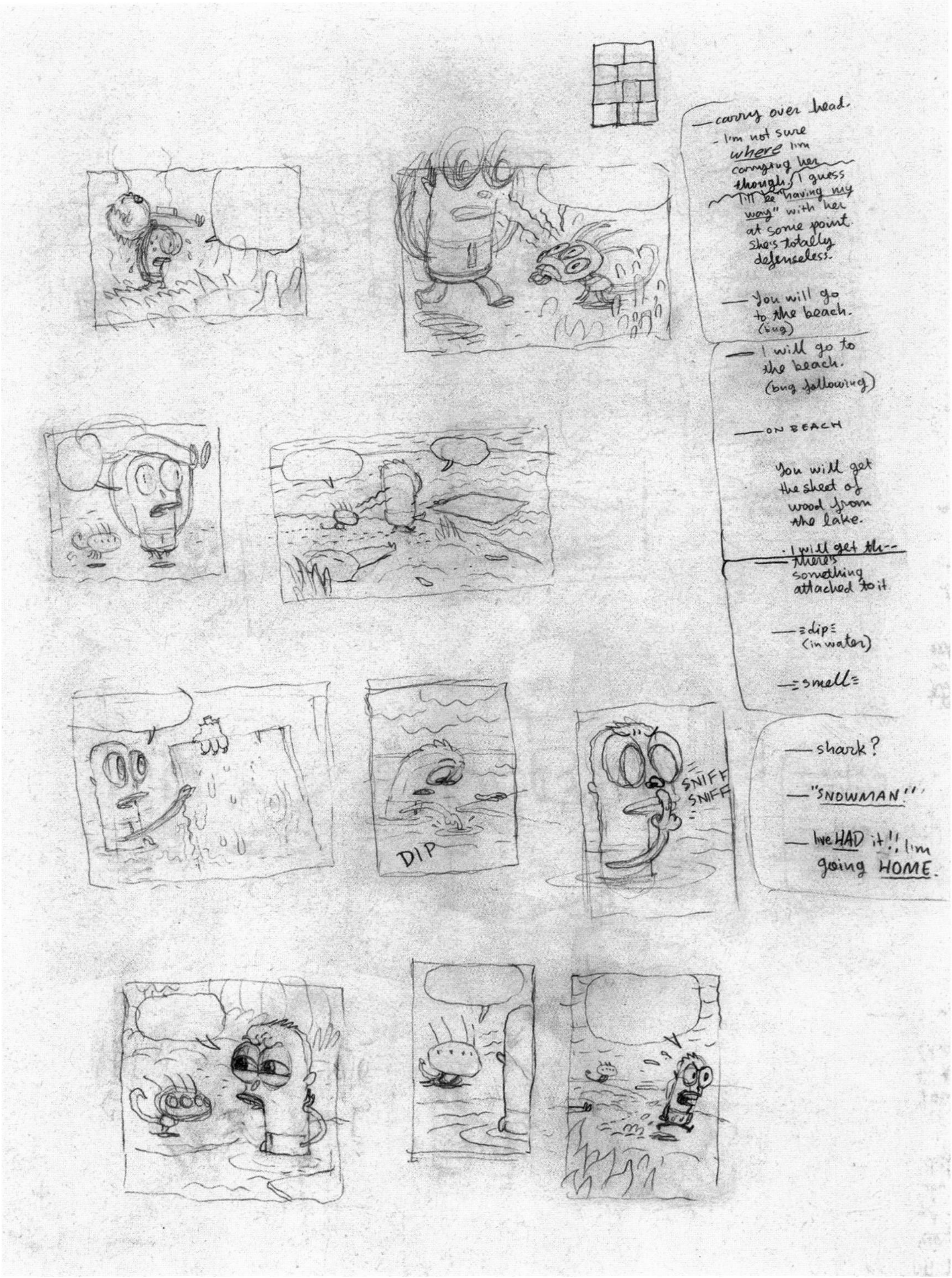
— carry over head.
- I'm not sure where I'm carrying her though. I guess I'll be "having my way" with her at some point. She's totally defenseless.
— You will go to the beach. (bug)
— I will go to the beach. (bug following)
— ON BEACH
You will get the sheet of wood from the lake.
I will get th--
— There's something attached to it.
— ≡dip≡ (in water)
— ≡smell≡
— shark?
— "SNOWMAN!"
— I've HAD it!! I'm going HOME.
DIP
SNIFF SNIFF

I'm not sure where I'm carrying her though. I guess I'll be "having my way with her" at some point. She's totally defenseless.
YOU WILL GO TO THE BEACH.
I will go to the beach...
YOU WILL FETCH THE SHEET OF WOOD FROM THE LAKE.
I will fetch thh--.
There's something attached to it.
DIP
SNIFF SNIFF
Shark?
SNOWMAN!
THAT DOES IT!! I'm going home!

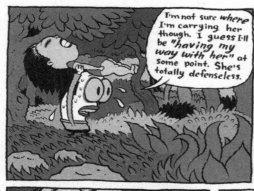

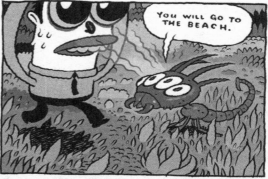

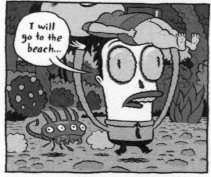

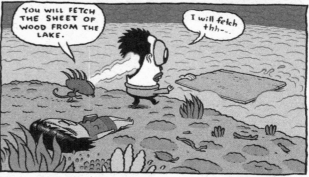

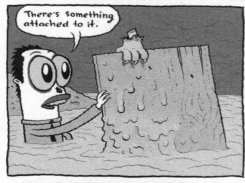

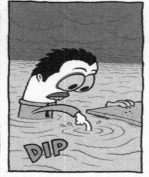

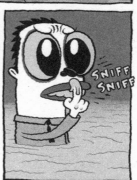

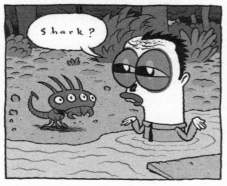

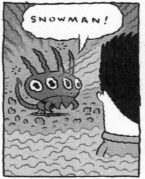

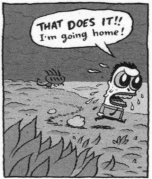

Previous pages: Dave Cooper's original artwork for a sequence from the Eddy Table strip "television program X-32 b" in Weasel *No. 5 (August 2002). On the left is Cooper's preliminary art and dialogue notes. The finished artwork is on the right. Copyright © Dave Cooper.*

Geigen-Miller (*Xeno's Arrow*), Craig Taillefer (*Wahoo Morris*), Steven Gilbert (*Colville*), Troy Little (*Chiaroscuro*), Steve Rolston (*Queen & Country* and *One Bad Day*), Michael Nicoll Yahgulanaas (*Tales of Raven*), Pia Guerra (*Y: The Last Man*), and Bryan Lee O'Malley (*Scott Pilgrim's Precious Little Life*). While several of these creators have followed the example of Dave Sim and successfully self-published their work, most publish primarily with U.S. comics firms such as Dark Horse Comics, Fantagraphics, Vertigo, Image Comics, and Oni Press, all of which have been very receptive to Canadian creators.

Most of the leading Canadian alternative-comics creators have appeared not only in comics periodicals, but also in graphic novels and book-length compilations, an increasingly popular form of comics. The graphic novel has given the medium long-overdue exposure in mainstream bookstores, thus broadening the audience for graphic narrative and further eroding the barriers in Canada between high and low culture.

Of course, alternative comics weren't the only alternative to mainstream comics. English Canada's lively small-press milieu remained a vibrant source of new, sometimes daring graphic-narratives. In fact, since the early 1990s, encouraged in part by the emergence of *Broken Pencil*, an important Canadian review journal devoted to zine culture, small-press comics have become an even more widespread phenomenon.[10] During the past decade, as well, many visual artists in Canada have turned to the creation of "artists' books" which, in some instances, closely resemble small-press comics in terms of format and graphic-narrative techniques.

Another key source of encouragement for many small-press publishers has been the emergence of innovative comic-book retailers such as The Beguiling in Toronto and Strange Adventures in Halifax. These booksellers and other retailers across the country have actively supported alternative approaches to comics and have generously provided small-press creators with a venue where they can sell their comics and connect with other artists and writers.

While the expansion of small-press comics publishing has resulted in dozens of local zine communities and the publication of hundreds of comics, fewer small-press creators have had a national impact. Much of the small-press comic art, in fact, has been exceedingly amateurish and/or self-indulgent. Nevertheless, the field represents an important underground current within Canada's comic art, offering creators complete freedom of expression independent from virtually any commercial considerations (even alternative-comics publishers have to contend with the realities of the marketplace). It has also been, since its inception more than twenty years ago, a crucial recruiting ground for alternative comics.

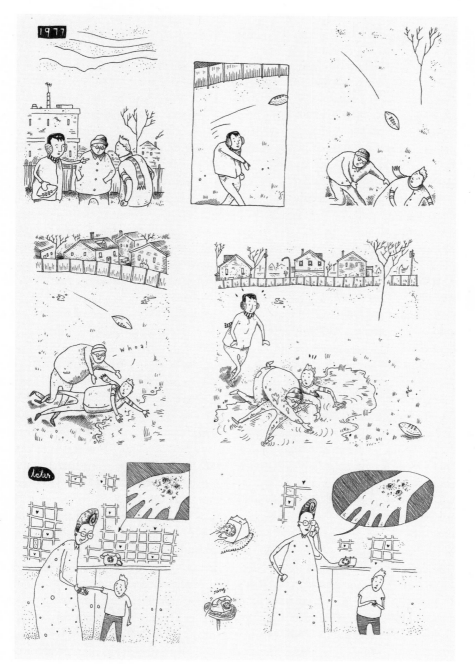

Original art by Christopher Hutsul for page 14 of Canal D'Amour No. 1 (1999). Copyright © Christopher Hutsul.

7

Facing page: Poster advertising an autograph session at a comic shop in the United Kingdom in 2006. Art by Hope Larson and Bryan Lee O'Malley. Copyright © Hope Larson and Bryan Lee O'Malley.

Many notable creators have been associated with the Canadian small-press field at various times during the past decade and a half, including Colin Upton, Julie Doucet, Rick Trembles (the son of Golden Age artist Jack Tremblay), Bernie Mireault, Greg Hyland, Jeff Wasson, Chris Howard, Luc Giard, Marc Bell, Peter Sandmark, Leanne Franson, Greg Kerr, Jean-Guy Brin, Tim Brown, Joe Gravel, Dave Howard, Dave Lapp, Christopher Hutsul, Shane Simmons, Mike White, Dave Howlett, Marc Ngui, Ken Boesem, Matthew Daley, and Diana Tamblyn. In the past few years, some of these creators, as well as various other small-press artists, have turned to the Web in order to promote their print publications or to create original webcomics. Among the most significant creators to take advantage of this new medium are Hope Larson (*Salamander Dream*), Kean Soo (*Jellaby*), and Jason Turner (*The Jason Turner Project*).[11] This trend is one that will certainly increase in the future, though many creators in the milieu are still very much attached to the hands-on production of mini- and digest-size comics.

The Web has also allowed for the development of several Canadian blogs devoted to graphic narrative, including the excellent *Sequential: Canadian Comix News & Culture* (*http://spiltink.dreamhost.com/blogs/Sequential.html*), founded by Max Douglas in 2002. In a sense, such blogs are the fanzines of the new millennium. The best blogs, however, are far more current, informative, and interactive than the comics fanzines of the past could ever hope to be. What's more, they have a global reach.

At the same time that Canadian alternative and small-press comics were thriving, English Canadian comic strips experienced an unexpected boom. Curiously, this phenomenon was happening just as newspaper comic-strip sections were shrinking, both in terms of the number of strips and the size at which strips were reproduced. Among the many new strips to run during the past decade or so were Vance Rodewalt's *Chubb & Chauncey*, Philip Street's *Fisher*, Sandra Bell Lundy's *Between Friends*, Graham Harrop's *Backbench*, Adrian Raeside's *The Coast*, Paul Gilligan's *Pooch Café*, Rina Picollo's *Tina's Groove*, and Gary Delainey and Gerry Rasmussen's *Betty*.[12] However, by far the most important Canadian strip of the period was Lynn Johnston's continuing domestic comedy *For Better or for Worse*, which remains one of the most popular comic strips in the world, enjoying syndication in nearly 2,000 papers in twenty-five countries. In 1993 the strip became an unlikely source of controversy when one of Johnston's characters, Lawrence, revealed he was gay.[13] The resulting brouhaha served to underscore the fact that comic strips have remained a mass medium, even

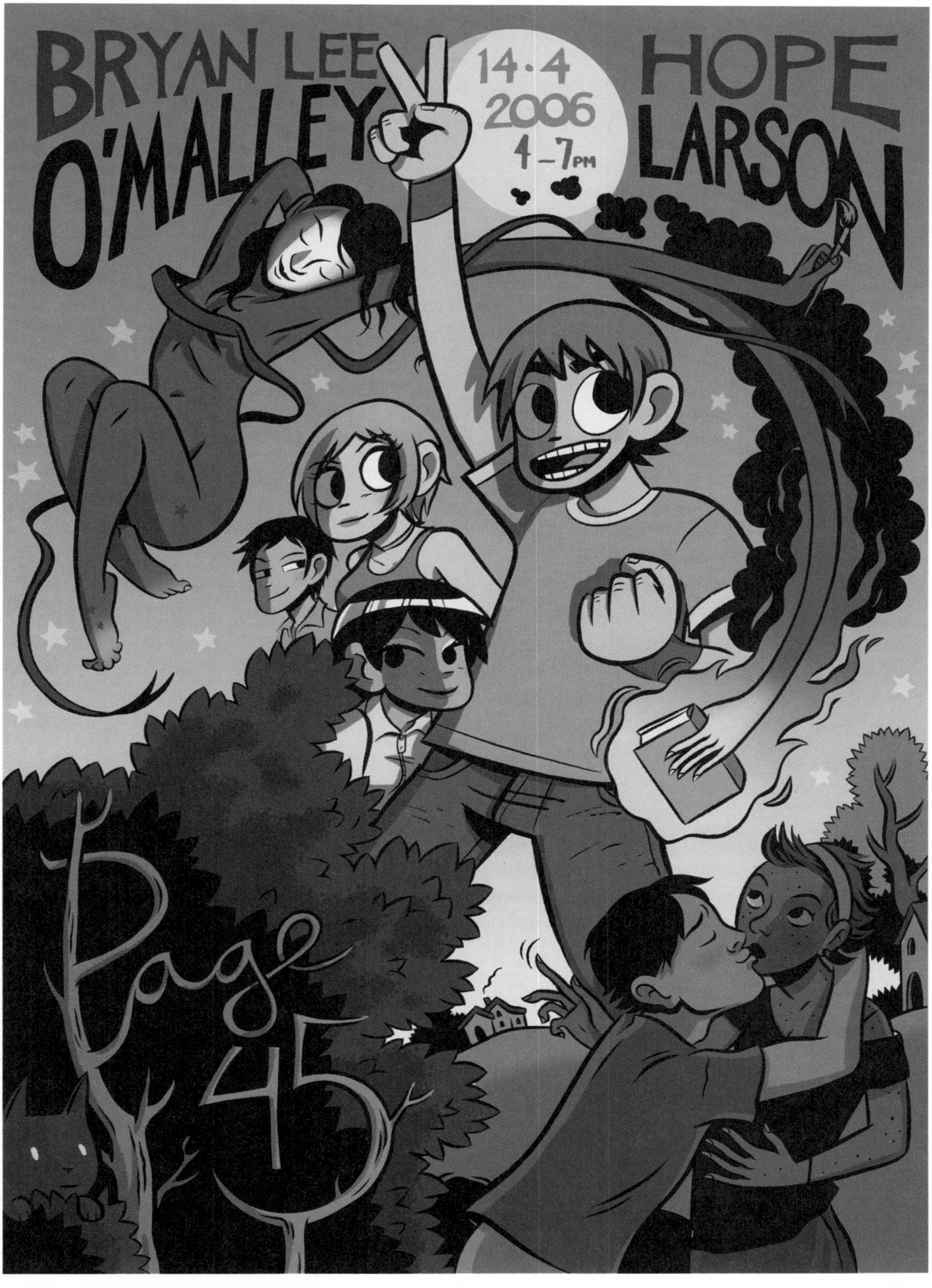
BRYAN LEE O'MALLEY
14·4
2006
4–7PM
HOPE LARSON
Page 45

Facing page: Dave
Sim (left) and
Gerhard receive the
Shuster Award for
Outstanding
Canadian
Achievement for the
completion of their
epic Cerebus,
Toronto, 2005.
Photo by Paul
Stockton. Copyright
© Paul Stockton.

The Road to
Palooka-Ville:
New Directions,
1989-2006

if their offspring, mainstream comic books, have not. Johnston's strip is also featured in countless reprint collections and in an animated television series. Recently, in 2003, she became the first cartoonist to receive a star on Canada's Walk of Fame in Toronto.[14]

Of course, comic strips aren't confined to mainstream newspapers. During the past decade or so, English Canada's energetic alternative press has contributed to the development of underground visions within the comic-strip field. Marc Bell, Greg Kerr, Dave Cooper, Tony Walsh, Peter Sandmark, Vesna Mostovac, Gareth Lind, Hope Larson, and many other notable alternative and small-press artists have produced strips for alternative papers (mostly weeklies) such as Vibe, The Georgia Straight, Exclaim!, X-Press, NOW, the Montreal Mirror, and The Coast.[15]

In addition to the growth of comic strips and non-mainstream comics, further scholarship relating to Canadian comics history was undertaken between 1989 and 2006. In 1992 I served as the curator of a Canadian Museum of Caricature (Ottawa) exhibition entitled Guardians of the North: The National Superhero in Canadian Comic Art, which was accompanied by a book of the same title. As already mentioned, Guardians of the North, which represented the first attempt to examine a particular theme within the English Canadian graphic-narrative tradition, inspired Canada Post

to issue a popular set of superhero stamps in 1995, featuring Superman and four Canadian national superheroes. In 2001 a substantially revised Web version of the exhibition became part of Library and Archives Canada's Digital Library of Canada.[16]

Another important scholarly work to appear during this period was Michel Viau's landmark BDQ: Répertoire des publications de bandes dessinées au Québec des origines à nos jours (2000). Although the focus of this French-language study was largely on francophone comics, it also provided useful information on English-language comics published in Quebec.

In 2002, Viau and I collaborated on Beyond the Funnies: The History of Comics in English Canada and Quebec, a Library and Archives Canada website that explores the development of Canada's two comic-art traditions.[17]

The past decade has also witnessed a considerable degree of academic interest in the Canadian anti-crime-comics campaign of the late 1940s and 1950s. Much of this research was undertaken by feminist scholars such as Mary Louise Adams, Mona Gleason, and Janice Dickin McGinnis, who were less concerned with comics history as such and more interested in the era's anti-comics hysteria as a notable example of moral panic worth exploring from the point of view of social and legal history or the history and sociology of sexuality.[18]

Academic interest in Canadian comics will probably increase markedly in the years to come as more and more scholars discover the obvious: Canada's popular culture merits serious attention, both for its own sake and as an invaluable and fascinating barometer of social attitudes and values.

Recently, the growth of interest in English Canada's comics heritage has led to the launch of two new awards recognizing achievements in Canadian comic art: the Shusters (named for Joe Shuster, the co-creator of Superman), which recognize excellence in the comic-book field, particularly main-stream comics; and the Doug Wright Awards, which focus more on contributions to cartooning, comic strips, and alternative comics. These awards, which commemorate two giants of Canadian comic art, are a welcome development and have already served to raise the profile of Canadian comics. During the past decade or so, numerous comics creators from Canada have been the recipients of the two leading American comic-art awards, the Harveys and the Eisners. But now Canadians can also vie for their own national awards.

Most of the academic attention devoted to Canadian comics to date has focused on the era when comic books were a hugely popular mass form of entertainment intended primarily for children and adolescents, but contemporary Canadian comics have evolved in another direction entirely, becoming a serious art form aimed at a much smaller but adult audience. Not surprisingly, this maturation has been a difficult process. Adult comics have proven to be controversial and have, at times, been the target of censorship and repression. The new comics also had the misfortune of emerging at a time when the comic-book industry in North America was beset by economic difficulties that resulted in the demise of numerous publishers, distributors, and retailers.[1]

Despite these and other obstacles, Canadian comic art continues to receive significant recognition within the international comic-book community. Mainstream critical acceptance of comics has been much harder to achieve. Increasingly, though, more and more critics have come to recognize not only that this hybrid art form affords an opportunity to create unique and powerful narratives, but also that there is a large body of impressive Canadian graphic storytelling worthy of serious attention. The Montreal-based publisher Drawn & Quarterly in particular has been successful in encouraging this new critical acceptance of comics. Furthermore, projects such as Chester Brown's *Louis Riel* graphic novel, for which Brown won two Harvey Awards in 2004, have allowed Drawn & Quarterly to expand the audience for comics in Canada markedly. As a result, positive stories about comics now regularly appear in the Canadian media, especially the

Brad Mackay (left), Seth (centre), and Chris Oliveros examine original artwork by the cartoonist Doug Wright at Library and Archives Canada in Gatineau, Quebec, in 2006. (Drawn & Quarterly will be publishing a major new work on Wright by Mackay and Seth in 2007.) Copyright © Drawn & Quarterly.

national newspaper the *National Post*. Also encouraging is the fact that most bookstores and libraries in Canada now feature sections devoted to graphic novels — and the increasingly popular *manga* (Japanese comics).

At the beginning of the new millennium, after a century of comics, the very best Canadian comic artists are combining art and literature in new ways, exploring the limits of graphic narrative, and calling into question our preconceptions relating to the boundary between so-called fine art and popular culture. The major challenge now facing these creators and their publishers is to continue to bring the resulting comics in all forms — comic books, comix, small-press zines, graphic novels, webcomics, artists' books, and comic strips — from

the artistic and literary margins to a more central place in Canadian culture where they can reach a much larger audience and gain further acceptance as a legitimate form of storytelling.

Just as Canada has found its own unique and powerful voice in literature and other arts, it is now creating its own distinct visions within the field of graphic narrative.[2] Furthermore, as the acceptance of comics as an art form expands, more and more Canadians will discover what many comics readers around the world already know: Canada produces some of the best and most sophisticated graphic narratives available today. After more than six decades, during which their very right to exist was at times contested, comic books in English Canada have finally come of age.

Acknowledgements

1. Slightly revised versions of Chapters 3 and 4 of this book were combined and published under the title "The Golden Age of Canadian Comic Books and Its Aftermath: Super-Heroes & Others in English Canada, 1941–1966," in *Alter Ego* 36 (May 2004): 3–26.

Introduction

1. Marshall McLuhan, *Understanding Media: The Extensions of Man* (Cambridge, MA: MIT Press, 1994), 168. McLuhan misdates the precise birth of the comic book. Nevertheless, his observations about the challenges of learning the "language" of comics are typically discerning.

2. Harold Town, "Can You Forget Mole, Giant Escargot, 88 Keys & B.O. Plenty? Tracy Is the Literary Steal of the Century," *Toronto Life* 3, no. 4 (February 1969): 22.

3. Useful surveys of comics history include: Dick Lupoff and Don Thompson, eds., *All in Color for a Dime* (New Rochelle, NY: Arlington House, 1970); Trina Robbins and Catherine Yronwode, *Women and the Comics* (Forestville, CA: Eclipse Books, 1985); Mike Benton, *The Comic Book in America: An Illustrated History* (Dallas: Taylor Publishing, 1989); Ron Goulart, *Over 50 Years of American Comic Books* (Lincolnwood, IL: Mallard Press, 1991); Robert C. Harvey, *The Art of the Comic Book: An Aesthetic History* (Jackson: University of Mississippi Press, 1996); and Roger Sabin, *Comics, Comix, & Graphic Novels: A History of Comic Art* (London: Phaidon, 1996).

4. McLuhan, *Understanding Media*, 165.

5. The structure, syntax, and aesthetic conventions of the comics medium are discussed in numerous studies, including Scott McCloud, *Understanding Comics* (Northampton, MA: Kitchen Sink Press, 1993); Philip Fry and Ted Poulos, *Steranko: Graphic Narrative; Storytelling in the Comics and the Visual Novel* (Winnipeg: Winnipeg Art Gallery, 1977); Will Eisner, *Comics and Sequential Art* (Princeton, WI: Kitchen Sink Press, 1992); and David Carrier, *The Aesthetics of Comics* (University Park, PA: Pennsylvania State University Press, 2000). Also of interest are Marshall McLuhan's reflections on the medium in *Understanding Media* and *The Mechanical Bride: Folklore of Industrial Man* (New York: Vanguard Press, 1951).

6. See the Selected Bibliography in this book for information on scholarship relating to the history of English Canadian comic art.

7. While the primary focus of the historical survey is on comic books, it also touches on the history of English Canadian comic strips.

Chapter 1: Of Brownies and Doo Dads

1. For more information on the history of the newspaper comic strip, see David Kunzle, *The Early Comic Strip* (Berkeley, CA: University of California Press, 1973); Bill Blackbeard and Martin Williams, eds., *The Smithsonian Collection of Newspaper Comics* (New York: Harry N. Abrams with Smithsonian Institution Press, 1977); Bill Blackbeard and Dale Crain, eds., *The Comic Strip Century: Celebrating 100 Years of an American Art Form* (Northampton, MA: Kitchen Sink Press, 1995); and Pascal Lefèvre and Dierick Charles, *Forging a New Medium: The Comic Strip in the 19th Century* (Brussels: VUB University Publishers, 1998). The intriguing link between comic strips and the expansion of American consumerism is examined by Ian Gordon in *Comic Strips and Consumer Culture, 1890–1945* (Washington, DC: Smithsonian Institution Press, 1998).

2. Peter Desbarats and Terry Mosher, *The Hecklers: A History of Canadian Political Cartooning and a Cartoonists' History of Canada* (Toronto: McClelland & Stewart, 1979), 40–44, 240–53; Fraser Sutherland, *The Monthly Epic: A History of Canadian Magazines* (Markham, ON: Fitzhenry & Whiteside, 1989), 46–58.

3. Desbarats and Mosher, *The Hecklers*, 44–52, 228–29; Sutherland, *The Monthly Epic*, 69–79. For a useful account of John Wilson Bengough's role as a social critic and reformer, see Ramsay Cook, *The Regenerators: Social Criticism in Late Victorian English Canada* (Toronto: University of Toronto Press, 1985), 123–51.

4. Desbarats and Mosher, *The Hecklers*, 61–68, 240. See also David R. Spencer, "Double Vision: The Victorian Bi-Cultural World of Henri Julien," *International Journal of Comic Art* 2, no. 2 (Fall 2000): 1–32.

5. Richard Marschall, "Cox, Palmer," Maurice Horn, ed., *The World Encyclopedia of Cartoons* (New York: Chelsea House, 1980), 173–74; Charlotte Spivak, "Palmer Cox," *Dictionary of Literary Biography*, vol. 42 (Detroit, MI: Gale Research Company, 1985), 133–38. See also Roger W. Cummins, *Humorous but Wholesome: A History of Palmer Cox and the Brownies* (Watkins Glen, NY: Century House, 1973).

6. Desbarats and Mosher, *The Hecklers*, 78–80, 248. See also A.G. Racey, *The Englishman in Canada* (Montreal: Montreal News Co., 1902).

7. Desbarats and Mosher, *The Hecklers*, 80–81, 236.

8. *Ibid.*, 82; Robert Thomas Allen, *A Treasury of Canadian Humour* (Toronto: McClelland & Stewart, 1967), 21–26. For more on Edwards, see Grant MacEwan, *Eye Opener Bob: The Story of Bob Edwards* (Saskatoon: Western Producer Prairie Books, 1974), and Hugh A. Dempsey, *The Best of Bob Edwards* (Edmonton, AB: Hurtig Publishers, 1975).

9. This aspect of Carl Barks's career is documented in Bruce Hamilton, ed., *The Unexpurgated Carl Barks* (Prescott, AZ: Hamilton Comics, 1997). Also of interest is a related reprint: *Coo-Coo Facsimile Edition* (Prescott, AZ: Bruce Hamilton Company, 1998).

10. Coulton Waugh, *The Comics* (New York: Macmillan, 1947), 18, 22–23, 63–64; J. Ernest Kerr, *Imprint of the Maritimes: Highlights in the Lives of 100 Interesting Americans Whose Roots Are in Canada's Atlantic Provinces* (Boston: Christopher Publishing House, 1959), 131; Dave Strickler, *Syndicated Comic Strips and Artists, 1924–1995: The Complete Index* (Cambria, CA: Comics Access, 1995), 176. Some sources utilize a variant spelling of Harold MacGill's surname, i.e., "McGill." For information on the Hall-Room Boys films, see *Camera* 4, no. 31 (November 12, 1921): 6; *Camera* 4, no. 32 (November 19, 1921): 7.

11. Maurice Horn, "Patterson, Russell," Maurice Horn, ed., *The World Encyclopedia of Comics*, vol. 2 (New York: Chelsea House, 1976), 540–41; Desbarats and Mosher, *The Hecklers*, 247. Interestingly, Patterson was an influence on Joe Shuster, the Canadian artist who co-created Superman. See Shel Dorf, "Remembering the 30's; Shel Dorf Interviews: Jerry Siegel, Joe Shuster & Joanne Siegel," *Siegel and Shuster: Dateline 1930's* 1, no. 1 (November 1984): [33].

12. Serge Jongué, "Barré, Raoul," Horn, ed., *The World Encyclopedia of Cartoons*, 101–02; Karen Mazurkewich, *Cartoon Capers: The History of Canadian Animators* (Toronto: McArthur & Company, 1999), 18–20. See also André Martin, *Barré l'introuvable/In search of Raoul Barré* (Montreal: Cinémathèque québécoise, 1976).

13. Desbarats and Mosher, *The Hecklers*, 86–91, 234–35; Allen, *A Treasury of Canadian Humour*, 58–59. For information on the short-lived *Adventures of Dicky Dare* strip, see *http://yesterdays-papers.blogspot.com/2006/04/adventures-of-dicky-dare-by-winnipeg.html*.

14. Gene Walz, *Cartoon Charlie: The Life and Times of Animation Pioneer Charles Thorson* (Winnipeg: Great Plains Publications, 1998), 20, 43–44, 51–52, 138–41.

15. Craig Layng, "Cartoons and Comic Strips," *Canadian Encyclopedia Year 2000 Edition* (Toronto: McClelland & Stewart, 1999), 413; Allen, *A Treasury of Canadian Humour*, 59–61; Gregory Clark, "Frise," Jimmy Frise, *Birdseye Centre* (Toronto: McClelland & Stewart, 1965), [9-16]; Peter Harris, "Frise, James Llewelyn," Horn, ed., *The World Encyclopedia of Comics*, vol. 1, 266.

16. Layng, "Cartoons and Comic Strips," 413; Desbarats and Mosher, *The Hecklers*, 254; Doug Kendig, "Wright, Doug," Horn, ed., *The World Encyclopedia of Cartoons*, 586–87.

17. Allen, *A Treasury of Canadian Humour*, 56–57; Layng, "Cartoons and Comic Strips," 412–13.

18. Bill Blackbeard, "Williams, James Robert," Horn, ed., *The World Encyclopedia of Comics*, vol. 2, 700–01.

Chapter 2: Up, Up, and Away

1. From an unpublished draft (circa 1930) found in the Archibald MacMechan fonds (Dalhousie University Archives), as quoted in John Bell, *Canuck Comics: A Guide to Comic Books Published in Canada* (Montreal: Matrix Books, 1986), 19.

2. For a useful survey of the adventure strips, see Ron Goulart, *The Adventurous Decade: Comic Strips in the Thirties* (New Rochelle, NY: Arlington House Publishers, 1975).

3. Harold Foster discussed his formative years in Canada in his last interview, which was conducted by the Canadian comics creator and historian Arn Saba. See Arn Saba, "Drawing Upon History: Arn Saba Interviews Harold Foster," *The Comics Journal* 102 (September 1985), 61–84. See also Brian M. Kane, *Hal Foster: Prince of Illustrators, Father of the Adventure Strip* (Lebanon, NJ: Vanguard Productions/Watson-Guptill Publications, 2001).

4. For more on the portrayal of Mounties in popular culture, see Dick Harrison, ed., *Best Mounted Police Stories* (Edmonton, AB: University of Alberta Press, 1978); Bernard A. Drew, *Lawmen in Scarlet: An Annotated Guide to Royal Canadian Mounted Police in Print and Performance* (Metuchen, N.J.: Scarecrow Press, 1990); Michael Dawson, *The Mountie from Dime Novel to Disney* (Toronto: Between the Lines, 1998); and Don Hutchison, ed., *The Scarlet Riders: Action-Packed Mountie Stories from the Fabulous Pulps* (Oakville, ON: Mosaic Press, 1998). During the Canadian Golden Age of Comics, most of the major comics publishers offered Royal Canadian Mounted Police stories.

5. Robert MacMillan, "The War Years: Anglo-American Publishing Ltd.," Bell, *Canuck Comics*, 93–94.

6. Maurice Horn, "Robin Hood and Company," Horn, ed., *The World Encyclopedia of Comics*, vol. 2, 585; MacMillan, "The War Years: Anglo-American Publishing Ltd.," 94; Robert Fulford, "Notebook: Krazy Kat at Last Joins the Kanon," *National Post* (February 15, 2005).

7. For more on the "pre-history" of the comic book and the form's early evolution, see Denis Gifford, *The American Comic Book Catalogue: The Evolutionary Era, 1884–1939* (London: Mansell, 1990); Charles Wooley, *Wooley's History of the Comic Book, 1899–1936* (Lake Buena Vista, FL: Charles Wooley, 1986); Robert L. Beerbohm, Doug Wheeler, and Richard D. Olson, "The American Comic Book: 1900–1938," Robert M. Overstreet, comp., *The Official Overstreet Comic Book Price Guide, 32nd Edition* (New York: House of Collectibles, 2002), 281–87; and Robert

L. Beerbohm and Richard D. Olson, "The American Comic Book: 1933–Present," Overstreet, *The Official Overstreet Comic Book Price Guide, 32nd Edition*, 303–09.

8. Denis Gifford, *The British Comic Catalogue* (Westport, CT: Greenwood Press, 1975), 36–37, 67; Alan Abrams, *Why Windsor: An Anecdotal History of the Jews of Windsor and Essex County* (Windsor, ON: Black Moss Press, 1981), 52–62.

9. Jerry Siegel and Joe Shuster's early collaborations are reprinted in the Eclipse Comics publication *Siegel and Shuster: Dateline 1930's* 1, nos. 1–2 (November 1984–85).

10. Thomas Andrae, "Of Supermen and Kids with Dreams: An Interview with Jerry Siegel and Joe Shuster," Robert M. Overstreet, comp., *The Official Overstreet Comic Book Price Guide No. 18* (New York: House of Collectibles, 1988), A78–A98. See also Les Daniels, *Superman: The Complete History* (San Francisco: Chronicle Books, 1998).

11. Mordecai Richler, "The Great Comic Book Heroes," *Hunting Tigers Under Glass: Essays and Reports* (Toronto: McClelland & Stewart, 1968), 80.

12. Maurice Horn, "Chartier, Albert," Horn, ed., *The World Encyclopedia of Comics*, vol. 1, 166–67; Jerry Bails, *The Who's Who of American Comic Books*, vols. 1–4 (Detroit: Jerry Bails, 1973–76), 31, 275.

Chapter 3: Smashing the Axis

1. Alan Walker, "Historical Perspective," Michael Hirsh and Patrick Loubert, *The Great Canadian Comic Books* (Toronto: Peter Martin Associates, 1971), 6; A.F.W. Plumptre, *Three Decades of Decision: Canada and the World Monetary System, 1944–75* (Toronto: McClelland & Stewart, 1977), 90–93.

2. For more on the Canadian pulps, see John Robert Colombo, ed., *Years of Light: A Celebration of Leslie A. Croutch* (Toronto: Hounslow Press, 1982), 136–40; and John Bell, *The Far North and Beyond: An Index to Canadian Science Fiction and Fantasy in Genre Magazines and Other Selected Periodicals of the Pulp Era, 1896–1955* (Halifax: Dalhousie University School of Library and Information Studies/London, Eng.: Vine Press, 1998), 57–58. Also see Carolyn Strange and Tina Loo, *True Crime, True North: The Golden Age of Canadian Pulp Magazines* (Vancouver: Raincoast Books, 2004).

3. The principal source, in this and all subsequent chapters, for information on specific comics and the output of various comics publishers is the John Bell Canadian Comic Book Collection, Rare Books Collection, Library and Archives Canada (hereafter LAC).

4. Not all comics readers eagerly embraced the new Canadian comic books. Bruce McCall remembers dismissing them as "black-and-white, vapid, and hopelessly

wholesome." See Bruce McCall, *Thin Ice: Coming of Age in Canada* (Toronto: Random House of Canada, 1997), 8.

5. John Bell, *Guardians of the North: The National Superhero in Canadian Comic-Book Art* (Ottawa: National Archives of Canada, 1992), 3–4.

6. The most extensive public holdings of Maple Leaf comics are found in the John Bell Canadian Comic Book Collection, LAC.

7. MacMillan, "The War Years: Anglo-American Publishing Ltd.," 91–101.

8. Gary Carter, "Letter from the Editor: A Weird Discovery!" *Comic Book Marketplace* 2, no. 27 (September 1995): 6, 44; Kirk Wallace, "Canadian Weird #12" [letter to the editor], *Comic Book Marketplace* 2, no. 48 (June 1997): 77.

9. MacMillan, "The War Years: Anglo-American Publishing Ltd.," 97.

10. Harold Town, "Afterword," Hirsh and Loubert, *The Great Canadian Comic Books*, 263–64.

11. Walker, "Historical Perspective," 16; Dave Sim, "A Conversation with Adrian and Pat Dingle and Bill Thomas," *Now and Then Times* 1, no. 2 (October 1973): [27–28]; Peter Harris, "Dingle, Adrian," Horn, ed., *The World Encyclopedia of Comics*, vol. 1, 208. Dave Sim's interview with the Dingles and Thomas was recently reprinted in *Alter Ego* 36 (May 2004): 27–35. The issue also includes the text of an interview (probably conducted by Sim) with the Bell Features artist Jerry Lazare.

12. Sim, "A Conversation with Adrian and Pat Dingle and Bill Thomas," [28–29]; Bell, *Guardians of the North*, 5–10.

13. Walker, "Historical Perspective," 7–11.

14. The John Bell Canadian Comic Book Collection, LAC, contains a nearly complete run of Bell Features comics. The Bell Features portion of the collection combines issues acquired by John Bell with the publisher's original file copies. These latter copies had previously formed part of an archival collection, the Bell Features fonds.

15. Bell, *Guardians of the North*, 10–13.

16. Alexander Ross, "The Wild World of Wartime Comic Books," *Maclean's* 77, no. 18 (September 19, 1964): 28.

17. Bell, *Guardians of the North*, 13–15.

18. *Ibid.*, 13–17.

19. *Ibid.*, 15.

20. Rik Offenberger, "A Brief History of Canadian Golden Age Archie Comics," (*http://www.mightycrusaders.net/canada.htm*).

21. Until very recently, it was assumed that the "whites" were strictly an English Canadian phenomenon. However, a single issue of a French-language "white,"

Comiques Bravo, was recently discovered by the author. Probably published in Montreal (the publisher and place of publication aren't explicitly indicated), the comic book is undated but likely appeared in the fall of 1945. *Comiques Bravo* isn't recorded in Michel Viau's authoritative guide *BDQ: Répertoire des publications de bandes dessinées au Québec des origines à nos jours* (Laval, QC: Éditions Mille-Îles, 2000).

22. The relaxation of foreign-exchange controls relating to non-essential goods actually started in the latter part of 1944, so it is likely that U.S. comics began to trickle back into Canada months before the end of World War II. It is also during this period that early Canadian reprints of U.S. comics probably appeared. See Plumptre, *Three Decades of Decision*, 95.

23. Bell, *Canuck Comics*, 85–87.

24. MacMillan, "The War Years: Anglo-American Publishing Ltd.," 99–100. See also Harlan Ellison, "Dreams of Joy Recaptured," Bell, *Canuck Comics*, 4–10.

25. Walker, "Historical Perspective," 17–19.

26. Over the course of the Golden Age, tens of thousands of pages of original comic art were created by Canadian artists. Not surprisingly, given the marginality of early comics publishing, most of this artwork has been lost to posterity. However, due primarily to the efforts of Michael Hirsh and Patrick Loubert in the early 1970s, several hundred pages of Bell Features artwork did survive and are now held by LAC (Bell Features fonds). See Walker, "Historical Perspective," 20–21.

27. Additional information on the post-war careers of many of the Canadian Golden Age creators can be found in Bails, *The Who's Who of American Comic Books*, vols.1–4, and Colin S. MacDonald, *A Dictionary of Canadian Artists*, vols. 1–7 (Ottawa: Canadian Paperbacks, 1967–90). Bails's biographical dictionary is now available online (*http://www.bailsprojects.com/(S(ofhugyju2ddg2gydvi1hld45))/about.html*).

28. For a useful and entertaining study of this era in American comics publishing, see William Savage, Jr., *Comic Books and America, 1945–1954* (Norman, OK: University of Oklahoma Press, 1990).

Spotlight: Johnny Canuck and the Search for Canadian Superheroes

1. McLuhan, *The Mechanical Bride*, 103.

2. Ron Goulart, *Over 50 Years of American Comic Books* (Lincolnwood, IL: Publications International, 1991), 128–30.

3. For a more detailed discussion of the Canadian national superheroes, see the website *Guardians of the North* (*www.collectionscanada.ca/superheroes*), and John

Bell, *Guardians of the North: The National Superhero in Canadian Comic-Book Art* (Ottawa: National Archives of Canada, 1992).

4. Sim, "A Conversation with Adrian and Pat Dingle and Bill Thomas," [28–29].

5. For detailed summaries of the adventures of Nelvana and the other Canadian national superheroes, see the Superhero Profiles section of the *Guardians of the North* website.

6. This account of Johnny Canuck's origin is based on an interview with Leo Bachle conducted by the author by telephone in 1991.

7. Although Johnny Canuck disappeared from comics, he has made occasional appearances in other media, including the theatre. Most recently, he appeared in the play *Johnny Canuck and the Last Burlesque* in which he is enlisted to save a Montreal burlesque house. See the *National Post* (January 26, 2006).

8. See the Shuster Awards website (*www.shusterawards.com*).

9. Based on an interview with George M. Rae conducted by the author by telephone in 1991.

10. For an interesting study of the post-war period in U.S. comics, see William Savage, Jr.'s *Comic Books and America, 1945–1954* (Norman, OK: University of Oklahoma Press, 1990).

11. For a discussion of this era in Canadian comics history, see Chapter 6.

12. Bell, *Guardians of the North*, 37–41.

13. Based on an interview with James Waley conducted by the author by telephone in 1991.

14. See the *Captain Canuck Official Website* (*www.captaincanuck.com*) for Richard Comely's account of Captain Canuck's origin. For an academic take on Comely's superhero, see Ryan Edwardson, "The Many Lives of Captain Canuck: Nationalism, Culture, and the Creation of a Canadian Comic Book Superhero," *The Journal of Popular Culture* 37, no. 2 (2003): 184–201.

15. Larry Mitchell, "John L. Byrne Looks at the New Canadian Comics," *The Melting Pot* 5 (Winter 1972–73): 7–9.

Chapter 4: Crackdown on Comics

1. Another contributor to the early Superior Publishers titles was Bill Thomas, whose work had previously appeared in various Bell Features titles. See Sim, "A Conversation with Adrian and Pat Dingle and Bill Thomas," [27].

2. Ross, "The Wild World of Wartime Comic Books," 28. Examples of 1946–48 Canadian comics that were exported to the United Kingdom are regularly offered for auction by British sellers on the on-line auction site eBay (*www.ebay.com*). The comics often feature a U.K. price sticker or price stamp. In

some instances, they are coverless, which suggests they were remaindered in the United Kingdom.

3. John Bell, "Superior Publications," *Books Are Everything!* 1, no. 6 (November 1988): 9.

4. Plumptre, *Three Decades of Decision*, 97–101.

5. For the most part, the plethora of 1948–51 reprint comics hasn't been documented in a systematic fashion, probably because the task would be daunting, if not impossible. One notable exception is the Canadian Gilberton publications. See Dan Malan, *The Complete Guide to Classics Collectibles*, vol. 2 (St. Louis, MO: Malan Classical Enterprises, 1993), 11–14. For less authoritative and exhaustive information on some of the other reprint titles, see the brief notes on Canadian reprints in Robert M. Overstreet, *The Official Overstreet Comic Book Price Guide*, no. 23 (New York, NY: House of Collectibles, 1993), A-41-A-42. For more information on vintage Canadian paperback publications, see Jon Warren, *The Official Price Guide: Paperbacks* (New York: House of Collectibles, 1991).

6. For a listing of the Iger Shop personnel, see Bails, *The Who's Who of American Comic Books*, vol. 4, 339. For a useful overview of the history of the Iger Shop, see Jay Edward Disbrow, *The Iger Comics Kingdom* (El Cajon, CA: Blackthorne, 1985). A revised version of Disbrow's text recently appeared in *Alter Ego* 3, no. 21 (February 2003): 3–45. After the demise of Superior Publishers, the firm's original comic art (mostly created by the Iger Shop) was acquired by the New York publisher Sol Cohen, who was likely involved in some capacity with the production in New York of Superior's later comic-book titles. In the late 1960s, Cohen sold the Superior artwork to Jane and Ron Howard, two leading American collectors of science-fiction and fantasy art. Not long after, the Howards apparently sold most of the pages to The Million Year Picnic, a comic-book store in Cambridge, Massachusetts. Since that time the art has slowly been acquired and dispersed by a variety of collectors and dealers. Most recently, some Superior precode horror stories were featured in a Sotheby's auction. Library and Archives Canada holds some original Superior pages (John Bell collection).

7. McLuhan, *Understanding Media*, 168.

8. "U.S. Senate Hearings; Official Facsimile Excerpts from the Record, U.S. Senate Subcommittee of the Committee to Investigate Juvenile Delinquency, April 21, 22, and June 4, 1954, New York, New York," Horn, ed., *The World Encyclopedia of Comics*, vol. 2, 778–80; Frederic Wertham, *Seduction of the Innocent* (New York: Rinehart, 1954), 277–79.

9. Wertham, *Seduction of the Innocent*, 274–76.

10. *Ibid.*, 273–76.

11. LAC, William Lyon Mackenzie King fonds, MG 26 J 13, Diaries Series, entry for June 9, 1948, 2.

12. *Ibid.*

13. Rae Murphy, Robert Chodos, and Nick Auf der Maur, *Brian Mulroney: The Boy from Baie-Comeau* (Toronto: James Lorimer, 1984), 21.

14. "U.S. Senate Hearings," 782.

15. Canada, House of Commons, *Debates*, October 4, 1949, 514.

16. "U.S. Senate Hearings," 782–83.

17. *Ibid.*, 784; Wertham, *Seduction of the Innocent*, 282–83.

18. For an interesting examination of the cultural nationalism and elitism implicit in the Fulton Bill and Canada's decade-long anti-comics campaign, see Bart Beaty, "High Treason: Canadian Nationalism and the Regulation of American Crime Comic Books," *Essays on Canadian Writing* 62 (Fall 1997): 85–107.

19. "Canadian Reprints (ECs: by J.B. Clifford)," Overstreet, *The Official Overstreet Comic Book Price Guide No. 23*, A-41. For an image of the cover of *Weird Suspense Stories* No. 1, see Frank "Ephemera" Motler, "Printed in Canada," *From the Tomb* 3 (October 2000): 7.

20. Wertham, *Seduction of the Innocent*, 283; LAC, Honourable E. Davie Fulton fonds, MG 32 B 11, MP for Kamloops, British Columbia Series, vol. 16, file "Literature: Crime Comics, 1950–51," Mannie Brown to Fulton, September 22, 1950.

21. Plumptre, *Three Decades of Decision*, 102–103; LAC, Fulton fonds, vol. 16, file "Literature: Crime Comics, 1950–51," Brown to Fulton, September 22, 1950.

22. See George Suarez, "Terrology; Chapter 6: Superior," *Tales Too Terrible to Tell* 6 (Fall 1992): 32–38. For more on the shift to horror comics, see "U.S. Senate Hearings," Horn, ed., *The World Encyclopedia of Comics*, vol. 2, 785.

23. "U.S. Senate Hearings," Horn, ed., *The World Encyclopedia of Comics*, vol. 2, 785–88.

24. *Ibid.*, 776–89.

25. Amy Kiste Nyberg offers a balanced, scholarly study of the infamous code in her *Seal of Approval: The History of the Comics Code* (Jackson, MS: University Press of Mississippi, 1998). See also "Appendix A: Code of the Comics Magazine Association of America, Inc.," Horn, ed., *The World Encyclopedia of Comics*, vol. 2, 819–21.

26. LAC, Fulton fonds, vol. 17, file "Literature: Speech Material — Crime Comics, Vol. 1, 1953–1955."

27. *Ottawa Citizen* (September 27, 1958); Bob Blakey, "Arrrrrgh … Horror Comics Creep Back from the Crypt," *Comic Cellar* 1 (1980): 18; LAC, Fulton fonds, vol.

16, file "Correspondence: Crime Comics, 1954–1956," James P. Leonard to Fulton, August 9, 1956.

28. Perhaps the most vehement expression of this alienation is found in Bruce McCall's rather vitriolic memoir of his Canadian childhood. See, McCall, *Thin Ice*, 8–10. For a more dispassionate and sustained examination of Canada's ambivalent relationship with American popular culture, see David Flaherty and Frank E. Manning, eds., *The Beaver Bites Back?: American Popular Culture in Canada* (Montreal and Kingston: McGill-Queen's University Press, 1993). Unfortunately, the latter book ignores comics.

29. Numerous examples of Canadian giveaway comics are found in the John Bell Canadian Comic Book Collection, LAC.

30. Layng, "Cartoons and Comic Strips," 413.

31. For a useful discussion of the woodcut novel, including Lawrence Hyde's work, see David A. Beronä and Chris Lanier, "A Season of Silent Novels," *The Comics Journal* 208 (November 1998): 95–103. Also see Patricia Ainslie, *Images of the Land: Canadian Block Prints, 1919–1945* (Calgary: Glenbow Museum, 1984), 54–55, 138–40.

Chapter 5: Harold Hedd and Fuddle Duddle

1. For background on Canada's underground newspapers, see Ron Verzuh, *Underground Times: Canada's Flower-Child Revolutionaries* (Toronto: Deneau Publishers, 1989). Regrettably, Verzuh gives short shrift to the graphic content of these publications.

2. In 2000, bpNichol's experiments in visual poetry and graphic narrative were examined in an interesting exhibition, *St. Art: The Visual Poetry of bpNichol*, curated by Gil McElroy. See the exhibition catalogue *St. Art: The Visual Poetry of bpNichol; Curated by Gil McElroy* (Charlottetown, PEI: Confederation Centre Art Gallery and Museum, 2000). More recently, Nichol's comics have been collected by Carl Peters in a substantial compilation: bpNichol, *bpNichol Comics* (Vancouver: Talonbooks, 2001).

3. Martin Vaughn-James, who now lives in France, was probably the first comic artist to be taken seriously by the literary establishment in Canada. In 1982 a special issue of *Canadian Fiction Magazine* was devoted to his work. See "After 'The Cage': Martin Vaughn-James Issue," *Canadian Fiction Magazine* 42 (1982).

4. For more on the underground period, see Jay Kennedy, *The Official Underground and Newave Comix Price Guide* (Cambridge, MA: Boatner-Norton Press, 1982); Roger Sabin, *Adult Comics: An Introduction* (London: Routledge, 1993); and Patrick Rosenkranz, *Rebel Visions: The Underground*

Comix Revolution 1963–1975 (Seattle: Fantagraphic Books, 2002).

5. Bell, *Guardians of the North*, 37–41; John Robert Colombo, ed., *Colombo's Canadian Quotations* (Edmonton, AB: Hurtig Publishers,1974), 186b.

6. See the catalogue/kit *Comic Art Traditions in Canada, 1941–45/Les grands courants de la bande illustrée au Canada, 1941–45* (Ottawa: National Gallery of Canada/Galerie national du Canada, 1972).

7. For more on this era, see Dave Sim, "Memoir: Why an Aardvark?" *Cerebus* 200 (November 1995): [36–37]. Also see Alan Hewetson, *The Complete Illustrated History of the Skywald Horror-Mood* (Manchester, Eng.: Headpress, 2004).

8. Layng, "Cartoons and Comic Strips," 413.

9. For information on the early Marvel cartoons, see the websites *Spyder-25: The Ultimate Resource for Spidey Fans* (*www.spyder-25.com/60s.html*) and *The Big Cartoon Database* (*www.bcdb.com*).

Chapter 6: An Aardvark Leads the Way

1. Bell, *Guardians of the North*, 24–26.

2. *Ibid.*, 20–24.

3. For a useful account of the origins of the direct-sales market, see Robert Beerbohm's "Comics Reality" column (nos. 1–2), which appeared in 1997–98 on the web-based *Comic Book Network Electronic Magazine* (*members.aol.com/ComicBkNet/reality.htm*).

4. Greg W. Myers, "Flashback: 15 Years Ago," *The Comics Buyer's Guide* 641 (February 28, 1986): 28; "Captain George Henderson," *The Comics Journal* 150 (May 1992): 24. For a very early profile of Henderson in the mainstream press, see Mike Cowley, "Old Comic Books: A Funny Business," *Weekend Magazine* 16, no. 39 (September 24, 1966): 31–33.

5. In 2001, Dave Sim inaugurated the Howard Eugene Day Memorial Award to commemorate Gene Day's signal contribution to comics. The award recognizes excellence in the field of self-published comics. Day was one of Sim's early mentors. For an amusing and insightful commentary on Day's intense dedication to his small-press career, see Sim's early comics narrative "A Day in the Life of Gene Day," *Comic Report* 1, no. 3 (1976): 6–8.

6. See Fry and Poulos, *Steranko: Graphic Narrative*.

7. Bell, *Guardians of the North*, 27–29.

8. For a very useful overview of the early small-press-comics milieu, see Dale Luciano, "Newave Comics Survey" [seven parts], *The Comics Journal* 96 (March 1985): 51–78; 97 (April 1985): 33–40; 98 (May 1985): 80–84; 99 (June 1985): 82–93; 100 (July 1985): 197–213; 101 (August 1985): 80–86; 102 (September 1985): 91–98.

9. For a revealing discussion of this period in Barry Blair's career, see Pat McEown, "The Dave Cooper Interview," *The Comics Journal* 245 (August 2002): 81–84.

10. Bell, *Guardians of the North*, 32–36.

11. Bell, *Canuck Comics*, 61, 68–69, 88.

12. McEown, "The Dave Cooper Interview," 85–88.

13. For citations to articles in the comics press about the boom-and-bust cycle that rocked alternative-comics publishing in the late 1980s, see the heading "Black and White Explosion" in the Michigan State University Libraries Special Collections Division's on-line bibliographical tool *Reading Room Index: An Index to the Holding of the Michigan State University Libraries Comic Art Collection*: *www.lib.msu.edu/comics/rri/index.htm*.

14, Arjun Basu, "Julie Doucet: Comic Stripper/Julie Doucet: Débauche d'encre," *enRoute* (March/mars 2001), 46.

15. See *Casual Casual* 19/20 (1987), which served as the catalogue for the *Casual Casual Cultural Exchange* exhibition.

16. Layng, "Cartoons and Comic Strips," 413.

17. See the *Comic Legends Legal Defense Fund Information Page*: *www.mypage.uniserve.ca/~lswong/CLLDF.html*.

18. Mark Nichols, "The Crime-Comic Wars," *Maclean's* 101, no. 36 (August 29, 1988): 44; "Strict Obscenity Law Proposed in Canada," *The Comics Journal* 124 (October 1988): 10; Dave Burns, "Cracking Down on Comic Smut," *Alberta Report* 16, no. 7 (January 30, 1989): [39–40]. Not all Canadian feminists supported the new pornography legislation. One dissenting voice was that of Varda Burstyn, who argued that the legislation — and the intense lobbying that had preceded it — contributed to a "chill on oppositional culture." See Varda Burstyn, "The Left and the Porn Wars: A Case Study in Sexual Politics," *Who's on Top: The Politics of Heterosexuality* (Toronto: Garamond Press, 1987), 13–46.

19. Janice Dickin McGinnis, "Bogeymen and the Law: Crime Comics and Pornography," *Ottawa Law Review/Revue de Droit d'Ottawa* 20, no. 1 (1988): 3–23. The lead article by McGinnis is followed by comments by the Honourable E.D. Fulton, Maureen Forrester, Reval Landau, Tina Head, John G. Ince, Jan Bauer, E. Ratushny, John McLaren, and Alan Walker.

20. The Honourable E.D. Fulton, PC, QC, "Comment on Crime Comics and Pornography," *Ottawa Law Review/Revue de Droit d'Ottawa* 20, no. 1 (1988): 25–31.

21. See Carl Horak and Todd Goldberg, *A Prince Valiant Companion* (Mountain Home, TN: Manuscript Press, 1992). The book is now available online at *www.members.aol.com/TGoldberg/pvcompanion.htm*.

Spotlight: Chester Brown and the Search for New Narratives

1. See the first part of the "Getting *Riel*" dialogue from *Cerebus* available at the *Cerebus Fangirl Site* (*www.cerebusfangirl.com/artists/louisriel1.html*)

2. Jay Torres, "Chester Brown," *Comics Interview* 93 (1991), 29.

3. See the profile of Brown at the *Read Yourself Raw* website (*www.readyourselfraw.com*).

4. Reg Hartt, "The Art of William Chester David Brown," ANIMAzine 18 (January 17, 1985): 28–29, 40.

5. See the RAMP interview with Brown on the Toronto Public Library website (*http:/ramp.torontopubliclibrary.ca/pdfs/chester_brown_interview.pdf*).

6. Andrew D. Arnold, "Keeping It 'Riel,'" *Time Viewpoint* (*www.time.com*), April 12, 2004.

7. Jeet Heer, "Beguiled by the Beguiling," *National Post* (May 17, 2002).

8. See Chester Brown's profile at the *Read Yourself Raw* website.

9. Chester Brown and Dave Sim's collaboration is found in *Cerebus World Tour Book 1995* (Kitchener, ON: Aardvark-Vanaheim, 1995).

10. Torres, "Chester Brown," 35.

11. Brad MacKay, "Special Ed," *cbc.ca Arts & Entertainment* (*www.cbc.ca/art/books/edclown.html*).

12. Torres, "Chester Brown," 28.

13. As quoted on the back cover of Chester Brown, *Ed the Happy Clown: The Definitive Ed Book* (Toronto, Vortex Comics, 1992).

14. *Read Yourself Raw.*

15. Andrea Juno, ed., *Dangerous Drawings: Interviews with Comix & Graphix Artists* (New York: Juno Books, 1997), 136.

16. Darrell Epp, "Two-Handed Man Interviews Cartoonist Chester Brown," *Two-Handed Man* website (*www.twohandedman.com/Interviews/Chester/Index.html*).

17. Nancy Tousley, "Chester Brown Meets Louis Riel," *Canadian Art* 21, no. 3 (Fall 2004): 128–29.

18. This strip was first published in *Underwater* No. 4 (September 1995) and was then issued by Chester Brown as a mini-comic, which he distributed in bus shelters and other public venues in Toronto. The strip was later collected in Brown's *The Little Man: Short Strips, 1980–1995* (Montreal: Drawn & Quarterly, 1998).

19. Gerald Hannon, "Retro Man," *Toronto Life* website (*www.torontolife.com/features/retro-man*).

20. Epp, "Two-Handed Man Interviews Cartoonist Chester Brown."

21. For the Eddie Campbell quote, see *Read Yourself Raw*. For the Gilbert Hernandez quote, see the discussion between Craig Thompson and Hernandez (excerpted

from *The Comics Journal* No. 258) found on *The Comics Journal* website (*http://www.tcj.com/258/i_craigbeto.html*).

22. Flannery O'Connor, *Wise Blood* (London: Faber and Faber, 1996), 11.
23. Torres, "Chester Brown," 23.
24. Juno, ed., *Dangerous Drawings*, 146.
25. *Ibid.*, 144, 147.
26. Chester Brown's response to a letter, *Underwater* 6 (May 1996): back cover.
27. Bill Wray letter, *Underwater* 2 (December 1994): 13.
28. Epp, "Two-Handed Man Interviews Cartoonist Chester Brown."
29. Tousley, "Chester Brown Meets Louis Riel," 128.
30. Epp, "Two-Handed Man Interviews Cartoonist Chester Brown."
31. Nicholas Hune-Brown, "Comics: Sketching Chester Brown," *McGill Daily* website (*http://www.mcgilldaily.com/view.php?aid=3697*).
32. First part of "Getting *Riel*."
33. *Ibid.*
34. Chester Brown, *Louis Riel* (Montreal: Drawn & Quarterly, 2003), 258.
35. Jeet Heer, "Little Orphan Louis," *National Post* (November 6, 2003); Daniel Epstein, "Chronicling the Revolutionary: Chester Brown on Louis Riel," *newsarama.com* (*http://newsarama.com/forums/showthread.php?s=&threadid=7360*).
36. Epp, "Two-Handed Man Interviews Cartoonist Chester Brown"; Tousley, "Chester Brown Meets Louis Riel," 128.
37. First part of "Getting *Riel*."
38. Brown, *Louis Riel*, 259.

Chapter 7: The Road to Palooka-Ville

1. Torres, "Chester Brown," 35. Also see Tousley, "Chester Brown Meets Louis Riel," 126–29.
2. In 2000, Todd McFarlane's media empire was the subject of a lead article in one of Canada's major business periodicals. See Bruce Hutchinson, "Rich, Famous — and Furious," *Report on Business* (May 2000): 32–42. For an interesting profile emphasizing McFarlane's remarkable success as a toy manufacturer, see Bruce Handy, "Small Is Beautiful," *Vanity Fair* 520 (December 2003): 208, 210, 212, 214, 217–18. Transcripts and other material relating to the McFarlane-Gaiman trial are found in *The Comics Journal* 250 (January 2003).
3. See the News Archive section of the website *www.spawn.com* for information on the Tony Twist lawsuit.
4. See Michael Dean, "State of the Comics Industry 2002: Recovery or Decline?" *The Comics Journal* 245 (August 2002): 6–14.

5. See the Captain Canuck profile in the "Superhero Profiles" section of Library and Archives Canada's *Guardians of the North* website at *www.collectionscanada.ca/superheroes*.

6. For a typical example of the comics community's somewhat bewildered response to Dave Sim's provocations, particularly his strident critiques of feminism, see Michael Dean and Staff, "In the Company of Sim," *The Comics Journal* 234 (May 2001): 10–11.

7. Dave Sim, letter in the "Blood and Thunder" column, *The Comics Journal* 258 (February 2004): 11. For an interesting overview of Dave Sim's controversial views and his many accomplishments as an artist, see Christopher Shulgan, "Comic-Book Anti-Hero," *Saturday Night* 118, no. 6 (November 2003): 48–50, 52–54.

8. Ian McGillis, "A Graphic Tale; Drawn & Quarterly: A Comix Empire Grows in Montreal," *Montreal Review of Books* 6, no. 1 (Fall and Winter 2002): 4–5. Also see the Drawn & Quarterly website at *www.drawnandquarterly.com*.

9. Seth recently contributed his first *New Yorker* cover (August 23, 2004).

10. See the *Broken Pencil* website at *www.brokenpencil.com*. In 2003, *Broken Pencil* published a special issue (No. 22) devoted to comics. For an overly tendentious but nevertheless useful overview of contemporary zine culture, see Stephen Duncombe, *Notes from the Underground: Zines and the Politics of Alternative Culture* (London: Verso, 1997).

11. Hope Larson and Kean Soo's work can be viewed at *http://www.friendlyuser.org/saniweb.php?saniUrl=http://www.secretfriendsociety.com*. Jason Turner's work can be found at *www.jasonturnerproject.com*. The *Sequential* website is an excellent source for information on other Canadian webcomics.

12. Layng, "Cartoons and Comic Strips," 413–14.

13. Doug Ogg, "Caught in Controversy: For Better or for Worse," *The Comics Journal* 159 (May 1993): 10–11.

14. See the Funbag Animation Studios website *www.funbag.com*. See also the on-line entry on the *For Better or for Worse* strip on the website *Don Markstein's Toonopedia*: *http://www.toonopedia.com/forbettr.htm*; *National Post* (June 26, 2003).

15. Layng, "Cartoons and Comic Strips," 413.

16. The website's URL is *www.collectionscanada.ca/superheroes*.

17. The website's URL is *www.collectionscanada.ca/comics*.

18. See the Selected Bibliography of this book.

Afterword

1. Dean, "State of the Comic Industry 2002: Recovery or Decline?" 6–14.

2.	Some of Canada's leading modern literary figures have had significant connections with comics. Among the most notable are Mordecai Richler, who wrote fondly about his childhood reading of comics (see the Selected Bibliography of this book); bpNichol, who experimented with the medium throughout his career (see Note 2, Chapter 5); and Margaret Atwood, who has contributed numerous strips to periodicals such as *This Magazine* and *Brick*. Another important Canadian writer, Michael Ondaatje, made use of comics as a source for his celebrated narrative poem *The Collected Works of Billy the Kid* (Toronto: House of Anansi, 1970). See Dominick M. Grace, "Ondaatje and Charlton Comics' *Billy the Kid*," *Canadian Literature* 133 (Summer 1992): 199–203. For another study of comics as a literary source for a major Canadian author (in this instance for the Canadian poet E.J. Pratt during the 1920s), see Brian Trehearne, "A Source for Pratt's Truant?" *Canadian Poetry: Studies, Document, Reviews* 7 (Fall/Winter 1980): 73–79. Unfortunately, Trehearne's article is overly speculative and not very convincing.

Notes

PRIMARY SOURCES

Library and Archives Canada Archival Holdings: John Bell collection, Bell Features fonds, and Honourable E. Davie Fulton fonds. Library and Archives Canada Library Holdings: John Bell Canadian Comic Book Collection and Bell Features Comic Book Collection.

Interviews: Leo Bachle (1991); Stanley Berneche (1991); Richard Comely (1991, 2001); Pierre Fournier (1991, 2001); Owen McCarron (1980); Gabriel Morrissette (1991, 2001); George M. Rae (1991); Mark Shainblum (1991, 2001); and James Waley (1991, 2001).

SECONDARY SOURCES

Websites

BD Québec — Le site actuel de la bande dessinée québécoise (*www.bdquebec.qc.ca/index.htm*); *Beyond the Funnies: The History of Comics in English Canada and Quebec/Au Delà de l'humour: L'histoire de la bande dessinée au Canada anglais et au Québec* (*www.collectionscanada.ca/comics*); *Comics Research Bibliography* (*www.rpi.edu/~bulloj/comxbib.html*); *Comics Scholarship Annotated Bibliographies* (*www.comicsresearch.org*); *Don Markstein's Toonopdedia* (*www.toonopedia.com/index.htm*); *Guardians of the North: The National Superhero in Canadian Comic-Book Art/Protecteurs de nord: Le superhéros national dans la bande dessinée canadienne* (*www.collectionscanada.ca/superheroes*); *Lambiek Comiclopedia* (*www.lambiek.net/artists*); *Michigan State University Libraries Comic Art Collection Reading Room Index* (*www.lib.msu.edu/comics/rri/index.htm*); *Sequential: Canadian Comix News & Culture* (*http://sequential.spiltink.org*); *The Word Balloon* (*http://wb.sparehed.com*).

Publications

Abrams, Alan. *Why Windsor: An Anecdotal History of the Jews of Windsor and Essex County*. Windsor, ON: Black Moss Press, 1981.

Adams, Mary Louise. *The Trouble with Normal: Postwar Youth and the Making of Heterosexuality*. Toronto: University of Toronto Press, 1997.

Allen, Robert Thomas. *A Treasury of Canadian Humour*. Toronto: McClelland & Stewart, 1967.

Anonymous. *Comic Art Traditions in Canada, 1941–45/Les grands courants de la bande illustrée au Canada, 1941–44*. Ottawa: National Gallery of Canada/Galerie national du Canada, 1972.

Bails, Jerry. *The Who's Who of American Comic Books*. 4 vols. Detroit: Jerry Bails, 1973–76.

Barker, Kenneth S. "An Introduction to the Canadian Newspaper Comic," *Inks* 4, no. 2 (May 1997): 18–25.

Barker, Martin. *The Haunt of Fears: The Strange History of the British Horror Comics Campaign*. London: Pluto Press, 1984.

Beaty, Bart. "High Treason: Canadian Nationalism and the Regulation of American Crime Comic Books," *Essays on Canadian Writing* 62 (Fall 1997): 85–107.

Bell, John. "Canada," *BD Guide 2005 — Encyclopédie de la bande dessinée internationale*, eds. Claude Moliterni, Philippe Mellot, Laurent Turpin, Michel Denni, and Nathalie Michel-Szelechowska. Paris: Omnibus, 2004: 214–21.

____. *Canuck Comics: A Guide to Comic Books Published in Canada*. Foreword by Harlan Ellison. Montreal: Matrix Books, 1986.

____. "Comic Books in English Canada," *Canadian Encyclopedia Year 2000 Edition*, ed. James H. Marsh. Toronto: McClelland & Stewart, 1999: 513–14.

____. "Foreword," *Northguard; Book One — Manifest Destiny*. Westland, MI: Caliber Press, 1990: [5–6].

____. "French Canadian Classics," *The Classics Collector* 9 (September 1989): 18–19.

____. "The Golden Age of Canadian Comic Books and Its Aftermath: Super-Heroes and Others in English Canada, 1941–1966," *Alter Ego* 36 (May 2004): 3–35.

____. *Guardians of the North: The National Superhero in Canadian Comic-Book Art*. Ottawa: National Archives of Canada, 1992.

____. *Protecteurs du Nord: Le superhéros national dans la bande dessinée canadienne*. Ottawa: Archives nationales du Canada, 1992.

Blackmore, Tim. "*Cerebus*: From Aardvark to Vanaheim, Reaching for Creative Heaven in Dave Sim's Hellish World," *Canadian Children's Literature* 71 (1993): 57–78.

Branigan, Augustine. "Mystification of the Innocents: Crime Comics and Delinquency in Canada, 1931–1949," *Criminal Justice History* 7 (1986): 111–44.

Charpentier, André. *La Bande Dessinée Kébécoise* [comprising *La Barre du Jour* 46–49]. Bois-des-Filion, QC: La Barre du Jour, 1975.

Daniels, Les. *Comix: A History of Comic Books in America*. New York: Outerbridge & Dienstfrey, 1971.

Desbarats, Peter, and Terry Mosher. *The Hecklers: A History of Canadian Political Cartooning and a Cartoonists' History of Canada*. Toronto: McClelland & Stewart, 1979.

Disbrow, Jay Edward. *The Iger Comics Kingdom*. El Cajon, CA: Blackthorne, 1985.

Dubois, Bernard. *Bande dessinée québécoise: répertoire bibliographique à suivre*. Sillery, QC: Éditions D.B.K., 1996.

Duncombe, Stephen. *Notes from the Underground: Zines and the Politics of Alternative Culture*. London: Verso, 1997.

Edwardson, Ryan. "The Many Lives of Captain Canuck: Nationalism, Culture, and the Creation of a Canadian Comic Book Superhero," *Journal of Popular Culture* 37, no. 2 (November 2003): 184–201.

Eisner, Will. *Comics and Sequential Art*. Princeton, WI: Kitchen Sink Press, 1992.

Ellison, Harlan. "Dreams of Joy Recaptured," *Canuck Comics: A Guide to Comic Books Published in Canada*, ed. John Bell. Montreal: Matrix Books, 1986: 5–10.

Falardeau, Mira. *La Bande dessinée au Québec*. Montréal: Les Éditions du Boréal, 1994.

Flaherty, David, and Frank E. Manning, eds. *The Beaver Bites Back?: American Popular Culture in Canada*. Montreal: McGill-Queen's University Press, 1993.

Fry, Philip, and Ted Poulos. *Steranko: Graphic Narrative; Storytelling in the Comics and the Visual Novel*. Winnipeg: Winnipeg Art Gallery, 1977.

Fulton, E.D., "Comment on Crime Comics and Pornography," *Ottawa Law Review/Revue de Droit d'Ottawa* 20, no. 1 (1988): 25–31.

Gerber, Ernst, and Mary Gerber, comps. *The Photo-Journal Guide to Comic Books*. 2 vols. Minden, NV: Gerber Enterprises, 1989.

Gifford, Denis. *The American Comic Book Catalogue: The Evolutionary Era, 1884–1939*. London: Mansell, 1990.

_____. *The British Comic Catalogue*. Westport, CT: Greenwood Press, 1975.

_____. *The Complete Catalogue of British Comics*. Exeter, Eng.: Webb and Bower, 1985.

_____. *The International Book of Comics*. New York: Crescent Books, 1984.

Goldberg, Todd H., and Carl J. Horak. *A Prince Valiant Companion*. Mountain Home, TN: Manuscript Press, 1992.

Goulart, Ron. *The Adventurous Decade: Comic Strips in the Thirties*. New Rochelle, NY: Arlington House Publishers, 1975.

_____. *Over 50 Years of American Comic Books*. Lincolnwood, IL: Publications International, 1991.

Hirsh, Michael, and Patrick Loubert. *The Great Canadian Comic Books*. Toronto: Peter Martin Associates, 1971.

Horn, Maurice, ed. *The World Encyclopedia of Cartoons*. New York: Chelsea House, 1980.

____. *The World Encyclopedia of Comics*. 2 vols. New York: Chelsea House, 1976.

Howe, Sean, ed. *Give Our Regards to the Atomsmashers! Writers on Comics*. New York: Pantheon Books, 2004.

Jacobs, Will, and Gerard Jones. *The Comic Book Heroes*. New York: Crown Publishers, 1985.

Juno, Andrea, ed. *Dangerous Drawings: Interviews with Comix & Graphix Artists*. New York: Juno Books, 1997.

Keltner, Howard. *Golden Age Comic Books Index, 1935–1955*. revised ed. Gainesville, TX: Howard Keltner, 1998.

Kennedy, Jay. *The Official Underground and Newave Comix Price Guide*. Cambridge, MA: Boatner-Norton Press, 1982.

Langlois, Richard, ed., "La Bande dessinee" [special issue], *La nouvelle barre du jour* 110–11 (février 1982).

Layng, Craig. "Cartoons and Comic Strips," *Canadian Encyclopedia Year 2000 Edition*. Toronto: McClelland & Stewart, 1999: 412–14.

Lent, John A., comp. *Animation, Caricature, and Gag and Political Cartoons in the United States and Canada: An International Bibliography*. Foreword by Maurice Horn. Westport, CT: Greenwood Press, 1994.

Lent, John A., ed. *Pulp Demons: International Dimensions of the Postwar Anti-Comics Campaign*. Madison and Teaneck, NJ: Fairleigh Dickinson University Press/Associated University Presses, 1999.

Letovsky, Cliff. "Komiks Kebek," *Le Beaver* 23–25 (June/August 1973): 87–93.

Luciano, Dale. "Newave Comics Survey" [seven parts], *The Comics Journal* 96 (Mar. 1985): 51–78; 97 (April 1985): 33–40; 98 (May 1985): 80–84; 99 (June 1985): 82–93; 100 (July 1985): 197–213; 101 (August 1985): 80–86; 102 (September 1985): 91–98.

Lupoff, Dick, and Don Thompson, eds. *All in Color for a Dime*. New Rochelle, NY: Arlington House, 1970.

McCall, Bruce. *Thin Ice: Coming of Age in Canada*. Toronto: Random House of Canada, 1997.

McCloud, Scott. *Understanding Comics*. Northampton, MA: Kitchen Sink Press, 1993.

MacDonald, Colin S. *A Dictionary of Canadian Artists*. 7 vols. Ottawa: Canadian Paperbacks, 1967–90.

McGinnis, Janice Dickin. "Bogeymen and the Law: Crime Comics and Pornography," *Ottawa Law Review/Revue de Droit d'Ottawa* 20, no. 1 (1988): 3–23.

McLuhan, Marshall. *The Mechanical Bride: Folklore of Industrial Man.* New York: Vanguard Press, 1951.

_____. *Understanding Media: The Extensions of Man.* Cambridge, MA: MIT Press, 1994.

MacMillan, Robert. "The War Years: Anglo-American Publishing Ltd.," *Canuck Comics: A Guide to Comic Books Published in Canada,* ed. John Bell. Montreal: Matrix Books, 1986: 92–101.

Malan, Dan. *The Complete Guide to Classics Collectibles.* 2 vols. St. Louis, MO: Malan Classical Enterprises, 1991, 1993.

Mazurkewich, Karen. *Cartoon Capers: The History of Canadian Animators.* Toronto: McArthur & Company, 1999.

Miller, John Jackson, and Maggie Thompson, Peter Bickford, and Brent Frankenhoff, comps. *The Standard Catalogue of Comic Books.* Iola, WI: Krause Publications, 2002.

Nyberg, Amy Kiste. *Seal of Approval: The History of the Comics Code.* Jackson, MS: University Press of Mississippi, 1998.

Overstreet, Robert M, comp. *The Official Overstreet Comic Book Price Guide No. 18.* New York: House of Collectibles, 1988.

_____. *The Official Overstreet Comic Book Price Guide No. 20.* New York: House of Collectibles, 1990.

_____. *The Official Overstreet Comic Book Price Guide No. 23.* New York: House of Collectibles, 1993.

_____. *The Official Overstreet Comic Book Price Guide, 32nd Edition.* New York: House of Collectibles, 2002.

Plumptre, A.F.W. *Three Decades of Decision: Canada and the World Monetary System, 1944–75.* Toronto: McClelland & Stewart, 1977.

Pomerleau, Luc. "La BD Québécoise: Bref Historique," *Canuck Comics: A Guide to Comic Book Published in Canada,* ed. John Bell. Montreal: Matrix Books, 1986: 116–23.

_____. "Quebec Comics: A Short History," *Canuck Comics: A Guide to Comic Books Published in Canada,* ed. John Bell. Montreal: Matrix Books, 1986: 102–15.

Richler, Mordecai. "The Great Comic Book Heroes," *Hunting Tigers Under Glass: Essays and Reports.* Toronto: McClelland & Stewart, 1968.

Rosenkranz, Patrick. *Rebel Visions: The Underground Comix Revolution 1963–1975.* Seattle: Fantagraphic Books, 2002.

Ross, Alexander. "The Wild World of Wartime Comic Books," *Maclean's* 77, no. 18 (September 19, 1964): 27–30.

Sabin, Roger. *Adult Comics: An Introduction*. London: Routledge, 1993.

_____. *Comics, Comix, & Graphic Novels: A History of Comic Art*. London: Phaidon, 1996.

Samson, Jacques, and André Carpentier, comp. *Actes — Premier colloque de bande dessinée de Montréal*. Montréal: Analogon, 1986.

Savage, Jr., William. *Comic Books and America, 1945–1954*. Norman, OK: University of Oklahoma Press, 1990.

Scalded, Frederik L. *Manga! Manga!: The World of Japanese Comics*. Tokyo: Kodansha International, 1983.

Shainblum, Mark. "Captain Canuck: The Triumphant Return of the Canadian Hero." *Orion, The Canadian Magazine of Time and Space* 1, no. 1 (Summer 1981): 8–11.

_____. "Orion Interview: A Conversation with Canada's Own Richard Comely." *Orion, The Canadian Magazine of Time and Space* 1, no. 1 (Summer 1981): 16–22.

Sim, Dave. "A Conversation with Adrian and Pat Dingle and Bill Thomas," *Now and Then Times* 1, no. 2 (October 1973): [27–29].

Strickler, Dave. *Syndicated Comic Strips and Artists, 1924–1995: The Complete Index*. Cambria, CA: Comics Access, 1995.

Suarez, George. "Terrology; Chapter 6: Superior," *Tales Too Terrible to Tell* 6 (Fall 1992): 32–38.

Sutherland, Fraser. *The Monthly Epic: A History of Canadian Magazines*. Markham, ON: Fitzhenry & Whiteside, 1989.

Town, Harold. "Afterword," Michael Hirsh and Patrick Loubert, *The Great Canadian Comic Books*. Toronto: Peter Martin Associates, 1971: 260–64.

Town, Harold. "Can You Forget Mole, Giant Escargot, 88 Keys & B.O. Plenty? Tracy Is the Literary Steal of the Century," *Toronto Life* 3, no. 4 (February 1969): 22–23.

Tratt, Grace. *Check List of Canadian Small Presses: English Language*. Halifax, NS: Dalhousie University School of Library Science, 1974.

Verzuh, Ron. *Underground Times: Canada's Flower-Child Revolutionaries*. Toronto: Deneau Publishers, 1989.

Viau, Michel. *BDQ: Répertoire des publications de bandes dessinées au Québec des origines à nos jours*. Laval, QC: Éditions Mille-Îles, 2000.

Waugh, Coulton. *The Comics*. New York: Macmillan, 1947.

Wertham, Frederic. *Seduction of the Innocent*. New York: Rinehart, 1954.

Wooley, Charles. *Wooley's History of the Comic Book, 1899–1936*. Lake Buena Vista, FL: Charles Wooley, 1986.

Page numbers in italics refer to images.